TensorFlow Deep Learning Projects

10 real-world projects on computer vision, machine translation, chatbots, and reinforcement learning

Luca Massaron
Alberto Boschetti
Alexey Grigorev
Abhishek Thakur
Rajalingappaa Shanmugamani

BIRMINGHAM - MUMBAI

TensorFlow Deep Learning Projects

Commissioning Editors: Amey Varangaonkar
Acquisition Editor: Viraj Madhav
Content Development Editors: Snehal Kolte
Technical Editor: Dharmendra Yadav
Copy Editor: Safis Editing
Project Coordinator: Manthan Patel
Proofreader: Safis Editing
Indexers: Rekha Nair
Graphics: Tania Dutta
Production Coordinator: Shraddha Falebhai

First published: March 2018

Production reference: 1270318

Published by Packt Publishing Ltd.
Livery Place
35 Livery Street
Birmingham
B3 2PB, UK.

ISBN 978-1-78839-806-0

www.packtpub.com

`mapt.io`

Mapt is an online digital library that gives you full access to over 5,000 books and videos, as well as industry leading tools to help you plan your personal development and advance your career. For more information, please visit our website.

Why subscribe?

- Spend less time learning and more time coding with practical eBooks and Videos from over 4,000 industry professionals

- Improve your learning with Skill Plans built especially for you

- Get a free eBook or video every month

- Mapt is fully searchable

- Copy and paste, print, and bookmark content

PacktPub.com

Did you know that Packt offers eBook versions of every book published, with PDF and ePub files available? You can upgrade to the eBook version at `www.PacktPub.com` and as a print book customer, you are entitled to a discount on the eBook copy. Get in touch with us at `service@packtpub.com` for more details.

At `www.PacktPub.com`, you can also read a collection of free technical articles, sign up for a range of free newsletters, and receive exclusive discounts and offers on Packt books and eBooks.

Contributors

About the authors

Luca Massaron is a data scientist and marketing research director specialized in multivariate statistical analysis, machine learning, and customer insight, with 10+ years experience of solving real-world problems and generating value for stakeholders using reasoning, statistics, data mining, and algorithms. Passionate about everything on data analysis and demonstrating the potentiality of data-driven knowledge discovery to both experts and non-experts, he believes that a lot can be achieved by understanding in simple terms and practicing the essentials of any discipline.

I would like to thank Yukiko and Amelia for their continued support, help, and loving patience.

Alberto Boschetti is a data scientist with strong expertise in signal processing and statistics. He holds a PhD in telecommunication engineering and lives and works in London. In his work, he faces daily challenges spanning natural language processing, machine learning, and distributed processing. He is very passionate about his job and always tries to stay up to date on the latest development in data science technologies, attending meetups, conferences, and other events.

Alexey Grigorev is a skilled data scientist, machine learning engineer, and software developer with more than 8 years of professional experience. He started his career as a Java developer working at a number of large and small companies, but after a while he switched to data science. Right now, Alexey works as a data scientist at Simplaex, where, in his day-to-day job, he actively uses Java and Python for data cleaning, data analysis, and modeling. His areas of expertise are machine learning and text mining.

I would like to thank my wife, Larisa, and my son, Arkadij, for their patience and support while I was working on the book.

Abhishek Thakur is a data scientist. His focus is mainly on applied machine learning and deep learning, rather than theoretical aspects. He completed his master's in computer science at the University of Bonn in early 2014. Since then, he has worked in various industries, with a research focus on automatic machine learning. He likes taking part in machine learning competitions and has attained a third place in the worldwide rankings on the popular website Kaggle.

Rajalingappaa Shanmugamani is currently a deep learning lead at SAP, Singapore. Previously, he worked and consulted at various startups, developing computer vision products. He has a master's from IIT Madras, his thesis having been based on the applications of computer vision in manufacturing. He has published articles in peer-reviewed journals, and spoken at conferences, and applied for a few patents in machine learning. In his spare time, he coaches programming and machine learning to school students and engineers.

I thank my spouse Ezhil, family and friends for their immense support. I thank all the teachers, colleagues, managers and mentors from whom I have learned a lot.

About the reviewer

Marvin Bertin is an online course author and technical book editor focused on deep learning, computer vision, and NLP with TensorFlow. He holds a bachelor's in mechanical engineering and a master's in data science. He has worked as an ML engineer and data scientist in the Bay Area, focusing on recommender systems, NLP, and biotech applications. He currently works at a start-up that develops deep learning (AI) algorithms for early cancer detection.

Packt is searching for authors like you

If you're interested in becoming an author for Packt, please visit authors.packtpub.com and apply today. We have worked with thousands of developers and tech professionals, just like you, to help them share their insight with the global tech community. You can make a general application, apply for a specific hot topic that we are recruiting an author for, or submit your own idea.

Table of Contents

Preface

TensorFlow is one of the most popular frameworks used for machine learning and, more recently, deep learning. It provides a fast and efficient framework for training different kinds of deep learning models with very high accuracy. This book is your guide to mastering deep learning with TensorFlow with the help of 12 real-world projects.

TensorFlow Deep Learning Projects starts with setting up the right TensorFlow environment for deep learning. You'll learn to train different types of deep learning models using TensorFlow, including CNNs, RNNs, LSTMs, and generative adversarial networks. While doing so, you will build end-to-end deep learning solutions to tackle different real-world problems in image processing, enterprise AI, and natural language processing, to name a few. You'll train high-performance models to generate captions for images automatically, predict the performance of stocks, and create intelligent chatbots. Some advanced aspects, such as recommender systems and reinforcement learning, are also covered in this book.

By the end of this book, you will have mastered all the concepts of deep learning and their implementation with TensorFlow, and will be able to build and train your own deep learning models with TensorFlow to tackle any kind of problem.

Who this book is for

This book is for data scientists, machine learning and deep learning practitioners, and AI enthusiasts who want a go-to guide to test their knowledge and expertise in building real-world intelligent systems. If you want to master the different deep learning concepts and algorithms associated with it by implementing practical projects in TensorFlow, this book is what you need!

What this book covers

Chapter 1, *Recognizing traffic signs using Convnets,* shows how to extract the proper features from images with all the necessary preprocessing steps. For our convolutional neural network, we will use simple shapes generated with matplotlib. For our image preprocessing exercises, we will use the Yale Face Database.

Chapter 2, *Annotating Images with Object Detection API*, details a the building of a real-time object detection application that can annotate images, videos, and webcam captures using TensorFlow's new object detection API (with its selection of pretrained convolutional networks, the so-called TensorFlow detection model zoo) and OpenCV.

Chapter 3, *Caption Generation for Images*, enables readers to learn caption generation with or without pretrained models.

Chapter 4, *Building GANs for Conditional Image Creation*, guides you step by step through building a selective GAN to reproduce new images of the favored kind. The used datasets that GANs will reproduce will be of handwritten characters (both numbers and letters in Chars74K).

Chapter 5, *Stock Price Prediction with LSTM*, explores how to predict the future of a mono-dimensional signal, a stock price. Given its past, we will learn how to forecast its future with an LSTM architecture, and how we can make our prediction's more and more accurate.

Chapter 6, *Create and Train Machine Translation Systems*, shows how to create and train a bleeding-edge machine translation system with TensorFlow.

Chapter 7, *Train and Set up a Chatbot, Able to Discuss Like a Human*, tells you how to build an intelligent chatbot from scratch and how to *discuss* with it.

Chapter 8, *Detecting Duplicate Quora Questions*, discusses methods that can be used to detect duplicate questions using the Quora dataset. Of course, these methods can be used for other similar datasets.

Chapter 9, *Building a TensorFlow Recommender System*, covers large-scale applications with practical examples. We'll learn how to implement cloud GPU computing capabilities on AWS with very clear instructions. We'll also utilize H2O's wonderful API for deep networks on a large scale.

Chapter 10, *Video Games by Reinforcement Learning*, details a project where you build an AI capable of playing *Lunar Lander* by itself. The project revolves around the existing OpenAI Gym project and integrates it using TensorFlow. OpenAI Gym is a project that provides different gaming environments to explore how to use AI agents that can be powered by, among other algorithms, TensorFlow neural models.

To get the most out of this book

The examples covered in this book can be run with Windows, Ubuntu, or Mac. All the installation instructions are covered. You will need basic knowledge of Python, machine learning and deep learning, and familiarity with TensorFlow.

Download the example code files

You can download the example code files for this book from your account at www.packtpub.com. If you purchased this book elsewhere, you can visit www.packtpub.com/support and register to have the files emailed directly to you.

You can download the code files by following these steps:

1. Log in or register at www.packtpub.com.
2. Select the **SUPPORT** tab.
3. Click on **Code Downloads & Errata**.
4. Enter the name of the book in the **Search** box and follow the onscreen instructions.

Once the file is downloaded, please make sure that you unzip or extract the folder using the latest version of:

- WinRAR/7-Zip for Windows
- Zipeg/iZip/UnRarX for Mac
- 7-Zip/PeaZip for Linux

The code bundle for the book is also hosted on GitHub at https://github.com/PacktPublishing/TensorFlow-Deep-Learning-Projects. We also have other code bundles from our rich catalog of books and videos available at https://github.com/PacktPublishing/. Check them out!

Conventions used

There are a number of text conventions used throughout this book.

CodeInText: Indicates code words in text, database table names, folder names, filenames, file extensions, pathnames, dummy URLs, user input, and Twitter handles. Here is an example: "The class TqdmUpTo is just a tqdm wrapper that enables the use of the progress display also for downloads."

A block of code is set as follows:

```
import numpy as np
import urllib.request
import tarfile
import os
import zipfile
import gzip
import os
from glob import glob
from tqdm import tqdm
```

Any command-line input or output is written as follows:

```
epoch 01: precision: 0.064
epoch 02: precision: 0.086
epoch 03: precision: 0.106
epoch 04: precision: 0.127
epoch 05: precision: 0.138
epoch 06: precision: 0.145
epoch 07: precision: 0.150
epoch 08: precision: 0.149
epoch 09: precision: 0.151
epoch 10: precision: 0.152
```

Bold: Indicates a new term, an important word, or words that you see onscreen. For example, words in menus or dialog boxes appear in the text like this. Here is an example: "Select **System info** from the **Administration** panel."

Warnings or important notes appear like this.

Tips and tricks appear like this.

Get in touch

Feedback from our readers is always welcome.

General feedback: Email `feedback@packtpub.com` and mention the book title in the subject of your message. If you have questions about any aspect of this book, please email us at `questions@packtpub.com`.

Errata: Although we have taken every care to ensure the accuracy of our content, mistakes do happen. If you have found a mistake in this book, we would be grateful if you would report this to us. Please visit `www.packtpub.com/submit-errata`, selecting your book, clicking on the Errata Submission Form link, and entering the details.

Piracy: If you come across any illegal copies of our works in any form on the Internet, we would be grateful if you would provide us with the location address or website name. Please contact us at `copyright@packtpub.com` with a link to the material.

If you are interested in becoming an author: If there is a topic that you have expertise in and you are interested in either writing or contributing to a book, please visit `authors.packtpub.com`.

Reviews

Please leave a review. Once you have read and used this book, why not leave a review on the site that you purchased it from? Potential readers can then see and use your unbiased opinion to make purchase decisions, we at Packt can understand what you think about our products, and our authors can see your feedback on their book. Thank you!

For more information about Packt, please visit `packtpub.com`.

Recognizing traffic signs using Convnets

1

As the first project of the book, we'll try to work on a simple model where deep learning performs very well: traffic sign recognition. Briefly, given a color image of a traffic sign, the model should recognize which signal it is. We will explore the following areas:

- How the dataset is composed
- Which deep network to use
- How to pre-process the images in the dataset
- How to train and make predictions with an eye on performance

The dataset

Since we'll try to predict some traffic signs using their images, we will use a dataset built for the same purpose. Fortunately, researchers of Institute für Neuroinformatik, Germany, created a dataset containing almost 40,000 images, all different and related to 43 traffic signs. The dataset we will use is part of a competition named **German Traffic Sign Recognition Benchmark (GTSRB)**, which attempted to score the performance of multiple models for the same goal. The dataset is pretty old—2011! But it looks like a nice and well-organized dataset to start our project from.

The dataset used in this project is freely available at `http://benchmark.ini.rub.de/Dataset/GTSRB_Final_Training_Images.zip`.

Before you start running the code, please download the file and unpack it in the same directory as the code. After decompressing the archive, you'll have a new folder, named GTSRB, containing the dataset.

The authors of the book would like to thank those who worked on the dataset and made it open source.
Also, refer `http://cs231n.github.io/convolutional-networks/` to learn more about CNN.

Let's now see some examples:

"Speed limit 20 km/h":

"go straight or turn right":

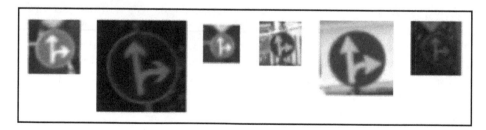

"roundabout":

As you can see, the signals don't have a uniform brightness (some are very dark and some others are very bright), they're different in size, the perspective is different, they have different backgrounds, and they may contain pieces of other traffic signs.

The dataset is organized in this way: all the images of the same label are inside the same folder. For example, inside the path `GTSRB/Final_Training/Images/00040/`, all the images have the same label, `40`. For the images with another label, `5`, open the folder `GTSRB/Final_Training/Images/00005/`. Note also that all the images are in PPM format, a lossless compression format for images with many open source decoders/encoders.

The CNN network

For our project, we will use a pretty simple network with the following architecture:

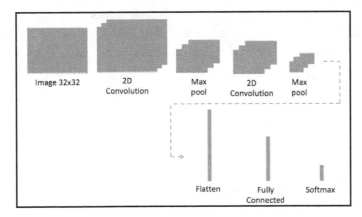

In this architecture, we still have the choice of:

- The number of filters and kernel size in the 2D convolution
- The kernel size in the **Max pool**
- The number of units in the **Fully Connected** layer
- The batch size, optimization algorithm, learning step (eventually, its decay rate), activation function of each layer, and number of epochs

Image preprocessing

The first operation of the model is reading the images and standardizing them. In fact, we cannot work with images of variable sizes; therefore, in this first step, we'll load the images and reshape them to a predefined size (32x32). Moreover, we will one-hot encode the labels in order to have a 43-dimensional array where only one element is enabled (it contains a 1), and we will convert the color space of the images from RGB to grayscale. By looking at the images, it seems obvious that the information we need is not contained in the color of the signal but in its shape and design.

Let's now open a Jupyter Notebook and place some code to do that. First of all, let's create some final variables containing the number of classes (43) and the size of the images after being resized:

```
N_CLASSES = 43
RESIZED_IMAGE = (32, 32)
```

Next, we will write a function that reads all the images given in a path, resize them to a predefined shape, convert them to grayscale, and also one-hot encode the label. In order to do that, we'll use a named tuple named `dataset`:

```
import matplotlib.pyplot as plt
import glob
from skimage.color import rgb2lab
from skimage.transform import resize
from collections import namedtuple
import numpy as np
np.random.seed(101)
%matplotlib inline
Dataset = namedtuple('Dataset', ['X', 'y'])
def to_tf_format(imgs):
    return np.stack([img[:, :, np.newaxis] for img in imgs],
axis=0).astype(np.float32)
def read_dataset_ppm(rootpath, n_labels, resize_to):
```

```
images = []
labels = []
for c in range(n_labels):
    full_path = rootpath + '/' + format(c, '05d') + '/'
    for img_name in glob.glob(full_path + "*.ppm"):
        img = plt.imread(img_name).astype(np.float32)
        img = rgb2lab(img / 255.0)[:,:,0]
        if resize_to:
            img = resize(img, resize_to, mode='reflect')
        label = np.zeros((n_labels, ), dtype=np.float32)
        label[c] = 1.0
       images.append(img.astype(np.float32))
        labels.append(label)
return Dataset(X = to_tf_format(images).astype(np.float32),
               y = np.matrix(labels).astype(np.float32))
dataset = read_dataset_ppm('GTSRB/Final_Training/Images', N_CLASSES,
RESIZED IMAGE)
print(dataset.X.shape)
print(dataset.y.shape)
```

Thanks to the skimage module, the operation of reading, transforming, and resizing is pretty easy. In our implementation, we decided to convert the original color space (RGB) to lab, then retaining only the luminance component. Note that another good conversion here is YUV, where only the "Y" component should be retained as a grayscale image.

Running the preceding cell gives this:

```
(39209, 32, 32, 1)
(39209, 43)
```

One note about the output format: the shape of the observation matrix X has four dimensions. The first indexes the observations (in this case, we have almost 40,000 of them); the other three dimensions contain the image (which is 32 pixel, by 32 pixels grayscale, that is, one-dimensional). This is the default shape when dealing with images in TensorFlow (see the code _tf_format function).

As for the label matrix, the rows index the observation, while the columns are the one-hot encoding of the label.

In order to have a better understanding of the observation matrix, let's print the feature vector of the first sample, together with its label:

```
plt.imshow(dataset.X[0, :, :, :].reshape(RESIZED_IMAGE)) #sample
print(dataset.y[0, :]) #label
```

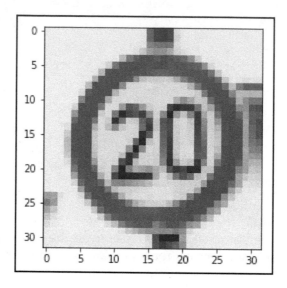

```
[[1. 0. 0. 0. 0. 0. 0. 0. 0. 0. 0. 0. 0. 0. 0. 0. 0. 0. 0. 0. 0. 0. 0. 0.
  0. 0. 0. 0. 0. 0. 0. 0. 0. 0. 0. 0. 0. 0. 0. 0. 0.]]
```

You can see that the image, that is, the feature vector, is 32x32. The label contains only one 1 in the first position.

Let's now print the last sample:

```
plt.imshow(dataset.X[-1, :, :, :].reshape(RESIZED_IMAGE)) #sample
print(dataset.y[-1, :]) #label
```

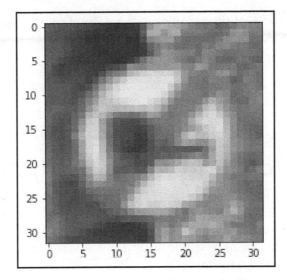

```
[[0. 0. 0. 0. 0. 0. 0. 0. 0. 0. 0. 0. 0. 0. 0. 0. 0. 0. 0. 0. 0. 0. 0. 0.
0. 0. 0. 0. 0. 0. 0. 0. 0. 0. 0. 0. 0. 0. 0. 0. 0. 1.]]
```

The feature vector size is the same (32x32), and the label vector contains one 1 in the last position.

These are the two pieces of information we need to create the model. Please, pay particular attention to the shapes, because they're crucial in deep learning while working with images; in contrast to classical machine learning observation matrices, here the X has four dimensions!

The last step of our preprocessing is the train/test split. We want to train our model on a subset of the dataset, and then measure the performance on the leftover samples, that is, the test set. To do so, let's use the function provided by `sklearn`:

```
from sklearn.model_selection import train_test_split
idx_train, idx_test = train_test_split(range(dataset.X.shape[0]),
test_size=0.25, random_state=101)
X_train = dataset.X[idx_train, :, :, :]
X_test = dataset.X[idx_test, :, :, :]
y_train = dataset.y[idx_train, :]
y_test = dataset.y[idx_test, :]
print(X_train.shape)
print(y_train.shape)
print(X_test.shape)
print(y_test.shape)
```

In this example, we'll use 75% of the samples in the dataset for training and the remaining 25% for testing. In fact, here's the output of the previous code:

```
(29406, 32, 32, 1)
(29406, 43)
(9803, 32, 32, 1)
(9803, 43)
```

Train the model and make predictions

The first thing to have is a function to create minibatches of training data. In fact, at each training iteration, we'd need to insert a minibatch of samples extracted from the training set. Here, we'll build a function that takes the observations, labels, and batch size as arguments and returns a minibatch generator. Furthermore, to introduce some variability in the training data, let's add another argument to the function, the possibility to shuffle the data to have different minibatches of data for each generator. Having different minibatches of data in each generator will force the model to learn the in-out connection and not memorize the sequence:

```python
def minibatcher(X, y, batch_size, shuffle):
    assert X.shape[0] == y.shape[0]
    n_samples = X.shape[0]
    if shuffle:
        idx = np.random.permutation(n_samples)
    else:
        idx = list(range(n_samples))
    for k in range(int(np.ceil(n_samples/batch_size))):
        from_idx = k*batch_size
        to_idx = (k+1)*batch_size
        yield X[idx[from_idx:to_idx], :, :, :], y[idx[from_idx:to_idx], :]
```

To test this function, let's print the shapes of minibatches while imposing `batch_size=10000`:

```python
for mb in minibatcher(X_train, y_train, 10000, True):
    print(mb[0].shape, mb[1].shape)
```

That prints the following:

```
(10000, 32, 32, 1) (10000, 43)
(10000, 32, 32, 1) (10000, 43)
(9406, 32, 32, 1) (9406, 43)
```

Unsurprisingly, the 29,406 samples in the training set are split into two minibatches of 10,000 elements, with the last one of `9406` elements. Of course, there are the same number of elements in the label matrix too.

It's now time to build the model, finally! Let's first build the blocks that will compose the network. We can start creating the fully connected layer with a variable number of units (it's an argument), without activation. We've decided to use Xavier initialization for the coefficients (weights) and 0-initialization for the biases to have the layer centered and scaled properly. The output is simply the multiplication of the input tensor by the weights, plus the bias. Please take a look at the dimensionality of the weights, which is defined dynamically, and therefore can be used anywhere in the network:

```
import tensorflow as tf
def fc_no_activation_layer(in_tensors, n_units):
w = tf.get_variable('fc_W',
    [in_tensors.get_shape()[1], n_units],
    tf.float32,
    tf.contrib.layers.xavier_initializer())
b = tf.get_variable('fc_B',
    [n_units, ],
    tf.float32,
    tf.constant_initializer(0.0))
return tf.matmul(in_tensors, w) + b
```

Let's now create the fully connected layer with activation; specifically, here we will use the leaky ReLU. As you can see, we can build this function using the previous one:

```
def fc_layer(in_tensors, n_units):
return tf.nn.leaky_relu(fc_no_activation_layer(in_tensors, n_units))
```

Finally, let's create a convolutional layer that takes as arguments the input data, kernel size, and number of filters (or units). We will use the same activations used in the fully connected layer. In this case, the output passes through a leaky ReLU activation:

```
def conv_layer(in_tensors, kernel_size, n_units):
w = tf.get_variable('conv_W',
    [kernel_size, kernel_size, in_tensors.get_shape()[3], n_units],
    tf.float32,
    tf.contrib.layers.xavier_initializer())
b = tf.get_variable('conv_B',
    [n_units, ],
    tf.float32,
    tf.constant_initializer(0.0))
return tf.nn.leaky_relu(tf.nn.conv2d(in_tensors, w, [1, 1, 1, 1], 'SAME') +
b)
```

Now, it's time to create a `maxpool_layer`. Here, the size of the window and the strides are both squares (quadrates):

```
def maxpool_layer(in_tensors, sampling):
    return tf.nn.max_pool(in_tensors, [1, sampling, sampling, 1], [1, sampling,
    sampling, 1], 'SAME')
```

The last thing to define is the dropout, used for regularizing the network. Pretty simple thing to create, but remember that dropout should only be used when training the network, and not when predicting the outputs; therefore, we need to have a conditional operator to define whether to apply dropouts or not:

```
def dropout(in_tensors, keep_proba, is_training):
    return tf.cond(is_training, lambda: tf.nn.dropout(in_tensors, keep_proba),
    lambda: in_tensors)
```

Finally, it's time to put it all together and create the model as previously defined. We'll create a model composed of the following layers:

1. 2D convolution, 5x5, 32 filters
2. 2D convolution, 5x5, 64 filters
3. Flattenizer
4. Fully connected later, 1,024 units
5. Dropout 40%
6. Fully connected layer, no activation
7. Softmax output

Here's the code:

```
def model(in_tensors, is_training):
# First layer: 5x5 2d-conv, 32 filters, 2x maxpool, 20% drouput
with tf.variable_scope('l1'):
    l1 = maxpool_layer(conv_layer(in_tensors, 5, 32), 2)
    l1_out = dropout(l1, 0.8, is_training)
# Second layer: 5x5 2d-conv, 64 filters, 2x maxpool, 20% drouput
with tf.variable_scope('l2'):
    l2 = maxpool_layer(conv_layer(l1_out, 5, 64), 2)
    l2_out = dropout(l2, 0.8, is_training)
with tf.variable_scope('flatten'):
    l2_out_flat = tf.layers.flatten(l2_out)
# Fully collected layer, 1024 neurons, 40% dropout
with tf.variable_scope('l3'):
    l3 = fc_layer(l2_out_flat, 1024)
    l3_out = dropout(l3, 0.6, is_training)
# Output
```

```
with tf.variable_scope('out'):
    out_tensors = fc_no_activation_layer(l3_out, N_CLASSES)
return out_tensors
```

And now, let's write the function to train the model on the training set and test the performance on the test set. Please note that all of the following code belongs to the function `train_model` function; it's broken down in to pieces just for simplicity of explanation.

The function takes as arguments (other than the training and test sets and their labels) the learning rate, the number of epochs, and the batch size, that is, number of images per training batch. First things first, some TensorFlow placeholders are defined: one for the minibatch of images, one for the minibatch of labels, and the last one to select whether to run for training or not (that's mainly used by the dropout layer):

```
from sklearn.metrics import classification_report, confusion_matrix
def train_model(X_train, y_train, X_test, y_test, learning_rate,
max_epochs, batch_size):
in_X_tensors_batch = tf.placeholder(tf.float32, shape = (None,
RESIZED_IMAGE[0], RESIZED_IMAGE[1], 1))
in_y_tensors_batch = tf.placeholder(tf.float32, shape = (None, N_CLASSES))
is_training = tf.placeholder(tf.bool)
```

Now, let's define the output, metric score, and optimizer. Here, we decided to use the `AdamOptimizer` and the cross entropy with `softmax(logits)` as loss:

```
logits = model(in_X_tensors_batch, is_training)
out_y_pred = tf.nn.softmax(logits)
loss_score = tf.nn.softmax_cross_entropy_with_logits(logits=logits,
labels=in_y_tensors_batch)
loss = tf.reduce_mean(loss_score)
optimizer = tf.train.AdamOptimizer(learning_rate).minimize(loss)
```

And finally, here's the code for training the model with minibatches:

```
with tf.Session() as session:
    session.run(tf.global_variables_initializer())
    for epoch in range(max_epochs):
     print("Epoch=", epoch)
      tf_score = []
      for mb in minibatcher(X_train, y_train, batch_size, shuffle = True):
        tf_output = session.run([optimizer, loss],
                           feed_dict = {in_X_tensors_batch : mb[0],
                                        in_y_tensors_batch :
b[1],
                                        is_training : True})
          tf_score.append(tf_output[1])
        print(" train_loss_score=", np.mean(tf_score))
```

After the training, it's time to test the model on the test set. Here, instead of sending a minibatch, we will use the whole test set. Mind it! `is_training` should be set as `False` since we don't want to use the dropouts:

```
print("TEST SET PERFORMANCE")
y_test_pred, test_loss = session.run([out_y_pred, loss],
                                    feed_dict = {in_X_tensors_batch :
X_test,
in_y_tensors_batch : y_test,
is_training : False})
```

And, as a final operation, let's print the classification report and plot the confusion matrix (and its `log2` version) to see the misclassifications:

```
print(" test_loss_score=", test_loss)
y_test_pred_classified = np.argmax(y_test_pred, axis=1).astype(np.int32)
y_test_true_classified = np.argmax(y_test, axis=1).astype(np.int32)
print(classification_report(y_test_true_classified,
y_test_pred_classified))
cm = confusion_matrix(y_test_true_classified, y_test_pred_classified)
plt.imshow(cm, interpolation='nearest', cmap=plt.cm.Blues)
plt.colorbar()
plt.tight_layout()
plt.show()
# And the log2 version, to enphasize the misclassifications
plt.imshow(np.log2(cm + 1), interpolation='nearest',
cmap=plt.get_cmap("tab20"))
plt.colorbar()
plt.tight_layout()
plt.show()
tf.reset_default_graph()
```

Finally, let's run the function with some parameters. Here, we will run the model with a learning step of 0.001, 256 samples per minibatch, and 10 epochs:

```
train_model(X_train, y_train, X_test, y_test, 0.001, 10, 256)
```

Here's the output:

```
Epoch= 0
train_loss_score= 3.4909246
Epoch= 1
train_loss_score= 0.5096467
Epoch= 2
train_loss_score= 0.26641673
Epoch= 3
train_loss_score= 0.1706828
```

```
Epoch= 4
train_loss_score= 0.12737551
Epoch= 5
train_loss_score= 0.09745725
Epoch= 6
train_loss_score= 0.07730477
Epoch= 7
train_loss_score= 0.06734192
Epoch= 8
train_loss_score= 0.06815668
Epoch= 9
train_loss_score= 0.060291935
TEST SET PERFORMANCE
test_loss_score= 0.04581982
```

This is followed by the classification report per class:

	precision	recall	f1-score	support
0	1.00	0.96	0.98	67
1	0.99	0.99	0.99	539
2	0.99	1.00	0.99	558
3	0.99	0.98	0.98	364
4	0.99	0.99	0.99	487
5	0.98	0.98	0.98	479
6	1.00	0.99	1.00	105
7	1.00	0.98	0.99	364
8	0.99	0.99	0.99	340
9	0.99	0.99	0.99	384
10	0.99	1.00	1.00	513
11	0.99	0.98	0.99	334
12	0.99	1.00	1.00	545
13	1.00	1.00	1.00	537
14	1.00	1.00	1.00	213
15	0.98	0.99	0.98	164
16	1.00	0.99	0.99	98
17	0.99	0.99	0.99	281
18	1.00	0.98	0.99	286
19	1.00	1.00	1.00	56
20	0.99	0.97	0.98	78
21	0.97	1.00	0.98	95
22	1.00	1.00	1.00	97
23	1.00	0.97	0.98	123
24	1.00	0.96	0.98	77
25	0.99	1.00	0.99	401
26	0.98	0.96	0.97	135
27	0.94	0.98	0.96	60
28	1.00	0.97	0.98	123
29	1.00	0.97	0.99	69

30	0.88	0.99	0.93	115
31	1.00	1.00	1.00	178
32	0.98	0.96	0.97	55
33	0.99	1.00	1.00	177
34	0.99	0.99	0.99	103
35	1.00	1.00	1.00	277
36	0.99	1.00	0.99	78
37	0.98	1.00	0.99	63
38	1.00	1.00	1.00	540
39	1.00	1.00	1.00	60
40	1.00	0.98	0.99	85
41	1.00	1.00	1.00	47
42	0.98	1.00	0.99	53
avg / total	0.99	0.99	0.99	9803

As you can see, we managed to reach a precision of 0.99 on the test set; also, recall and f1 score have the same score. The model looks stable since the loss in the test set is similar to the one reported in the last iteration; therefore, we're not over-fitting nor under-fitting.

And the confusion matrices:

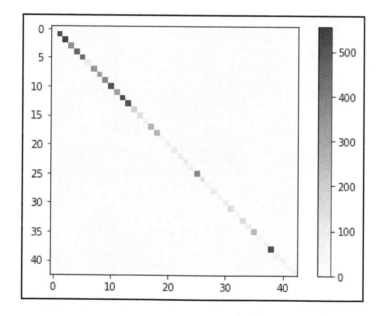

The following is the `log2` version of preceding screenshot:

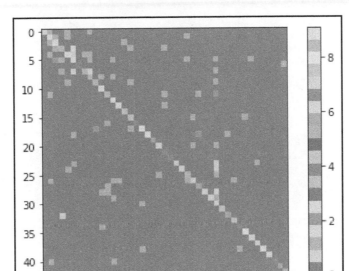

Follow-up questions

- Try adding/removing some CNN layers and/or fully connected layers. How does the performance change?
- This simple project is proof that dropouts are necessary for regularization. Change the dropout percentage and check the overfitting-underfitting in the output.
- Now, take a picture of multiple traffic signs in your city, and test the trained model in real life!

Summary

In this chapter, we saw how to recognize traffic signs using a convolutional neural network, or CNN. In the next chapter, we'll see something more complex that can be done with CNNs.

2
Annotating Images with Object Detection API

Computer vision has made great leaps forward in recent years because of deep learning, thus granting computers a higher grade in understanding visual scenes. The potentialities of deep learning in vision tasks are great: allowing a computer to visually perceive and understand its surroundings is a capability that opens the door to new artificial intelligence applications in both mobility (for instance, self-driving cars can detect if an appearing obstacle is a pedestrian, an animal or another vehicle from the camera mounted on the car and decide the correct course of action) and human-machine interaction in everyday-life contexts (for instance, allowing a robot to perceive surrounding objects and successfully interact with them).

After presenting ConvNets and how they operate in the first chapter, we now intend to create a quick, easy project that will help you to use a computer to understand images taken from cameras and mobile phones, using images collected from the Internet or directly from your computer's webcam. The goal of the project is to find the exact location and the type of the objects in an image.

In order to achieve such classification and localization, we will leverage the new TensorFlow object detection API, a Google project that is part of the larger TensorFlow models project which makes a series of pre-trained neural networks available off-the-shelf for you to wrap up in your own custom applications.

In this chapter, we are going to illustrate the following:

- The advantages of using the right data for your project
- A brief presentation of the TensorFlow object detection API
- How to annotate stored images for further use
- How to visually annotate a video using `moviepy`
- How to go real-time by annotating images from a webcam

The Microsoft common objects in context

Advances in application of deep learning in computer vision are often highly focalized on the kind of classification problems that can be summarized by challenges such as ImageNet (but also, for instance, PASCAL VOC - `http://host.robots.ox.ac.uk/pascal/VOC/voc2012/`) and the ConvNets suitable to crack it (Xception, VGG16, VGG19, ResNet50, InceptionV3, and MobileNet, just to quote the ones available in the well-known package Keras: `https://keras.io/applications/`).

Though deep learning networks based on ImageNet data are the actual state of the art, such networks can experience difficulties when faced with real-world applications. In fact, in practical applications, we have to process images that are quite different from the examples provided by ImageNet. In ImageNet the elements to be classified are clearly the only clear element present in the image, ideally set in an unobstructed way near the center of a neatly composed photo. In the reality of images taken from the field, objects are randomly scattered around, in often large number. All these objects are also quite different from each other, creating sometimes confusing settings. In addition, often objects of interest cannot be clearly and directly perceived because they are visually obstructed by other potentially interesting objects.

Please refer to the figure from the following mentioned reference:

Figure 1: A sample of images from ImageNet: they are arranged in a hierarchical structure, allowing working with both general or more specific classes.

SOURCE: DENG, Jia, et al. Imagenet: A large-scale hierarchical image database.
In: Computer Vision and Pattern Recognition, 2009. CVPR 2009. IEEE Conference on. IEEE, 2009. p. 248-255.

Realistic images contain multiple objects that sometimes can hardly be distinguished from a noisy background. Often you really cannot create interesting projects just by labeling an image with a tag simply telling you the object was recognized with the highest confidence.

In a real-world application, you really need to be able to do the following:

- Object classification of single and multiple instances when recognizing various objects, often of the same class
- Image localization, that is understanding where the objects are in the image
- Image segmentation, by marking each pixel in the images with a label: the type of object or background in order to be able to cut off interesting parts from the background.

The necessity to train a ConvNet to be able to achieve some or all of the preceding mentioned objectives led to the creation of the **Microsoft common objects in context (MS COCO)** dataset, as described in the paper: LIN, Tsung-Yi, et al. Microsoft coco: common objects in context. In: *European conference on computer vision.* Springer, Cham, 2014. p. 740-755. (You can read the original paper at the following link: https://arxiv.org/abs/1405.0312.) This dataset is made up of 91 common object categories, hierarchically ordered, with 82 of them having more than 5,000 labeled instances. The dataset totals 2,500,000 labeled objects distributed in 328,000 images.

Here are the classes that can be recognized in the MS COCO dataset:

```
{1: 'person', 2: 'bicycle', 3: 'car', 4: 'motorcycle', 5: 'airplane', 6:
'bus', 7: 'train', 8: 'truck', 9: 'boat', 10: 'traffic light', 11: 'fire
hydrant', 13: 'stop sign', 14: 'parking meter', 15: 'bench', 16: 'bird',
17: 'cat', 18: 'dog', 19: 'horse', 20: 'sheep', 21: 'cow', 22: 'elephant',
23: 'bear', 24: 'zebra', 25: 'giraffe', 27: 'backpack', 28: 'umbrella', 31:
'handbag', 32: 'tie', 33: 'suitcase', 34: 'frisbee', 35: 'skis', 36:
'snowboard', 37: 'sports ball', 38: 'kite', 39: 'baseball bat', 40:
'baseball glove', 41: 'skateboard', 42: 'surfboard', 43: 'tennis racket',
44: 'bottle', 46: 'wine glass', 47: 'cup', 48: 'fork', 49: 'knife', 50:
'spoon', 51: 'bowl', 52: 'banana', 53: 'apple', 54: 'sandwich', 55:
'orange', 56: 'broccoli', 57: 'carrot', 58: 'hot dog', 59: 'pizza', 60:
'donut', 61: 'cake', 62: 'chair', 63: 'couch', 64: 'potted plant', 65:
'bed', 67: 'dining table', 70: 'toilet', 72: 'tv', 73: 'laptop', 74:
'mouse', 75: 'remote', 76: 'keyboard', 77: 'cell phone', 78: 'microwave',
79: 'oven', 80: 'toaster', 81: 'sink', 82: 'refrigerator', 84: 'book', 85:
'clock', 86: 'vase', 87: 'scissors', 88: 'teddy bear', 89: 'hair drier',
90: 'toothbrush'}
```

Though the `ImageNet` dataset can present 1,000 object classes (as described at `https://gist.github.com/yrevar/942d3a0ac09ec9e5eb3a`) distributed in 14,197,122 images, MS COCO offers the peculiar feature of multiple objects distributed in a minor number of images (the dataset has been gathered using Amazon Mechanical Turk, a somehow more costly approach but shared by ImageNet, too). Given such premises, the MS COCO images can be considered very good examples of *contextual relationships and non-iconic object views*, since objects are arranged in realistic positions and settings. This can be verified from this comparative example taken from the MS COCO paper previously mentioned:

Figure 2: Examples of iconic and non-iconic images. SOURCE: *LIN, Tsung-Yi, et al. Microsoft coco: common objects in context. In: European conference on computer vision. Springer, Cham, 2014. p. 740-755.*

In addition, the image annotation of MS COCO is particularly rich, offering the coordinates of the contours of the objects present in the images. The contours can be easily translated into bounding boxes, boxes that delimit the part of the image where the object is located. This is a rougher way to locate objects than the original one used for training MS COCO itself, based on pixel segmentation.

In the following figure, a crowded row has been carefully segmented by defining notable areas in an image and creating a textual description of those areas. In machine learning terms, this translates to assigning a label to every pixel in the image and trying to predict the segmentation class (corresponding to the textual description). Historically this has been done with image processing until ImageNet 2012 when deep learning proved a much more efficient solution.

2012 marked a milestone in computer vision because for the first time a deep learning solution provided many superior results than any technique used before: *KRIZHEVSKY, Alex; SUTSKEVER, Ilya; HINTON, Geoffrey E. Imagenet classification with deep convolutional neural networks. In: Advances in neural information processing systems. 2012. p. 1097-1105* (`https://papers.nips.cc/paper/4824-imagenet-classification-with-deep-convolutional-neural-networks.pdf`).

Image segmentation is particularly useful for various tasks, such as:

- Highlighting the important objects in an image, for instance in medical applications detecting areas with illness
- Locating objects in an image so that a robot can pick them up or manipulate them
- Helping with road scene understanding for self-driving cars or drones to navigate
- Editing images by automatically extracting portions of an image or removing a background

This kind of annotation is very expensive (hence the reduced number of examples in MS COCO) because it has to be done completely by hand and it requires attention and precision. There are some tools to help with annotating by segmenting an image. You can find a comprehensive list at `https://stackoverflow.com/questions/8317787/image-labelling-and-annotation-tool`. However, we can suggest the following two tools, if you want to annotate by segmentation images by yourself:

- LabelImg `https://github.com/tzutalin/labelImg`
- FastAnnotationTool `https://github.com/christopher5106/FastAnnotationTool`

All these tools can also be used for the much simpler annotation by bounding boxes, and they really can come in handy if you want to retrain a model from MS COCO using a class of your own. (We will mention this again at the end of the chapter):

A pixel segmentation of an image used in MS COCO training phase

The TensorFlow object detection API

As a way of boosting the capabilities of the research community, Google research scientists and software engineers often develop state-of-the-art models and make them available to the public instead of keeping them proprietary. As described in the Google research blog post, `https://research.googleblog.com/2017/06/supercharge-your-computer-vision-models.html`, on October 2016, Google's in-house object detection system placed first in the COCO detection challenge, which is focused on finding objects in images (estimating the chance that an object is in this position) and their bounding boxes (you can read the technical details of their solution at `https://arxiv.org/abs/1611.10012`).

The Google solution has not only contributed to quite a few papers and been put to work in some Google products (Nest Cam - `https://nest.com/cameras/nest-aware/`, Image Search - `https://www.blog.google/products/search/now-image-search-can-jump-start-your-search-style/`, and Street View - `https://research.googleblog.com/2017/05/updating-google-maps-with-deep-learning.html`), but has also been released to the larger public as an open source framework built on top of TensorFlow.

The framework offers some useful functions and these five pre-trained different models (constituting the so-called pre-trained Model Zoo):

- Single Shot Multibox Detector (SSD) with MobileNets
- SSD with Inception V2
- Region-Based Fully Convolutional Networks (R-FCN) with Resnet 101
- Faster R-CNN with Resnet 101
- Faster R-CNN with Inception Resnet v2

The models are in growing order of precision in detection and slower speed of execution of the detection process. MobileNets, Inception and Resnet refer to different types of CNN network architectures (MobileNets, as the name suggests, it is the architecture optimized for mobile phones, smaller in size and faster in execution). We have discussed CNN architecture in the previous chapter, so you can refer there for more insight on such architectures. If you need a refresher, this blog post by Joice Xu can help you revise the topic in an easy way: `https://towardsdatascience.com/an-intuitive-guide-to-deep-network-architectures-65fdc477db41`.

Single Shot Multibox Detector (SSD), **Region-Based Fully convolutional networks (R-FCN)** and **Faster Region-based convolutional neural networks (Faster R-CNN)** are instead the different models to detect multiple objects in images. In the next paragraph, we are going to explain something about how they effectively work.

Depending on your application, you can decide on the most suitable model for you (you have to experiment a bit), or aggregate results from multiple models in order to get better results (as done by the researchers at Google in order to win the COCO competition).

Grasping the basics of R-CNN, R-FCN and SSD models

Even if you have clear in mind how a CNN can manage to classify an image, it could be less obvious for you how a neural network can localize multiple objects into an image by defining its bounding box (a rectangular perimeter bounding the object itself). The first and easiest solution that you may imagine could be to have a sliding window and apply the CNN on each window, but that could be really computationally expensive for most real-world applications (if you are powering the vision of a self-driving car, you do want it to recognize the obstacle and stop before hitting it).

You can find more about the sliding windows approach for object detection in this blog post by Adrian Rosebrock: `https://www.pyimagesearch.com/2015/03/23/sliding-windows-for-object-detection-with-python-and-opencv/` that makes an effective example by pairing it with image pyramid.

Though reasonably intuitive, because of its complexity and being computationally cumbersome (exhaustive and working at different image scales), the sliding window has quite a few limits, and an alternative preferred solution has immediately been found in the *region proposal* algorithms. Such algorithms use image segmentation (segmenting, that is dividing the image into areas based on the main color differences between areas themselves) in order to create a tentative enumeration of possible bounding boxes in an image. You can find a detailed explanation of how the algorithm works in this post by Satya Mallik: `https://www.learnopencv.com/selective-search-for-object-detection-cpp-python/`. The point is that region proposal algorithms suggest a limited number of boxes to be evaluated, a much smaller one than the one proposed by an exhaustive sliding windows algorithm. That allowed them to be applied in the first R-CNN, Region-based convolutional neural networks, which worked by:

1. finding a few hundreds or thousands of regions of interest in the image, thanks to a region proposal algorithm
2. Process by a CNN each region of interest, in order to create features of each area
3. Use the features to classify the region by a support vector machine and a linear regression to compute bounding boxes that are more precise.

The immediate evolution of R-CNN was Fast R-CNN which made things even speedier because:

1. it processed all the image at once with CNN, transformed it and applied the region proposal on the transformation. This cut down the CNN processing from a few thousand calls to a single one.
2. Instead of using an SVM for classification, it used a soft-max layer and a linear classifier, thus simply extending the CNN instead of passing the data to a different model.

In essence, by using a Fast R-CNN we had again a single classification network characterized by a special filtering and selecting layer, the region proposal layer, based on a non-neural network algorithm. Faster R-CNN even changed that layer, by replacing it with a region proposal neural network. That made the model even more complicated but most effective and faster than any previous method.

R-FCN, anyway, are even faster than Faster R-CNN, because they are fully convolutional networks, that don't use any fully connected layer after their convolutional layers. They are end-to-end networks: from input by convolutions to output. That simply makes them even faster (they have a much lesser number of weights than CNN with a fully connect layer at their end). But their speed comes at a price, they have not been characterized anymore by image invariance (CNN can figure out the class of an object, no matter how the object is rotated). Faster R-CNN supplements this weakness by a position-sensitive score map, that is a way to check if parts of the original image processed by the FCN correspond to parts of the class to be classified. In easy words, they don't compare to classes, but to part of classes. For instance, they don't classify a dog, but a dog-upper-left part, a dog-lower-right-part and so on. This approach allows to figure out if there is a dog in a part of the image, no matter how it is orientated. Clearly, this speedier approach comes at the cost of less precision, because position-sensitive score maps cannot supplement all the original CNN characteristics.

Finally, we have SSD (Single Shot Detector). Here the speed is even greater because the network simultaneously predicts the bounding box location and its class as it processes the image. SSD computes a large number of bounding boxes, by simply skipping the region proposal phase. It just reduces highly-overlapping boxes, but still, it processes the largest number of bounding boxes compared to all the model we mentioned up-so-far. Its speed is because as it delimits each bounding box it also classifies it: by doing everything in one shot, it has the fastest speed, though performs in a quite comparable way.

Another short article by Joice Xu can provide you with more details on the detection models we discussed up so far: `https://towardsdatascience.com/deep-learning-for-object-detection-a-comprehensive-review-73930816d8d9`

Summing up all the discussion, in order to choose the network you have to consider that you are combining different CNN architectures in classification power and network complexity and different detection models. It is their combined effect to determinate the capability of the network to spot objects, to correctly classify them, and to do all that in a timely fashion.

If you desire to have more reference in regard to the speed and precision of the models we have briefly explained, you can consult: *Speed/accuracy trade-offs for modern convolutional object detectors*. Huang J, Rathod V, Sun C, Zhu M, Korattikara A, Fathi A, Fischer I, Wojna Z, Song Y, Guadarrama S, Murphy K, CVPR 2017: `http://openaccess.thecvf.com/content_cvpr_2017/papers/Huang_SpeedAccuracy_Trade-Offs_for_CVPR_2017_paper.pdf` Yet, we cannot but advise to just test them in practice for your application, evaluating is they are good enough for the task and if they execute in a reasonable time. Then it is just a matter of a trade-off you have to best decide for your application.

Presenting our project plan

Given such a powerful tool made available by TensorFlow, our plan is to leverage its API by creating a class you can use for annotating images both visually and in an external file. By annotating, we mean the following:

- Pointing out the objects in an image (as recognized by a model trained on MS COCO)
- Reporting the level of confidence in the object recognition (we will consider only objects above a minimum probability threshold, which is set to 0.25, based on the *speed/accuracy trade-offs for modern convolutional object detector*s discussed in the paper previously mentioned)
- Outputting the coordinates of two opposite vertices of the bounding box for each image
- Saving all such information in a text file in JSON format
- Visually representing the bounding box on the original image, if required

In order to achieve such objectives, we need to:

1. Download one of the pre-trained models (available in `.pb` format - `protobuf`) and make it available in-memory as a TensorFlow session.
2. Reformulate the helper code provided by TensorFlow in order to make it easier to load labels, categories, and visualization tools by a class that can be easily imported into your scripts.
3. Prepare a simple script to demonstrate its usage with single images, videos, and videos captured from a webcam.

We start by setting up an environment suitable for the project.

Setting up an environment suitable for the project

You don't need any specialized environment in order to run the project, though we warmly suggest installing Anaconda `conda` and creating a separated environment for the project. The instructions to run if `conda` is available on your system are as follows:

```
conda create -n TensorFlow_api python=3.5 numpy pillow
activate TensorFlow_api
```

After activating the environment, you can install some other packages that require a `pip install` command or a `conda install` command pointing to another repository (`menpo`, `conda-forge`):

```
pip install TensorFlow-gpu
conda install -c menpo opencv
conda install -c conda-forge imageio
pip install tqdm, moviepy
```

In case you prefer another way of running this project, just consider that you need `numpy`, `pillow`, `TensorFlow`, `opencv`, `imageio`, `tqdm`, and `moviepy` in order to run it successfully.

For everything to run smoothly, you also need to create a directory for your project and to save in it the `object_detection` directory of the TensorFlow object detection API project (`https://github.com/tensorflow/models/tree/master/research/object_detection`).

You can simply obtain that by using the `git` command on the entire TensorFlow models' project and selectively pulling only that directory. This is possible if your Git version is 1.7.0 (February 2012) or above:

```
mkdir api_project
cd api_project
git init
git remote add -f origin https://github.com/tensorflow/models.git
```

These commands will fetch all the objects in the TensorFlow models project, but it won't check them out. By following those previous commands by:

```
git config core.sparseCheckout true
echo "research/object_detection/*" >> .git/info/sparse-checkout
git pull origin master
```

You will now have only the `object_detection` directory and its contents as *checked out* on your filesystem and no other directories or files present.

Just keep in mind that the project will need to access the `object_detection` directory, thus you will have to keep the project script in the very same directory of `object_detection` directory. In order to use the script outside of its directory, you will need to access it using a full path.

Protobuf compilation

The TensorFlow object detection API uses *protobufs*, protocol buffers -- Google's data interchange format (`https://github.com/google/protobuf`), to configure the models and their training parameters. Before the framework can be used, the protobuf libraries must be compiled, and that requires different steps if you are in a Unix (Linux or Mac) or Windows OS environment.

Windows installation

First, unpack the `protoc-3.2.0-win32.zip` that can be found at `https://github.com/google/protobuf/releases` into the project folder. Now you should have a new `protoc-3.4.0-win32` directory, containing a `readme.txt` and two directories, `bin`, and `include`. The folders contain a precompiled binary version of the protocol buffer compiler (*protoc*). All you have to do is add the `protoc-3.4.0-win32` directory to the system path.

After adding it to the system path, you can execute the following command:

```
protoc-3.4.0-win32/bin/protoc.exe object_detection/protos/*.proto --
python_out=.
```

That should be enough to allow the TensorFlow object detection API to work on your computer.

Unix installation

For Unix environments, the installation procedure can be done using shell commands, just follow the instructions available at `https://github.com/tensorflow/models/blob/master/ research/object_detection/g3doc/installation.md`.

Provisioning of the project code

We start scripting our project in the file `tensorflow_detection.py` by loading the necessary packages:

```
import os
import numpy as np
import tensorflow as tf
import six.moves.urllib as urllib
import tarfile
from PIL import Image
from tqdm import tqdm
from time import gmtime, strftime
import json
import cv2
```

In order to be able to process videos, apart from OpenCV 3, we also need the `moviepy` package. The package `moviepy` is a project that can be found at `http://zulko.github.io/ moviepy/` and freely used since it is distributed with an MIT license. As described on its home page, `moviepy` is a tool for video editing (that is cuts, concatenations, title insertions), video compositing (non-linear editing), video processing, or to create advanced effects.

The package operates with the most common video formats, including the GIF format. It needs the FFmpeg converter (https://www.ffmpeg.org/) in order to properly operate, therefore at its first usage it will fail to start and will download FFmpeg as a plugin using imageio:

```
try:
    from moviepy.editor import VideoFileClip
except:
    # If FFmpeg (https://www.ffmpeg.org/) is not found
    # on the computer, it will be downloaded from Internet
    # (an Internet connect is needed)
    import imageio
    imageio.plugins.ffmpeg.download()
    from moviepy.editor import VideoFileClip
```

Finally, we require two useful functions available in the object_detection directory from the TensorFlow API project:

```
from object_detection.utils import label_map_util
from object_detection.utils import visualization_utils as vis_util
```

We define the DetectionObj class and its init procedure. The initialization expects only a parameter and the model name (which is initially set to the less well performing, but faster and more lightweight model, the SSD MobileNet), but a few internal parameters can be changed to suit your use of the class:

- self.TARGET_PATH pointing out the directory where you want the processed annotations to be saved.
- self.THRESHOLD fixing the probability threshold to be noticed by the annotation process. In fact, any model of the suit will output many low probability detections in every image. Objects with too low probabilities are usually false alarms, for such reasons you fix a threshold and ignore such highly unlikely detection. As a rule of thumb, 0.25 is a good threshold in order to spot uncertain objects due to almost total occlusion or visual clutter.

```
class DetectionObj(object):
    """
    DetectionObj is a class suitable to leverage
    Google Tensorflow detection API for image annotation from
    different sources: files, images acquired by own's webcam,
    videos.
    """

    def __init__(self, model='ssd_mobilenet_v1_coco_11_06_2017'):
        """
```

```
The instructions to be run when the class is instantiated
"""

# Path where the Python script is being run
self.CURRENT_PATH = os.getcwd()

# Path where to save the annotations (it can be modified)
self.TARGET_PATH = self.CURRENT_PATH

# Selection of pre-trained detection models
# from the Tensorflow Model Zoo
self.MODELS = ["ssd_mobilenet_v1_coco_11_06_2017",
               "ssd_inception_v2_coco_11_06_2017",
               "rfcn_resnet101_coco_11_06_2017",
               "faster_rcnn_resnet101_coco_11_06_2017",
               "faster_rcnn_inception_resnet_v2_atrous_\
                coco_11_06_2017"]

# Setting a threshold for detecting an object by the models
self.THRESHOLD = 0.25 # Most used threshold in practice

# Checking if the desired pre-trained detection model is available
if model in self.MODELS:
    self.MODEL_NAME = model
else:
    # Otherwise revert to a default model
    print("Model not available, reverted to default",
self.MODELS[0])
    self.MODEL_NAME = self.MODELS[0]

# The file name of the Tensorflow frozen model
    self.CKPT_FILE = os.path.join(self.CURRENT_PATH,
'object_detection',
                                  self.MODEL_NAME,
                                  'frozen_inference_graph.pb')

# Attempting loading the detection model,
# if not available on disk, it will be
# downloaded from Internet
# (an Internet connection is required)
try:
    self.DETECTION_GRAPH = self.load_frozen_model()
except:
    print ('Couldn\'t find', self.MODEL_NAME)
    self.download_frozen_model()
    self.DETECTION_GRAPH = self.load_frozen_model()

# Loading the labels of the classes recognized by the detection
```

```
model
        self.NUM_CLASSES = 90
        path_to_labels = os.path.join(self.CURRENT_PATH,
                                'object_detection', 'data',
                                'mscoco_label_map.pbtxt')
        label_mapping = \
                label_map_util.load_labelmap(path_to_labels)
        extracted_categories = \
                label_map_util.convert_label_map_to_categories(
                label_mapping, max_num_classes=self.NUM_CLASSES,
                                use_display_name=True)
        self.LABELS = {item['id']: item['name'] \
                for item in extracted_categories}
        self.CATEGORY_INDEX = label_map_util.create_category_index\
(extracted_categories)

        # Starting the tensorflow session
        self.TF_SESSION = tf.Session(graph=self.DETECTION_GRAPH)
```

As a convenient variable to have access to, you have the `self.LABELS` containing a dictionary relating a class numerical code to its textual representation. Moreover, the `init` procedure will have the `TensorFlow` session loaded, open, and ready to be used at `self.TF_SESSION`.

The functions `load_frozen_model` and `download_frozen_model` will help the `init` procedure to load the chosen frozen model from disk and, if not available, will help to download it as a TAR file from the internet and unzip it in the proper directory (which is `object_detection`):

```
def load_frozen_model(self):
    """
    Loading frozen detection model in ckpt
    file from disk to memory
    """

    detection_graph = tf.Graph()
    with detection_graph.as_default():
        od_graph_def = tf.GraphDef()
        with tf.gfile.GFile(self.CKPT_FILE, 'rb') as fid:
            serialized_graph = fid.read()
            od_graph_def.ParseFromString(serialized_graph)
            tf.import_graph_def(od_graph_def, name='')

    return detection_graph
```

The function `download_frozen_model` leverages the `tqdm` package in order to visualize its progress as it downloads the new models from the internet. Some models are quite large (over 600 MB) and it may take a long time. Providing visual feedback on the progress and estimated time of completion will allow the user to be more confident about the progression of the operations:

```python
def download_frozen_model(self):
    """
    Downloading frozen detection model from Internet
    when not available on disk
    """
    def my_hook(t):
        """
        Wrapping tqdm instance in order to monitor URLopener
        """
        last_b = [0]

        def inner(b=1, bsize=1, tsize=None):
            if tsize is not None:
                t.total = tsize
            t.update((b - last_b[0]) * bsize)
            last_b[0] = b
        return inner

    # Opening the url where to find the model
    model_filename = self.MODEL_NAME + '.tar.gz'
    download_url = \
        'http://download.tensorflow.org/models/object_detection/'
    opener = urllib.request.URLopener()

    # Downloading the model with tqdm estimations of completion
    print('Downloading ...')
    with tqdm() as t:
        opener.retrieve(download_url + model_filename,
                        model_filename, reporthook=my_hook(t))

    # Extracting the model from the downloaded tar file
    print ('Extracting ...')
    tar_file = tarfile.open(model_filename)
    for file in tar_file.getmembers():
        file_name = os.path.basename(file.name)
        if 'frozen_inference_graph.pb' in file_name:
            tar_file.extract(file,
                os.path.join(self.CURRENT_PATH,
                             'object_detection'))
```

The following two functions, `load_image_from_disk` and `load_image_into_numpy_array`, are necessary in order to pick an image from disk and transform it into a Numpy array suitable for being processed by any of the TensorFlow models available in this project:

```
def load_image_from_disk(self, image_path):
    return Image.open(image_path)

def load_image_into_numpy_array(self, image):
    try:
        (im_width, im_height) = image.size
        return np.array(image.getdata()).reshape(
            (im_height, im_width, 3)).astype(np.uint8)
    except:
        # If the previous procedure fails, we expect the
        # image is already a Numpy ndarray
        return image
```

The `detect` function, instead, is the core of the classification functionality of the class. The function just expects lists of images to be processed. A Boolean flag, `annotate_on_image`, just tells the script to visualize the bounding box and the annotation directly on the provided images.

Such a function is able to process images of different sizes, one after the other, but it necessitates processing each one singularly. Therefore, it takes each image and expands the dimension of the array, adding a further dimension. This is necessary because the model expects an array of size: number of images * height * width * depth.

Note, we could pack all the batch images to be predicted into a single matrix. That would work fine, and it would be faster if all the images were of the same height and width, which is an assumption that our project does not make, hence the single image processing.

We then take a few tensors in the model by name (`detection_boxes`, `detection_scores`, `detection_classes`, `num_detections`), which are exactly the outputs we expect from the model, and we feed everything to the input tensor, `image_tensor`, which will normalize the image in a suitable form for the layers of the model to process.

The results are gathered into a list and the images are processed with the detection boxes and represented if required:

```
def detect(self, images, annotate_on_image=True):
    """
    Processing a list of images, feeding it
    into the detection model and getting from it scores,
```

```
bounding boxes and predicted classes present
in the images
"""
if type(images) is not list:
    images = [images]
results = list()
for image in images:
    # the array based representation of the image will
    # be used later in order to prepare the resulting
    # image with boxes and labels on it.
    image_np = self.load_image_into_numpy_array(image)

    # Expand dimensions since the model expects images
    # to have shape: [1, None, None, 3]
    image_np_expanded = np.expand_dims(image_np, axis=0)
    image_tensor = \
            self.DETECTION_GRAPH.get_tensor_by_name(
                                      'image_tensor:0')

    # Each box represents a part of the image where a
    # particular object was detected.
    boxes = self.DETECTION_GRAPH.get_tensor_by_name(
                                  'detection_boxes:0')

    # Each score represent how level of confidence
    # for each of the objects. Score could be shown
    # on the result image, together with the class label.
    scores = self.DETECTION_GRAPH.get_tensor_by_name(
                                  'detection_scores:0')
    classes = self.DETECTION_GRAPH.get_tensor_by_name(
                                  'detection_classes:0')
    num_detections = \
            self.DETECTION_GRAPH.get_tensor_by_name(
                                  'num_detections:0')

  # Actual detection happens here
  (boxes, scores, classes, num_detections) = \
            self.TF_SESSION.run(
            [boxes, scores, classes, num_detections],
            feed_dict={image_tensor: image_np_expanded})

if annotate_on_image:
    new_image = self.detection_on_image(
                    image_np, boxes, scores, classes)
    results.append((new_image, boxes,
                    scores, classes, num_detections))
else:
    results.append((image_np, boxes,
```

```
                                    scores, classes, num_detections))
        return results
```

The function `detection_on_image` just processes the results from the `detect` function and returns a new image enriched by bounding boxes which will be represented on screen by the function `visualize_image` (You can adjust the latency parameter, which corresponds to the seconds the image will stay on screen before the script passes to process another image).

```
    def detection_on_image(self, image_np, boxes, scores,
                        classes):
        """
        Put detection boxes on the images over
        the detected classes
        """
        vis_util.visualize_boxes_and_labels_on_image_array(
            image_np,
            np.squeeze(boxes),
            np.squeeze(classes).astype(np.int32),
            np.squeeze(scores),
            self.CATEGORY_INDEX,
            use_normalized_coordinates=True,
            line_thickness=8)
        return image_np
```

The function `visualize_image` offers a few parameters that could be modified in order to suit your needs in this project. First of all, `image_size` provides the desired size of the image to be represented on screen. Larger or shorter images are therefore modified in order to partially resemble this prescribed size. The `latency` parameter, instead, will define the time in seconds that each image will be represented on the screen, thus locking the object detection procedure, before moving to the next one. Finally, the `bluish_correction` is just a correction to be applied when images are offered in the **BGR** format (in this format the color channels are arranged in the order: **blue-green-red** and it is the standard for the OpenCV library: `https://stackoverflow.com/questions/14556545/why-opencv-using-bgr-colour-space-instead-of-rgb`), instead of the **RGB** (**red-green-blue**), which is the image format the model is expecting:

```
    def visualize_image(self, image_np, image_size=(400, 300),
                        latency=3, bluish_correction=True):
        height, width, depth = image_np.shape
        reshaper = height / float(image_size[0])
        width = int(width / reshaper)
        height = int(height / reshaper)
        id_img = 'preview_' + str(np.sum(image_np))
        cv2.startWindowThread()
```

```
cv2.namedWindow(id_img, cv2.WINDOW_NORMAL)
cv2.resizeWindow(id_img, width, height)
if bluish_correction:
    RGB_img = cv2.cvtColor(image_np, cv2.COLOR_BGR2RGB)
    cv2.imshow(id_img, RGB_img)
else:
    cv2.imshow(id_img, image_np)
cv2.waitKey(latency*1000)
```

Annotations are prepared and written to disk by the `serialize_annotations` function, which will create single JSON files containing, for each image, the data regarding the detected classes, the vertices of the bounding boxes, and the detection confidence. For instance, this is the result from a detection on a dog's photo:

```
"{"scores": [0.9092628359794617], "classes": ["dog"], "boxes":
[[0.025611668825149536, 0.22220897674560547, 0.9930437803268433,
0.7734537720680237]]}"
```

The JSON points out the detected class, a single dog, the level of confidence (about 0.91 confidence), and the vertices of the bounding box, and expresses as percentages the height and width of the image (they are therefore relative, not absolute pixel points):

```
    def serialize_annotations(self, boxes, scores, classes,
filename='data.json'):
        """
        Saving annotations to disk, to a JSON file
        """

        threshold = self.THRESHOLD
        valid = [position for position, score in enumerate(
                                        scores[0]) if score >
threshold]
        if len(valid) > 0:
            valid_scores = scores[0][valid].tolist()
            valid_boxes  = boxes[0][valid].tolist()
            valid_class = [self.LABELS[int(
                                a_class)] for a_class in
classes[0][valid]]
            with open(filename, 'w') as outfile:
                json_data = {'classes': valid_class,
                    'boxes':valid_boxes, 'scores': valid_scores})
                json.dump(json_data, outfile)
```

The function `get_time` conveniently transforms the actual time into a string that can be used in a filename:

```
def get_time(self):
    """
    Returning a string reporting the actual date and time
    """
    return strftime("%Y-%m-%d_%Hh%Mm%Ss", gmtime())
```

Finally, we prepare three detection pipelines, for images, videos, and webcam. The pipeline for images loads each image into a list. The pipeline for videos lets the `VideoFileClip` module from `moviepy` do all the heavy lifting after simply passing the `detect` function appropriately wrapped in the `annotate_photogram` function. Finally, the pipeline for webcam capture relies on a simple `capture_webcam` function that, based on OpenCV's VideoCapture, records a number of snapshots from the webcam returning just the last (the operation takes into account the time necessary for the webcam before adjusting to the light levels of the environment):

```
def annotate_photogram(self, photogram):
    """
    Annotating a video's photogram with bounding boxes
    over detected classes
    """
    new_photogram, boxes, scores, classes, num_detections =
self.detect(photogram)[0]
    return new_photogram
```

The `capture_webcam` function will acquire an image from your webcam using the `cv2.VideoCapture` functionality (http://docs.opencv.org/3.0-beta/modules/videoio/doc/reading_and_writing_video.html). As webcams have first to adjusts to the light conditions present in the environment where the picture is taken, the procedure discards a number of initial shots, before taking the shot that will be used in the object detection procedure. In this way, the webcam has all the time to adjust its light settings, :

```
def capture_webcam(self):
    """
    Capturing an image from the integrated webcam
    """

    def get_image(device):
        """
        Internal function to capture a single image
        from the camera and return it in PIL format
        """
```

```
        retval, im = device.read()
        return im

    # Setting the integrated webcam
    camera_port = 0

    # Number of frames to discard as the camera
    # adjusts to the surrounding lights
    ramp_frames = 30

    # Initializing the webcam by cv2.VideoCapture
    camera = cv2.VideoCapture(camera_port)

    # Ramping the camera - all these frames will be
    # discarded as the camera adjust to the right light levels
    print("Setting the webcam")
    for i in range(ramp_frames):
        _ = get_image(camera)

    # Taking the snapshot
    print("Now taking a snapshot ... ", end='')
    camera_capture = get_image(camera)
    print('Done')

    # releasing the camera and making it reusable
    del (camera)
    return camera_capture
```

The `file_pipeline` comprises all the steps necessary to load images from storage and visualize/annotate them:

1. Loading images from disk.
2. Applying object detection on the loaded images.
3. Writing the annotations for each image in a JSON file.
4. If required by the Boolean parameter `visualize`, represent the images with its bounding boxes on the computer's screen:

```
def file_pipeline(self, images, visualize=True):
    """
    A pipeline for processing and annotating lists of
    images to load from disk
    """
    if type(images) is not list:
        images = [images]
    for filename in images:
        single_image = self.load_image_from_disk(filename)
```

```
            for new_image, boxes, scores, classes, num_detections in
    self.detect(single_image):
                self.serialize_annotations(boxes, scores, classes,
                                            filename=filename + ".json")
            if visualize:
                self.visualize_image(new_image)
```

The `video_pipeline` simply arranges all the steps necessary to annotate a video with bounding boxes and, after completing the operation, saves it to disk:

```
def video_pipeline(self, video, audio=False):
    """
    A pipeline to process a video on disk and annotating it
    by bounding box. The output is a new annotated video.
    """
    clip = VideoFileClip(video)
    new_video = video.split('/')
    new_video[-1] = "annotated_" + new_video[-1]
    new_video = '/'.join(new_video)
    print("Saving annotated video to", new_video)
    video_annotation = clip.fl_image(self.annotate_photogram)
    video_annotation.write_videofile(new_video, audio=audio)
```

The `webcam_pipeline` is the function that arranges all the steps when you want to annotate an image acquired from your webcam:

1. Captures an image from the webcam.
2. Saves the captured image to disk (using `cv2.imwrite` which has the advantage of writing different image formats based on the target filename, see at: `http:// docs.opencv.org/3.0-beta/modules/imgcodecs/doc/reading_and_writing_ images.html`
3. Applies object detection on the image.
4. Saves the annotation JSON file.
5. Represents visually the image with bounding boxes:

```
def webcam_pipeline(self):
    """
    A pipeline to process an image acquired by the internal webcam
    and annotate it, saving a JSON file to disk
    """
    webcam_image = self.capture_webcam()
    filename = "webcam_" + self.get_time()
    saving_path = os.path.join(self.CURRENT_PATH, filename + ".jpg")
    cv2.imwrite(saving_path, webcam_image)
    new_image, boxes, scores, classes, num_detections =
                                    self.detect(webcam_image)[0]
```

```
        json_obj = {'classes': classes, 'boxes':boxes, 'scores':scores}
        self.serialize_annotations(boxes, scores, classes,
filename=filename+".json")
        self.visualize_image(new_image, bluish_correction=False)
```

Some simple applications

As a concluding paragraph of the code provisioning, we demonstrate just three simple scripts leveraging the three different sources used by our project: files, videos, webcam.

Our first testing script aims at annotating and visualizing three images after importing the class DetectionObj from the local directory (In cases where you operate from another directory, the import won't work unless you add the project directory to the Python path).

In order to add a directory to the Python path in your script, you just have to put sys.path.insert command before the part of the script that needs access to that directory:

```
import sys
sys.path.insert(0, '/path/to/directory')
```

Then we activate the class, declaring it using the SSD MobileNet v1 model. After that, we have to put the path to every single image into a list and feed it to the method file_pipeline:

```
from TensorFlow_detection import DetectionObj
if __name__ == "__main__":
    detection = DetectionObj(model='ssd_mobilenet_v1_coco_11_06_2017')
    images = ["./sample_images/intersection.jpg",
              "./sample_images/busy_street.jpg",
"./sample_images/doge.jpg"]
    detection.file_pipeline(images)
```

The output that we receive after our detection class has been placed on the intersection image and will return us another image enriched with bounding boxes around objects recognized with enough confidence:

Object detection by SSD MobileNet v1 on a photo of an intersection

After running the script, all three images will be represented with their annotations on the screen (each one for three seconds) and a new JSON file will be written on disk (in the target directory, which corresponds to the local directory if you have not otherwise stated it by modifying the class variable `TARGET_CLASS`).

In the visualization, you will see all the bounding boxes relative to objects whose prediction confidence is above 0.5. Anyway, you will notice that, in this case of an annotated image of an intersection (depicted in the preceding figure), not all cars and pedestrians have been spotted by the model.

By looking at the JSON file, you will discover that many other cars and pedestrians have been located by the model, though with lesser confidence. In the file, you will find all the objects detected with at least 0.25 confidence, a threshold which represents a common standard in many studies on object detection (but you can change it by modifying the class variable THRESHOLD).

Here you can see the scores generated in the JSON file. Only eight detected objects are above the visualization threshold of 0.5, whereas 16 other objects have lesser scores:

```
"scores": [0.9099398255348206, 0.8124723434448242, 0.7853631973266602,
0.709653913974762, 0.5999227166175842, 0.5942907929420471,
0.5858771800994873, 0.5656214952468872, 0.49047672748565674,
0.4781857430934906, 0.4467884600162506, 0.4043623208999634,
0.40048354864120483, 0.38961756229400635, 0.35605812072753906,
0.3488095998764038, 0.3194449841976166, 0.3000411093235016,
0.294520765542984, 0.2912806570529938, 0.2889115010394287,
0.2781482934951782, 0.2767323851585388, 0.2747304439544678]
```

And here you can find the relative class of the detected objects. Many cars have been spotted with lesser confidence. They actually may be cars in the image or errors. In accordance with your application of the Detection API, you may want to adjust your threshold or use another model and estimate an object only if it has been repeatedly detected by different models above a threshold:

```
"classes": ["car", "person", "person", "person", "person", "car", "car",
"person", "person", "person", "person", "person", "person", "person",
"car", "car", "person", "person", "car", "car", "person", "car", "car",
"car"]
```

Applying detection to videos uses the same scripting approach. This time you just point to the appropriate method, video_pipeline, the path to the video, and set whether the resulting video should have audio or not (by default audio will be filtered out). The script will do everything by itself, saving, on the same directory path as the original video, a modified and annotated video (you can spot it because it has the same filename but with the addition of annotated_ before it):

```
from TensorFlow_detection import DetectionObj
if __name__ == "__main__":
    detection = DetectionObj(model='ssd_mobilenet_v1_coco_11_06_2017')
    detection.video_pipeline(video="./sample_videos/ducks.mp4",
audio=False)
```

Finally, you can also leverage the exact same approach for images acquired by a webcam. This time you will be using the method `webcam_pipeline`:

```
from TensorFlow_detection import DetectionObj
if __name__ == "__main__":
    detection = DetectionObj(model='ssd_mobilenet_v1_coco_11_06_2017')
    detection.webcam_pipeline()
```

The script will activate the webcam, adjust the light, pick a snapshot, save the resulting snapshot and its annotation JSON file in the current directory, and finally represent the snapshot on your screen with bounding boxes on detected objects.

Real-time webcam detection

The previous `webcam_pipeline` is not a real-time detection system because it just takes snapshots and applies detection to the single taken image. This is a necessary limitation because dealing with webcam streaming requires intensive I/O data exchange. In particular, the problem is the queue of images arriving from the webcam to the Python interpreter that locks down Python until the transfer is completed. Adrian Rosebrock on his website pyimagesearch proposes a simple solution based on threads that you can read about at this Web address: http://www.pyimagesearch.com/2015/12/21/increasing-webcam-fps-with-python-and-opencv/.

The idea is very simple. In Python, because of the **global interpreter lock** (**GIL**), only one thread can execute at a time. If there is some I/O operation that blocks the thread (such as downloading a file or getting an image from the webcam), all the remaining commands are just delayed for it to complete causing a very slow execution of the program itself. It is then a good solution to move the blocking I/O operation to another thread. Since threads share the same memory, the program thread can proceed with its instructions and inquiry from time to time the I/O thread in order to check if it has completed its operations. Therefore, if moving images from the webcam to the memory of the program is a blocking operation, letting another thread dealing with I/O could be the solution. The main program will just inquiry the I/O thread, pick the image from a buffer containing only the latest received image and plot it on the screen.

```
from tensorflow_detection import DetectionObj
from threading import Thread
import cv2

def resize(image, new_width=None, new_height=None):
    """
    Resize an image based on a new width or new height
```

```
        keeping the original ratio
        """
    height, width, depth = image.shape
    if new_width:
        new_height = int((new_width / float(width)) * height)
    elif new_height:
        new_width = int((new_height / float(height)) * width)
    else:
        return image
    return cv2.resize(image, (new_width, new_height), \
                        interpolation=cv2.INTER_AREA)


class webcamStream:
    def __init__(self):
        # Initialize webcam
        self.stream = cv2.VideoCapture(0)
        # Starting TensorFlow API with SSD Mobilenet
        self.detection = DetectionObj(model=\
                        'ssd_mobilenet_v1_coco_11_06_2017')
        # Start capturing video so the Webca, will tune itself
        _, self.frame = self.stream.read()
        # Set the stop flag to False
        self.stop = False
        #
        Thread(target=self.refresh, args=()).start()

    def refresh(self):
        # Looping until an explicit stop is sent
        # from outside the function
        while True:
            if self.stop:
                return
            _, self.frame = self.stream.read()

    def get(self):
        # returning the annotated image
        return self.detection.annotate_photogram(self.frame)

    def halt(self):
        # setting the halt flag
        self.stop = True

if __name__ == "__main__":
    stream = webcamStream()
    while True:
        # Grabbing the frame from the threaded video stream
        # and resize it to have a maximum width of 400 pixels
        frame = resize(stream.get(), new_width=400)
```

```
cv2.imshow("webcam", frame)
# If the space bar is hit, the program will stop
if cv2.waitKey(1) & 0xFF == ord(" "):
    # First stopping the streaming thread
    stream.halt()
    # Then halting the while loop
    break
```

The above code implements this solution using a `webcamStream` class that instantiates a thread for the webcam I/O, allowing the main Python program to always have at hand the latest received image, processed by the TensorFlow API (using `ssd_mobilenet_v1_coco_11_06_2017`). The processed image is fluidly plotted on the screen using an `OpenCV` function, listening to the space bar keystroke in order to terminate the program.

Acknowledgements

Everything related to this project started from the following paper: *Speed/accuracy trade-offs for modern convolutional object detectors*(`https://arxiv.org/abs/1611.10012`) by Huang J, Rathod V, Sun C, Zhu M, Korattikara A, Fathi A, Fischer I, Wojna Z, Song Y, Guadarrama S, Murphy K, CVPR 2017. Concluding this chapter, we have to thank all the contributors of the TensorFlow object detection API for their great job programming the API and making it open-source and thus free and accessible to anyone: Jonathan Huang, Vivek Rathod, Derek Chow, Chen Sun, Menglong Zhu, Matthew Tang, Anoop Korattikara, Alireza Fathi, Ian Fischer, Zbigniew Wojna, Yang Song, Sergio Guadarrama, Jasper Uijlings, Viacheslav Kovalevskyi, Kevin Murphy. We also cannot forget to thank Dat Tran for his inspirational posts on medium of two MIT licensed projects on how to use the TensorFlow object detection API for real-time recognition even on custom (`https://towardsdatascience.com/building-a-real-time-object-recognition-app-with-tensorflow-and-opencv-b7a2b4ebdc32` and `https://towardsdatascience.com/how-to-train-your-own-object-detector-with-tensorflows-object-detector-api-bec72ecfe1d9`)

Summary

This project has helped you to start immediately classifying objects in images with confidence without much hassle. It helps you to see what a ConvNet could do for your problem, focusing more on the wrap up (possibly a larger application) you have in mind, and annotating many images for training more ConvNets with fresh images of a selected class.

During the project, you have learned quite a few useful technicalities you can reuse in many projects dealing with images. First of all, you now know how to process different kinds of visual inputs from images, videos, and webcam captures. You also know how to load a frozen model and put it to work, and also how to use a class to access a TensorFlow model.

On the other hand, clearly, the project has some limitations that you may encounter sooner or later, and that may spark the idea to try to integrate your code and make it shine even more. First of all, the models we have discussed will soon be surpassed by newer and more efficient ones (you can check here for newly available models: `https://github.com/tensorflow/models/blob/master/object_detection/g3doc/detection_model_zoo.md`), and you will need to incorporate new ones or create your own architecture (`https://github.com/tensorflow/models/blob/master/object_detection/g3doc/defining_your_own_model.md`). Then you may need to combine the model to reach the accuracy you need in your project (the paper *Speed/accuracy trade-offs for modern convolutional object detectors* reveals how researchers at Google have done it). Finally, you may need to tune a ConvNet to recognize a new class (you can read how to do that here, but beware, it is a long process and a project by itself: `https://github.com/tensorflow/models/blob/master/object_detection/g3doc/using_your_own_dataset.md`).

In the next chapter, we will look at state-of-the-art object detection in images, devising a project that will lead you to produce complete discursive captions describing submitted images, not just simple labels and bounding boxes.

Caption Generation for Images 3

Caption generation is one of the most important applications in the field of deep learning and has gained quite a lot of interest recently. Image captioning models involve a combination of both visual information along with natural language processing.

In this chapter, we will learn about:

- Recent advancements in the field of the caption generation
- How caption generation works
- Implementation of caption generation models

What is caption generation?

Caption generation is the task of describing an image with natural language. Previously, caption generation models worked on object detection models combined with templates that were used to generate text for detected objects. With all the advancements in deep learning, these models have been replaced with a combination of convolutional neural networks and recurrent neural networks.

An example is shown as follows:

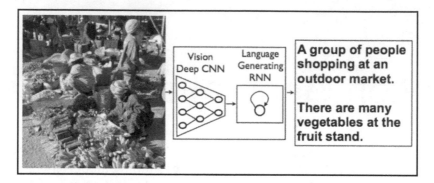

Source: https://arxiv.org/pdf/1609.06647.pdf

There are several datasets that help us create image captioning models.

Exploring image captioning datasets

Several datasets are available for captioning image task. The datasets are usually prepared by showing an image to a few persons and asking them to write a sentence each about the image. Through this method, several captions are generated for the same image. Having multiple options of captions helps in better generalization. The difficulty lies in the ranking of model performance. For each generation, preferably, a human has to evaluate the caption. Automatic evaluation is difficult for this task. Let's explore the `Flickr8` dataset.

Downloading the dataset

`Flickr8` is gathered from Flickr and is not permitted for commercial usage. Download the `Flickr8` dataset from `https://forms.illinois.edu/sec/1713398`. The descriptions can be found at `http://nlp.cs.illinois.edu/HockenmaierGroup/8k-pictures.html`. Download the text and images separately. Access to it can be obtained by filling in a form shown on the page:

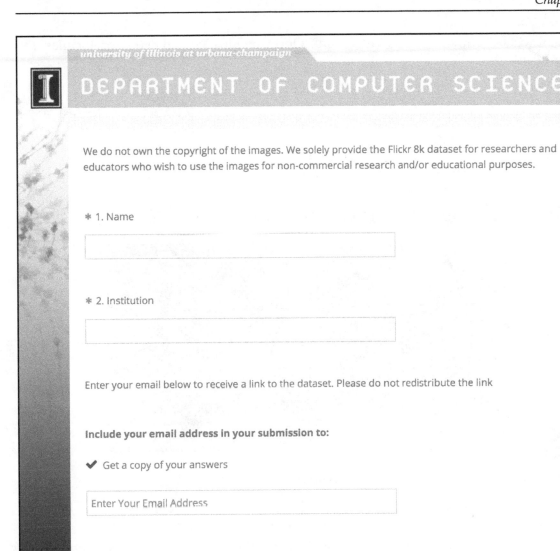

university of illinois at urbana-champaign

DEPARTMENT OF COMPUTER SCIENCE

We do not own the copyright of the images. We solely provide the Flickr 8k dataset for researchers and educators who wish to use the images for non-commercial research and/or educational purposes.

* 1. Name

* 2. Institution

Enter your email below to receive a link to the dataset. Please do not redistribute the link

Include your email address in your submission to:

✔ Get a copy of your answers

Enter Your Email Address

Submit Form

An email will be sent with the download link. Once downloaded and extracted, the files should be like this:

```
Flickr8k_text
CrowdFlowerAnnotations.txt
Flickr_8k.devImages.txt
ExpertAnnotations.txt
Flickr_8k.testImages.txt
Flickr8k.lemma.token.txt
Flickr_8k.trainImages.txt
Flickr8k.token.txt readme.txt
```

The following are a couple of examples given in the dataset:

The preceding figure shows the following components:

- A man in street racer armor is examining the tire of another racer's motor bike
- The two racers drove the white bike down the road
- Two motorists are riding along on their vehicle that is oddly designed and colored
- Two people are in a small race car driving by a green hill
- Two people in racing uniforms in a street car

The following is example two:

The preceding figure shows the following components:

- A man in a black hoodie and jeans skateboards down a railing
- A man skateboards down a steep railing next to some steps
- A person is sliding down a brick rail on a snowboard
- A person walks down the brick railing near a set of steps
- A snowboarder rides down a handrail without snow

As you can see, there are different captions provided for one image. The captions show the difficulty of the image captioning task.

Converting words into embeddings

English words have to be converted into embeddings for caption generation. An embedding is nothing but a vector or numerical representation of words or images. It is useful if words are converted to a vector form such that arithmetic can be performed using the vectors.

Such an embedding can be learned by two methods, as shown in the following figure:

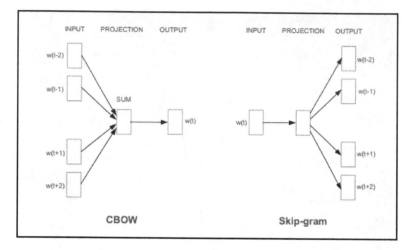

The **CBOW** method learns the embedding by predicting a word given the surrounding words. The **Skip-gram** method predicts the surrounding words given a word, which is the reverse of **CBOW**. Based on the history, a target word can be trained, as shown in the following figure:

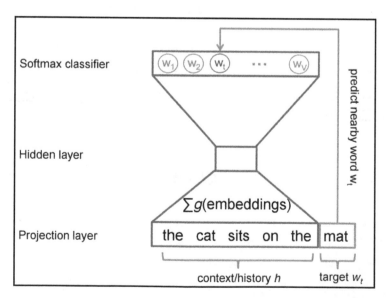

Once trained, the embedding can be visualized as follows:

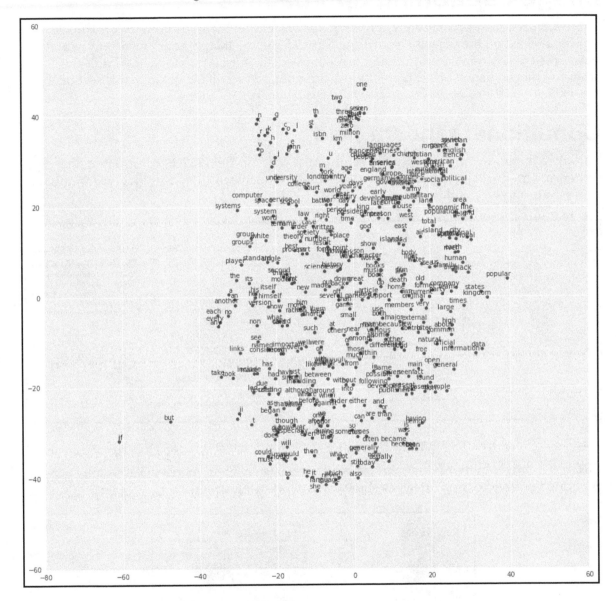

Visualization of words

This type of embedding can be used to perform vector arithmetic of words. This concept of word embedding will be helpful throughout this chapter.

Image captioning approaches

There are several approaches to captioning images. Earlier methods used to construct a sentence based on the objects and attributes present in the image. Later, **recurrent neural networks** (**RNN**) were used to generate sentences. The most accurate method uses the attention mechanism. Let's explore these techniques and results in detail in this section.

Conditional random field

Initially a method was tried with the **conditional random field** (**CRF**) constructing the sentence with the objects and attributes detected in the image. The steps involved in this process are shown as follows:

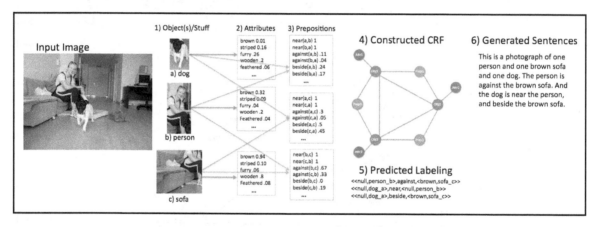

System flow for an example images (Source: http://www.tamaraberg.com/papers/generation_cvpr11.pdf)

CRF has limited ability to come up with sentences in a coherent manner. The quality of generated sentences is not great, as shown in the following screenshot:

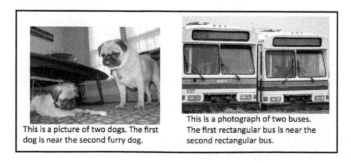

The sentences shown here are too structured despite getting the objects and attributes correct.

Kulkarni et al., in the paper `http://www.tamaraberg.com/papers/generation_cvpr11.pdf`, proposed a method of finding the objects and attributes from an image and using it to generate text with a **conditional random field (CRF)**.

Recurrent neural network on convolution neural network

A recurrent neural network can be combined with convolutional neural network features to produce new sentences. This enables end-to-end training of the models. The following is the architecture of such a model:

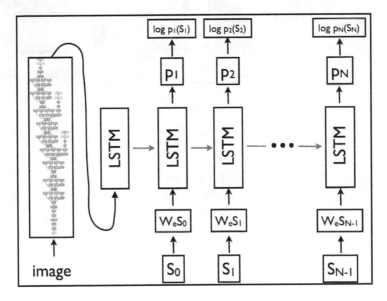

LSTM model (Source: https://arxiv.org/pdf/1411.4555.pdf)

There are several layers of **LSTM** used to produce the desired results. A few of the results produced by this model are shown in the following screenshot:

Source: https://arxiv.org/pdf/1411.4555.pdf

These results are better than the results produced by CRF. This shows the power of LSTM in generating sentences.

Reference: Vinyals et al., in the paper `https://arxiv.org/pdf/1411.4555.pdf`, proposed an end to end trainable deep learning for image captioning, which has CNN and RNN stacked back to back.

Caption ranking

Caption ranking is an interesting way of selecting a caption from a set of captions. First, the images are ranked according to their features and corresponding captions are picked, as shown in this screenshot:

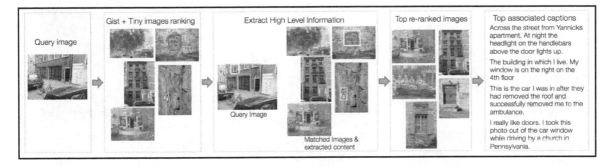

Source: http://papers.nips.cc/paper/4470-im2text-describing-images-using-1-million-captioned-photographs.pdf

The top images can be re-ranked using a different set of attributes. By getting more images, the quality can improve a lot as shown in the following screenshot:

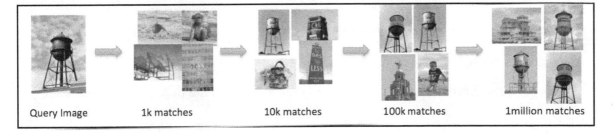

Source: http://papers.nips.cc/paper/4470-im2text-describing-images-using-1-million-captioned-photographs.pdf

The results are better with an increase in the number of images in the dataset.

 To learn more about caption ranking, refer: `http://papers.nips.cc/paper/4470-im2text-describing-images-using-1-million-captioned-photographs.pdf`

Dense captioning

Dense captioning is the problem of multiple captions on a single image. The following is the architecture of the problem:

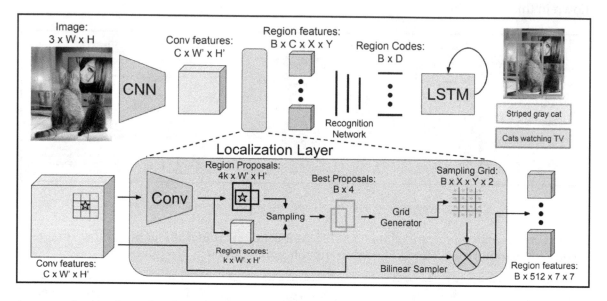

Source: https://www.cv-foundation.org/openaccess/content_cvpr_2016/papers/Johnson_DenseCap_Fully_Convolutional_CVPR_2016_paper.pdf

This architecture produces good results.

For more understanding refer: Johnson et al., in the paper `https://www.cv-foundation.org/openaccess/content_cvpr_2016/papers/Johnson_DenseCap_Fully_Convolutional_CVPR_2016_paper.pdf`, proposed a method for dense captioning.

RNN captioning

The visual features can be used with sequence learning to form the output.

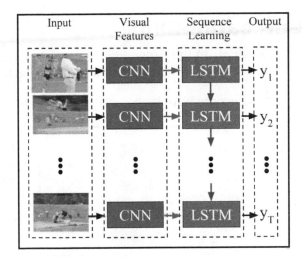

This is an architecture for generating captions.

 For details, refer: Donahue et al., in the paper `https://arxiv.org/pdf/1411.4389.pdf`, proposed **Long-term recurrent convolutional architectures** (**LRCN**) for the task of image captioning.

Multimodal captioning

Both the image and text can be mapped to the same embedding space to generate a caption.

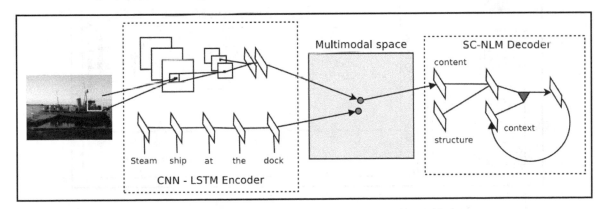

A decoder is required to generate the caption.

Attention-based captioning

For detailed learning, refer: Xu et al., in the paper, `https://arxiv.org/pdf/1502.03044.pdf`, proposed a method for image captioning using an **attention mechanism**.

Attention-based captioning has become popular recently as it provides better accuracy:

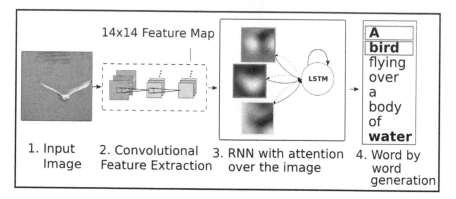

This method trains an attention model in the sequence of the caption, thereby producing better results:

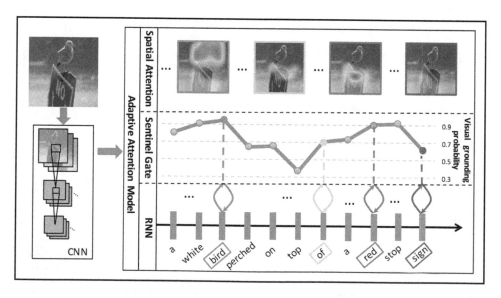

Here is a diagram of **LSTM** with attention-generating captions:

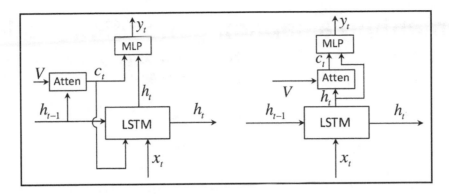

There are several examples shown here, with an excellent visualization of objects unfolding in a time series manner:

Unfolding objects in time series manner

The results are really excellent!

Implementing a caption generation model

First, let's read the dataset and transform it the way we need. Import the `os` library and declare the directory in which the dataset is present, as shown in the following code:

```
import os
annotation_dir = 'Flickr8k_text'
```

Next, define a function to open a file and return the lines present in the file as a list:

```
def read_file(file_name):
    with open(os.path.join(annotation_dir, file_name), 'rb') as
file_handle:
        file_lines = file_handle.read().splitlines()
    return file_lines
```

Read the image paths of the training and testing datasets followed by the captions file:

```
train_image_paths = read_file('Flickr_8k.trainImages.txt')
test_image_paths = read_file('Flickr_8k.testImages.txt')
captions = read_file('Flickr8k.token.txt')

print(len(train_image_paths))
print(len(test_image_paths))
print(len(captions))
```

This should print the following:

```
6000
1000
40460
```

Next, the image-to-caption map has to be generated. This will help in training for easily looking up captions. Also, unique words present in the caption dataset will help to create the vocabulary:

```
image_caption_map = {}
unique_words = set()
max_words = 0
for caption in captions:
    image_name = caption.split('#')[0]
    image_caption = caption.split('#')[1].split('\t')[1]
    if image_name not in image_caption_map.keys():
        image_caption_map[image_name] = [image_caption]
    else:
        image_caption_map[image_name].append(image_caption)
    caption_words = image_caption.split()
```

```
max_words = max(max_words, len(caption_words))
[unique_words.add(caption_word) for caption_word in caption_words]
```

Now, two maps have to be formed. One is word to index and the other is index to word map:

```
unique_words = list(unique_words)
word_to_index_map = {}
index_to_word_map = {}
for index, unique_word in enumerate(unique_words):
    word_to_index_map[unique_word] = index
    index_to_word_map[index] = unique_word
print(max_words)
```

The maximum number of words present in a caption is 38, which will help in defining the architecture. Next, import the libraries:

```
from data_preparation import train_image_paths, test_image_paths
from keras.applications.vgg16 import VGG16
from keras.preprocessing import image
from keras.applications.vgg16 import preprocess_input
import numpy as np
from keras.models import Model
import pickle
import os
```

Now create the `ImageModel` class for loading the VGG model with weights:

```
class ImageModel:
    def __init__(self):
        vgg_model = VGG16(weights='imagenet', include_top=True)
        self.model = Model(input=vgg_model.input,
                           output=vgg_model.get_layer('fc2').output)
```

The weights are downloaded and stored. It may take some time at the first attempt. Next, a separate model is created so that a second fully connected layer is predicted. The following is a method for reading an image from a path and preprocessing:

```
@staticmethod
def load_preprocess_image(image_path):
    image_array = image.load_img(image_path, target_size=(224, 224))
    image_array = image.img_to_array(image_array)
    image_array = np.expand_dims(image_array, axis=0)
    image_array = preprocess_input(image_array)
    return image_array
```

Next, define a method to load the image and do prediction. The predicted second fully connected layer can be reshaped to `4096`:

```
def extract_feature_from_imagfe_path(self, image_path):
    image_array = self.load_preprocess_image(image_path)
    features = self.model.predict(image_array)
    return features.reshape((4096, 1))
```

Go through a list of image paths and create a list of features:

```
def extract_feature_from_image_paths(self, work_dir, image_names):
    features = []
    for image_name in image_names:
        image_path = os.path.join(work_dir, image_name)
        feature = self.extract_feature_from_image_path(image_path)
        features.append(feature)
    return features
```

Next, store the extracted features as a pickle file:

```
def extract_features_and_save(self, work_dir, image_names, file_name):
    features = self.extract_feature_from_image_paths(work_dir,
image_names)
        with open(file_name, 'wb') as p:
            pickle.dump(features, p)
```

Next, initialize the class and extract both training and testing image features:

```
I = ImageModel()
I.extract_features_and_save(b'Flicker8k_Dataset',train_image_paths,
'train_image_features.p')
I.extract_features_and_save(b'Flicker8k_Dataset',test_image_paths,
'test_image_features.p')
```

Import the layers required to construct the model:

```
from data_preparation import get_vocab
from keras.models import Sequential
from keras.layers import LSTM, Embedding, TimeDistributed, Dense,
RepeatVector, Merge, Activation, Flatten
from keras.preprocessing import image, sequence
```

Get the vocabulary required:

```
image_caption_map, max_words, unique_words, \
word_to_index_map, index_to_word_map = get_vocab()
vocabulary_size = len(unique_words)
```

For the final caption generation model:

```
image_model = Sequential()
image_model.add(Dense(128, input_dim=4096, activation='relu'))
image_model.add(RepeatVector(max_words))
```

For the language, a model is created:

```
lang_model = Sequential()
lang_model.add(Embedding(vocabulary_size, 256, input_length=max_words))
lang_model.add(LSTM(256, return_sequences=True))
lang_model.add(TimeDistributed(Dense(128)))
```

The two different models are merged to form the final model:

```
model = Sequential()
model.add(Merge([image_model, lang_model], mode='concat'))
model.add(LSTM(1000, return_sequences=False))
model.add(Dense(vocabulary_size))
model.add(Activation('softmax'))
model.compile(loss='categorical_crossentropy', optimizer='rmsprop',
metrics=['accuracy'])
batch_size = 32
epochs = 10
total_samples = 9
model.fit_generator(data_generator(batch_size=batch_size),
steps_per_epoch=total_samples / batch_size,
                    epochs=epochs, verbose=2)
```

This model can be trained to generate captions.

Summary

In this chapter, we learned image captioning techniques. First, we understood the embedding space of word vectors. Then, several approaches for image captioning were learned. Then came the implementation of the image captioning model.

In the next chapter, we will take a look at the concept of **Generative Adversarial Networks (GAN)**. GANs are intriguing and useful for generating images for various purposes.

4
Building GANs for Conditional Image Creation

Yann LeCun, Director of Facebook AI, has recently stated that *"Generative Adversarial Networks is the most interesting idea in the last ten years in machine learning"*, and that is certainly confirmed by the elevated interest in academia about this deep learning solution. If you look at recent papers on deep learning (but also look at the leading trends on LinkedIn or Medium posts on the topic), there has really been an overproduction of variants of GANs.

You can get an idea of what a *zoo* the world of GANs has become just by glancing the continuously updated reference table, created by Hindu Puravinash, which can be found at `https://github.com/hindupuravinash/the-gan-zoo/blob/master/gans.tsv` or by studying the GAN timeline prepared by Zheng Liu, which can be found at `https://github.com/dongb5/GAN-Timeline` and can help you putting everything into time perspective.

GANs have the power to strike the imagination because they can demonstrate the creative power of AI, not just its computational strength. In this chapter, we are going to:

- Demystify the topic of GANs by providing you with all the necessary concepts to understand what GANs are, what they can do at the moment, and what they are expected to do
- Demonstrate how to generate images both based on the initial distribution of example images (the so-called unsupervised GANs)
- Explain how to condition the GAN to the kind of resulting image you expect them to generate for you
- Set up a basic yet complete project that can work with different datasets of handwritten characters and icons
- Provide you with basic instructions how to train your GANs in the Cloud (specifically on Amazon AWS)

The success of GANs much depends, besides the specific neural architecture you use, on the problem they face and the data you feed them with. The datasets we have chosen for this chapter should provide satisfactory results. We hope you will enjoy and be inspired by the creative power of GANs!

Introducing GANs

We'll start with some quite recent history because GANs are among the newest ideas you'll find around AI and deep learning.

Everything started in 2014, when Ian Goodfellow and his colleagues (there is also Yoshua Bengio closing the list of contributors) at the *Departement d'informatique et de recherche opérationnelle* at Montreal University published a paper on **Generative Adversarial Nets** (**GANs**), a framework capable of generating new data based on a set of initial examples:

 GOODFELLOW, Ian, et al. Generative Adversarial Nets. In: *Advances in Neural Information Processing Systems*. 2014. p. 2672-2680: `https://arxiv.org/abs/1406.2661`.

The initial images produced by such networks were astonishing, considering the previous attempts using Markov chains which were far from being credible. In the image, you can see some of the examples proposed in the paper, showing examples reproduced from MNIST, **Toronto Face Dataset** (**TFD**) a non-public dataset and CIFAR-10 datasets:

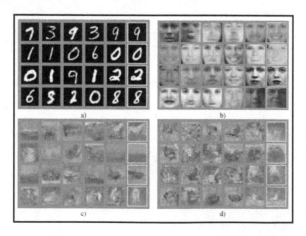

Figure 1: Samples from the first paper on GANs using different datasets for learning to generate fresh images: a) MNIST b) TFD c) and d) CIFAR-10
SOURCE: *GOODFELLOW*, Ian, et al. Generative Adversarial Nets. In: *Advances in Neural Information Processing Systems*. 2014. p. 2672-2680

The paper was deemed quite innovative because it put working together deep neural networks and game theory in a really smart architecture that didn't require much more than the usual back-propagation to train. GANs are generative models, models that can generate data because they have inscribed a model distribution (they learned it, for instance). Consequently when they generate something it is just like if they were sampling from that distribution.

The key is in the adversarial approach

The key to understanding how GANs can be such successful generative models resides in the term adversarial. Actually, the GANs architecture is made up of two distinct networks that are optimized based on the pooling of respective errors, and that's called an **adversarial process**.

You start with a real dataset, let's call it R, containing your images or your data of a different kind (GANs are not limited to images only, though they constitute the major application). You then set up a generator network, G, which tries to make fake data that looks like the genuine data, and you set up a discriminator, D, whose role is to compare the data produced by G mixed against the real data, R, and figures out which is genuine and which is not.

Goodfellow used the art forgers metaphor to describe the process, being, the generator the forgers, and the discriminator the detective (or the art critic) that has to disclose their misdeed. There is a challenge between the forgers and the detective because while the forgers have to become more skillful in order not to be detected, the detective has to become better at detecting fakes. Everything turns into an endless fight between the forgers and the detective until the forged artifacts are completely similar to the originals. When GANs overfit, in fact, they just reproduce the originals. It really seems an explanation of a competitive market, and it really is, because the idea comes from competitive game theory.

In GANs, the generator is incentivized to produce images that the discriminator cannot figure out if they are a fake or not. An obvious solution for the generator is simply to copy some training image or to just settle down for some produced image that seems successful with the discriminator. One solution is *one-sided label smoothing* a technique which we will be applying in our project. It is described in SALIMANS, Tim, et al. Improved techniques for training gans. In: *Advances in Neural Information Processing Systems. 2016. p. 2234-2242*: https://arxiv.org/abs/1606.03498.

Let's discuss how things actually work a little bit more. At first, the generator, *G*, is clueless and produces completely random data (it has actually never seen a piece of original data), it is therefore punished by the discriminator, *D*--an easy job figuring out the real versus the fake data. *G* takes full blame and starts trying something different to get better feedback from *D*. This is done completely randomly because the only data the generator sees is a random input called *Z*, it never touches the real data. After many trials and fails, hinted by the discriminator, the generator at last figures out what to do and starts to produce credible outputs. In the end, given enough time, the generator will exactly replicate all the original data without ever having seen a single example of it:

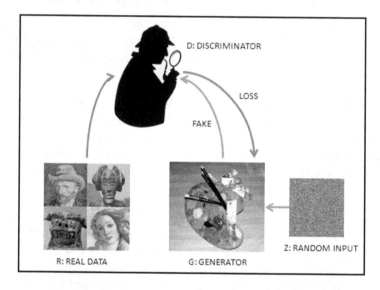

Figure 2: Illustrative example of how a vanilla GAN architecture works

A cambrian explosion

As mentioned, there are new papers on GANs coming out every month (as you can check on the reference table made by Hindu Puravinash that we mentioned at the beginning of the chapter).

Anyway, apart from the vanilla implementation described in the initial paper from Goodfellow and his colleagues, the most notable implementations to take notice of are **deep convolutional generative adversarial networks** (**DCGANs**) and **conditional GANs** (**CGANs**).

- DCGANs are GANs based on CNN architecture (*RADFORD, Alec; METZ, Luke; CHINTALA, Soumith. Unsupervised representation learning with deep convolutional generative adversarial networks. arXiv preprint arXiv:1511.06434, 2015:* https://arxiv.org/abs/1511.06434).

- CGANs are DCGANs which are conditioned on some input label so that you can obtain as a result an image with certain desired characteristics (*MIRZA, Mehdi; OSINDERO, Simon. Conditional generative adversarial nets. arXiv preprint arXiv:1411.1784, 2014:* https://arxiv.org/abs/1411.1784). Our project will be programming a CGAN class and training it on different datasets in order to prove its functioning.

But there are also other interesting examples around (which are not covered by our project) offering practical solutions to problems related to image creation or improvement:

- A CycleGAN translates an image into another (the classic example is the horse that becomes a zebra: *ZHU, Jun-Yan, et al. Unpaired image-to-image translation using cycle-consistent adversarial networks. arXiv preprint arXiv:1703.10593, 2017:* https://arxiv.org/abs/1703.10593)

- A StackGAN creates a realistic image from a text describing the image (*ZHANG, Han, et al. Stackgan: Text to photo-realistic image synthesis with stacked generative adversarial networks. arXiv preprint arXiv:1612.03242, 2016:* https://arxiv.org/abs/1612.03242)

- A Discovery GAN (DiscoGAN) transfers stylistic elements from one image to another, thus transferring texture and decoration from a fashion item such as a bag to another fashion item such as a pair of shoes (*KIM, Taeksoo, et al. Learning to discover cross-domain relations with generative adversarial networks. arXiv preprint arXiv:1703.05192, 2017:* https://arxiv.org/abs/1703.05192)

- A SRGAN can convert low-quality images into high-resolution ones (*LEDIG, Christian, et al. Photo-realistic single image super-resolution using a generative adversarial network. arXiv preprint arXiv:1609.04802, 2016:* https://arxiv.org/abs/1609.04802)

DCGANs

DCGANs are the first relevant improvement on the GAN architecture. DCGANs always successfully complete their training phase and, given enough epochs and examples, they tend to generate satisfactory quality outputs. That soon made them the baseline for GANs and helped to produce some amazing achievements, such as generating new Pokemon from known ones: https://www.youtube.com/watch?v=rs3aI7bACGc or creating faces of celebrities that actually never existed but are incredibly realistic (nothing uncanny), just as NVIDIA did: https://youtu.be/XOxxPcy5Gr4 using a new training approach called **progressing growing**: http://research.nvidia.com/sites/default/files/publications/karras2017gan-paper.pdf. They have their root in using the same convolutions used in image classification by deep learning supervised networks, and they use some smart tricks:

- Batch normalization in both networks
- No fully hidden connected layers
- No pooling, just stride-in convolutions
- ReLU activation functions

Conditional GANs

In **conditional GANs (CGANs)**, adding a vector of features controls the output and provides a better guide to the generator in figuring out what to do. Such a vector of features could encode the class the image should be derived be from (that is an image of a woman or a man if we are trying to create faces of imaginary actors) or even a set of specific characteristics we expect from the image (for imaginary actors, it could be the type of hair, eyes or complexion). The trick is done by incorporating the information into the images to be learned and into the Z input, which is not completely random anymore. The evaluation by the discriminator is done not only on the resemblance of fake data to the original data but also on the correspondence of the fake data image to its input label (or features):

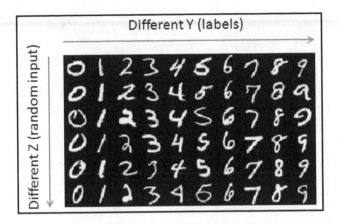

Figure 3: Combining Z input with Y input (a labeling feature vector) allows generating controlled images

The project

Importing the right libraries is where we start. Apart from `tensorflow`, we will be using `numpy` and math for computations, `scipy`, `matplolib` for images and graphics, and `warnings`, `random`, and `distutils` for support in specific operations:

```
import numpy as np
import tensorflow as tf
import math
import warnings
import matplotlib.pyplot as plt
from scipy.misc import imresize
from random import shuffle
from distutils.version import LooseVersion
```

Dataset class

Our first step is to provide the data. We will rely on datasets that have already been preprocessed, but our readers could use different kinds of images for their own GAN implementation. The idea is to keep separate a `Dataset` class that will have the task of providing batches of normalized and reshaped images to the GANs class we will build later.

In the initialization, we will deal with both images and their labels (if available). Images are first reshaped (if their shape differs from the one defined when instantiating the class), then shuffled. Shuffling helps GANs learning better if any order, for instance by class, is initially inscribed into the dataset - and this is actually true for any machine learning algorithm based on stochastic gradient descent: *BOTTOU, Léon. Stochastic gradient descent tricks. In: Neural networks: Tricks of the trade. Springer, Berlin, Heidelberg, 2012. p. 421-436:* `https://www.microsoft.com/en-us/research/wp-content/uploads/2012/01/tricks-2012.pdf.` Labels instead are encoded using one-hot encoding, that is, a binary variable is created for each one of the classes, which is set to one (whereas others are set to zero) to represent the label as a vector.

 For instance, if our classes are `{dog:0, cat:1}`, we will have these two one-hot encoded vectors to represent them: `{dog:[1, 0], cat:[0, 1]}`.

In such a way, we can easily add the vector to our image, as a further channel, and inscribe into it some kind of visual characteristic to be replicated by our GAN. Moreover, we could arrange the vectors in order to inscribe even more complex classes with special characteristics. For instance, we could specify the code for a class we prefer to be generated, and we can also specify some of its characteristics:

```python
class Dataset(object):
    def __init__(self, data, labels=None, width=28, height=28,
                            max_value=255, channels=3):
        # Record image specs
        self.IMAGE_WIDTH = width
        self.IMAGE_HEIGHT = height
        self.IMAGE_MAX_VALUE = float(max_value)
        self.CHANNELS = channels
        self.shape = len(data), self.IMAGE_WIDTH, \
                            self.IMAGE_HEIGHT, self.CHANNELS
        if self.CHANNELS == 3:
            self.image_mode = 'RGB'
            self.cmap = None
        elif self.CHANNELS == 1:
            self.image_mode = 'L'
            self.cmap = 'gray'

        # Resize if images are of different size
        if data.shape[1] != self.IMAGE_HEIGHT or \
                            data.shape[2] != self.IMAGE_WIDTH:
            data = self.image_resize(data,
                    self.IMAGE_HEIGHT, self.IMAGE_WIDTH)
```

```
    # Store away shuffled data
    index = list(range(len(data)))
    shuffle(index)
    self.data = data[index]

    if len(labels) > 0:
        # Store away shuffled labels
        self.labels = labels[index]
        # Enumerate unique classes
        self.classes = np.unique(labels)
        # Create a one hot encoding for each class
        # based on position in self.classes
        one_hot = dict()
        no_classes = len(self.classes)
        for j, i in enumerate(self.classes):
            one_hot[i] = np.zeros(no_classes)
            one_hot[i][j] = 1.0
        self.one_hot = one_hot
    else:
        # Just keep label variables as placeholders
        self.labels = None
        self.classes = None
        self.one_hot = None

def image_resize(self, dataset, newHeight, newWidth):
    """Resizing an image if necessary"""
    channels = dataset.shape[3]
    images_resized = np.zeros([0, newHeight,
                    newWidth, channels], dtype=np.uint8)
    for image in range(dataset.shape[0]):
        if channels == 1:
            temp = imresize(dataset[image][:, :, 0],
                            [newHeight, newWidth], 'nearest')
            temp = np.expand_dims(temp, axis=2)
        else:
            temp = imresize(dataset[image],
                            [newHeight, newWidth], 'nearest')
        images_resized = np.append(images_resized,
                        np.expand_dims(temp, axis=0), axis=0)
    return images_resized
```

The `get_batches` method will just release a batch subset of the dataset and normalize the data by dividing the pixel values by the maximum (256) and subtracting -0.5. The resulting images will have float values in the interval [-0.5, +0.5]:

```python
def get_batches(self, batch_size):
    """Pulling batches of images and their labels"""
    current_index = 0
    # Checking there are still batches to deliver
    while current_index < self.shape[0]:
        if current_index + batch_size > self.shape[0]:
            batch_size = self.shape[0] - current_index
        data_batch = self.data[current_index:current_index \
                               + batch_size]
        if len(self.labels) > 0:
            y_batch = np.array([self.one_hot[k] for k in \
            self.labels[current_index:current_index +\
            batch_size]])
        else:
            y_batch = np.array([])
        current_index += batch_size
        yield (data_batch / self.IMAGE_MAX_VALUE) - 0.5, y_batch
```

CGAN class

The CGAN class contains all the functions necessary for running a conditional GAN based on the CGAN model. The deep convolutional generative adversarial networks proved to have the performance in generating photo-like quality outputs. We have previously introduced CGANs, so just to remind you, their reference paper is:

RADFORD, Alec; METZ, Luke; CHINTALA, Soumith. Unsupervised representation learning with deep convolutional Generative Adversarial Networks. arXiv preprint arXiv:1511.06434, 2015 at https://arxiv.org/abs/1511.06434.

In our project, we will then add the conditional form of the CGAN that uses label information as in a supervised learning task. Using labels and integrating them with images (this is the trick) will result in much better images and in the possibility of deciding the characteristics of the generated image.

The reference paper for conditional GANs is:

 MIRZA, Mehdi; OSINDERO, Simon. *Conditional Generative Adversarial Nets*. arXiv preprint arXiv:1411.1784, 2014, `https://arxiv.org/abs/1411.1784.`

Our `CGAN` class expects as input a dataset class object, the number of epochs, the image `batch_size`, the dimension of the random input used for the generator (`z_dim`), and a name for the GAN (for saving purposes). It also can be initialized with different values for alpha and smooth. We will discuss later what these two parameters can do for the GAN network.

The instantiation sets all the internal variables and performs a performance check on the system, raising a warning if a GPU is not detected:

```python
class CGan(object):
    def __init__(self, dataset, epochs=1, batch_size=32,
                 z_dim=96, generator_name='generator',
                 alpha=0.2, smooth=0.1,
                 learning_rate=0.001, beta1=0.35):

        # As a first step, checking if the
        # system is performing for GANs
        self.check_system()

        # Setting up key parameters
        self.generator_name = generator_name
        self.dataset = dataset
        self.cmap = self.dataset.cmap
        self.image_mode = self.dataset.image_mode
        self.epochs = epochs
        self.batch_size = batch_size
        self.z_dim = z_dim
        self.alpha = alpha
        self.smooth = smooth
        self.learning_rate = learning_rate
        self.beta1 = beta1
        self.g_vars = list()
        self.trained = False

    def check_system(self):
        """
        Checking system suitability for the project
        """
        # Checking TensorFlow version >=1.2
```

```
version = tf.__version__
print('TensorFlow Version: %s' % version)

assert LooseVersion(version) >= LooseVersion('1.2'),\
('You are using %s, please use TensorFlow version 1.2 \
                                or newer.' % version)

# Checking for a GPU
if not tf.test.gpu_device_name():
    warnings.warn('No GPU found installed on the system.\
                It is advised to train your GAN using\
                a GPU or on AWS')
else:
    print('Default GPU Device: %s' % tf.test.gpu_device_name())
```

The `instantiate_inputs` function creates the TensorFlow placeholders for the inputs, both real and random. It also provides the labels (treated as images of the same shape of the original but for a channel depth equivalent to the number of classes), and for the learning rate of the training procedure:

```
def instantiate_inputs(self, image_width, image_height,
                        image_channels, z_dim, classes):
    """
    Instantiating inputs and parameters placeholders:
    real input, z input for generation,
    real input labels, learning rate
    """
    inputs_real = tf.placeholder(tf.float32,
                    (None, image_width, image_height,
                     image_channels), name='input_real')
    inputs_z = tf.placeholder(tf.float32,
                    (None, z_dim + classes), name='input_z')
    labels = tf.placeholder(tf.float32,
                    (None, image_width, image_height,
                     classes), name='labels')
    learning_rate = tf.placeholder(tf.float32, None)
    return inputs_real, inputs_z, labels, learning_rate
```

Next, we pass to work on the architecture of the network, defining some basic functions such as the `leaky_ReLU_activation` function (that we will be using for both the generator and the discriminator, contrary to what is prescribed in the original paper on deep convolutional GANs):

```
def leaky_ReLU_activation(self, x, alpha=0.2):
    return tf.maximum(alpha * x, x)

def dropout(self, x, keep_prob=0.9):
```

```
return tf.nn.dropout(x, keep_prob)
```

Our next function represents a discriminator layer. It creates a convolution using Xavier initialization, operates batch normalization on the result, sets a `leaky_ReLU_activation`, and finally applies `dropout` for regularization:

```
def d_conv(self, x, filters, kernel_size, strides,
           padding='same', alpha=0.2, keep_prob=0.5,
           train=True):
    """
    Discriminant layer architecture
    Creating a convolution, applying batch normalization,
    leaky rely activation and dropout
    """
    x = tf.layers.conv2d(x, filters, kernel_size,
                    strides, padding, kernel_initializer=\
                    tf.contrib.layers.xavier_initializer())
    x = tf.layers.batch_normalization(x, training=train)
    x = self.leaky_ReLU_activation(x, alpha)
    x = self.dropout(x, keep_prob)
    return x
```

Xavier initialization assures that the initial weights of the convolution are not too small, nor too large, in order to allow a better transmission of the signals through the network since the initial epochs.

 Xavier initialization provides a Gaussian distribution with a zero mean whose variance is given by 1.0 divided by the number of neurons feeding into a layer. It is because of this kind of initialization that deep learning moved away from pre-training techniques, previously used to set initial weights that could transmit back propagation even in the presence of many layers. You can read more about it and about the Glorot and Bengio's variant of the initialization in this post: http://andyljones. tumblr.com/post/110998971763/an-explanation-of-xavier-initialization.

Batch normalization is described by this paper:

 IOFFE, Sergey; SZEGEDY, Christian. Batch normalization: Accelerating deep network training by reducing internal covariate shift. In: *International Conference on Machine Learning*. 2015. p. 448-456.

As noted by the authors, the batch normalization algorithm for normalization deals with covariate shift (http://sifaka.cs.uiuc.edu/jiang4/domain_adaptation/survey/node8. html), that is, changing distribution in the inputs which could cause the previously learned weights not to work properly anymore. In fact, as distributions are initially learned in the first input layers, they are transmitted to all the following layers, and shifting later because suddenly the input distribution has changed (for instance, initially you had more input photos of cats than dogs, now it's the contrary) could prove quite daunting unless you have set the learning rate very low.

 Batch normalization solves the problem of changing distribution in the inputs because it normalizes each batch by both mean and variance (using batch statistics), as illustrated by the paper *IOFFE, Sergey; SZEGEDY, Christian.* Batch normalization: Accelerating deep network training by reducing internal covariate shift. *In: International Conference on Machine Learning. 2015. p. 448-456* (it can be found on the Internet at https://arxiv.org/abs/1502.03167).

g_reshaping and g_conv_transpose are two functions that are part of the generator. They operate by reshaping the input, no matter if it is a flat layer or a convolution. Practically, they just reverse the work done by convolutions, restoring back the convolution-derived features into the original ones:

```python
def g_reshaping(self, x, shape, alpha=0.2,
                keep_prob=0.5, train=True):
    """
    Generator layer architecture
    Reshaping layer, applying batch normalization,
    leaky rely activation and dropout
    """
    x = tf.reshape(x, shape)
    x = tf.layers.batch_normalization(x, training=train)
    x = self.leaky_ReLU_activation(x, alpha)
    x = self.dropout(x, keep_prob)
    return x

def g_conv_transpose(self, x, filters, kernel_size,
                     strides, padding='same', alpha=0.2,
                     keep_prob=0.5, train=True):
    """
    Generator layer architecture
    Transposing convolution to a new size,
    applying batch normalization,
    leaky rely activation and dropout
    """
    x = tf.layers.conv2d_transpose(x, filters, kernel_size,
```

```
                              strides, padding)
    x = tf.layers.batch_normalization(x, training=train)
    x = self.leaky_ReLU_activation(x, alpha)
    x = self.dropout(x, keep_prob)
    return x
```

The discriminator architecture operates by taking images as input and, by various convolutions, transforming them until the result is flattened and turned into logits and probabilities (using the sigmoid function). Practically, everything is the same as in an ordinal convolution:

```
def discriminator(self, images, labels, reuse=False):
    with tf.variable_scope('discriminator', reuse=reuse):
        # Input layer is 28x28x3 --> concatenating input
        x = tf.concat([images, labels], 3)

        # d_conv --> expected size is 14x14x32
        x = self.d_conv(x, filters=32, kernel_size=5,
                        strides=2, padding='same',
                        alpha=0.2, keep_prob=0.5)

        # d_conv --> expected size is 7x7x64
        x = self.d_conv(x, filters=64, kernel_size=5,
                        strides=2, padding='same',
                        alpha=0.2, keep_prob=0.5)

        # d_conv --> expected size is 7x7x128
        x = self.d_conv(x, filters=128, kernel_size=5,
                        strides=1, padding='same',
                        alpha=0.2, keep_prob=0.5)

        # Flattening to a layer --> expected size is 4096
        x = tf.reshape(x, (-1, 7 * 7 * 128))

        # Calculating logits and sigmoids
        logits = tf.layers.dense(x, 1)
        sigmoids = tf.sigmoid(logits)

        return sigmoids, logits
```

As for the generator, the architecture is exactly the opposite of the discriminator. Starting from an input vector, z, a dense layer is first created, then a series of transpositions aims to rebuild the inverse process of convolutions in the discriminator, ending in a tensor of the same shape of the input images, which undergoes a further transformation by a `tanh` activation function:

```
def generator(self, z, out_channel_dim, is_train=True):

    with tf.variable_scope('generator',
                            reuse=(not is_train)):
        # First fully connected layer
        x = tf.layers.dense(z, 7 * 7 * 512)

        # Reshape it to start the convolutional stack
        x = self.g_reshaping(x, shape=(-1, 7, 7, 512),
                            alpha=0.2, keep_prob=0.5,
                            train=is_train)

        # g_conv_transpose --> 7x7x128 now
        x = self.g_conv_transpose(x, filters=256,
                            kernel_size=5,
                            strides=2, padding='same',
                            alpha=0.2, keep_prob=0.5,
                            train=is_train)

        # g_conv_transpose --> 14x14x64 now
        x = self.g_conv_transpose(x, filters=128,
                            kernel_size=5, strides=2,
                            padding='same', alpha=0.2,
                            keep_prob=0.5,
                            train=is_train)

        # Calculating logits and Output layer --> 28x28x5 now
        logits = tf.layers.conv2d_transpose(x,
                            filters=out_channel_dim,
                            kernel_size=5,
                            strides=1,
                            padding='same')
        output = tf.tanh(logits)

    return output
```

The architecture is very similar to the one depicted in the paper introducing CGANs, depicting how to reconstruct a 64 x 64 x 3 image from an initial input of a vector of size 100:

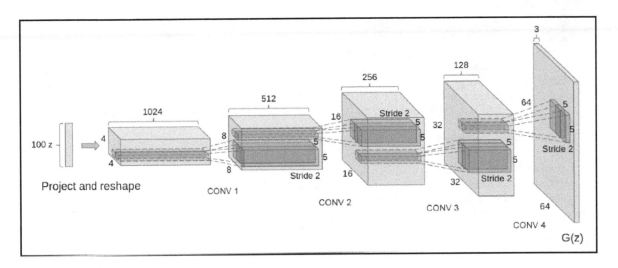

Figure 4: The DCGAN architecture of the generator.
SOURCE: arXiv, 1511.06434,2015

After defining the architecture, the loss function is the next important element to define. It uses two outputs, the output from the generator, which is pipelined into the discriminator outputting logits, and the output from the real images pipelined themselves into the discriminator. For both, a loss measure is then calculated. Here, the smooth parameter comes in handy because it helps to smooth the probabilities of the real images into something that is not 1.0, allowing a better, more probabilistic learning by the GAN network (with full penalization it could become more difficult for the fake images to have a chance against the real ones).

The final discriminator loss is simply the sum of the loss calculated on the fake and on the real images. The loss is calculated on the fake comparing the estimated logits against the probability of zero. The loss on the real images is calculated comparing the estimated logit against the smoothed probability (in our case it is 0.9), in order to prevent overfitting and having the discriminator learn simply to spot the real images because it memorized them. The generator loss is instead calculated from the logits estimated by the discriminator for the fake images against a probability of 1.0. In this way, the generator should strive to produce fake images that are estimated by the discriminator as most likely true (thus using a high probability). Therefore, the loss simply transmits from the discriminator evaluation on fake images to the generator in a feedback loop:

```
def loss(self, input_real, input_z, labels, out_channel_dim):

    # Generating output
    g_output = self.generator(input_z, out_channel_dim)
    # Classifying real input
```

```
        d_output_real, d_logits_real = self.discriminator(input_real,
labels, reuse=False)
        # Classifying generated output
        d_output_fake, d_logits_fake = self.discriminator(g_output, labels,
reuse=True)
        # Calculating loss of real input classification
        real_input_labels = tf.ones_like(d_output_real) * (1 - self.smooth)
# smoothed ones
        d_loss_real = tf.reduce_mean(
            tf.nn.sigmoid_cross_entropy_with_logits(logits=d_logits_real,
labels=real_input_labels))
        # Calculating loss of generated output classification
        fake_input_labels = tf.zeros_like(d_output_fake) # just zeros
        d_loss_fake = tf.reduce_mean(
            tf.nn.sigmoid_cross_entropy_with_logits(logits=d_logits_fake,
labels=fake_input_labels))
        # Summing the real input and generated output classification losses
        d_loss = d_loss_real + d_loss_fake # Total loss for discriminator
        # Calculating loss for generator: all generated images should have
been
        # classified as true by the discriminator
        target_fake_input_labels = tf.ones_like(d_output_fake) # all ones
        g_loss = tf.reduce_mean(
            tf.nn.sigmoid_cross_entropy_with_logits(logits=d_logits_fake,
labels=target_fake_input_labels))

        return d_loss, g_loss
```

Since the work of the GAN is visual, there are a few functions for visualizing a sample of the current production from the generator, as well as a specific set of images:

```
    def rescale_images(self, image_array):
        """
        Scaling images in the range 0-255
        """
        new_array = image_array.copy().astype(float)
        min_value = new_array.min()
        range_value = new_array.max() - min_value
        new_array = ((new_array - min_value) / range_value) * 255
        return new_array.astype(np.uint8)

    def images_grid(self, images, n_cols):
        """
        Arranging images in a grid suitable for plotting
        """
        # Getting sizes of images and defining the grid shape
        n_images, height, width, depth = images.shape
        n_rows = n_images // n_cols
```

```
        projected_images = n_rows * n_cols
        # Scaling images to range 0-255
        images = self.rescale_images(images)
        # Fixing if projected images are less
        if projected_images < n_images:
            images = images[:projected_images]
        # Placing images in a square arrangement
        square_grid = images.reshape(n_rows, n_cols,
                                 height, width, depth)
        square_grid = square_grid.swapaxes(1, 2)
        # Returning a image of the grid
        if depth >= 3:
            return square_grid.reshape(height * n_rows,
                                 width * n_cols, depth)

        else:
            return square_grid.reshape(height * n_rows,
                                 width * n_cols)


    def plotting_images_grid(self, n_images, samples):
        """
        Representing the images in a grid
        """
        n_cols = math.floor(math.sqrt(n_images))
        images_grid = self.images_grid(samples, n_cols)
        plt.imshow(images_grid, cmap=self.cmap)
        plt.show()


    def show_generator_output(self, sess, n_images, input_z,
                            labels, out_channel_dim,
                            image_mode):
        """
        Representing a sample of the
        actual generator capabilities
        """
        # Generating z input for examples
        z_dim = input_z.get_shape().as_list()[-1]
        example_z = np.random.uniform(-1, 1, size=[n_images, \
                                 z_dim - labels.shape[1]])
        example_z = np.concatenate((example_z, labels), axis=1)
        # Running the generator
        sample = sess.run(
            self.generator(input_z, out_channel_dim, False),
            feed_dict={input_z: example_z})
        # Plotting the sample
        self.plotting_images_grid(n_images, sample)


    def show_original_images(self, n_images):
        """
```

```
Representing a sample of original images
"""
# Sampling from available images
index = np.random.randint(self.dataset.shape[0],
                               size=(n_images))
sample = self.dataset.data[index]
# Plotting the sample
self.plotting_images_grid(n_images, sample)
```

Using the Adam optimizer, both the discriminator loss and the generator one are reduced, starting first from the discriminator (establishing how good is the generator's production against true images) and then propagating the feedback to the generator, based on the evaluation of the effect the fake images produced by the generator had on the discriminator:

```
def optimization(self):
    """
    GAN optimization procedure
    """
    # Initialize the input and parameters placeholders
    cases, image_width, image_height,\
    out_channel_dim = self.dataset.shape
    input_real, input_z, labels, learn_rate = \
                    self.instantiate_inputs(image_width,
                                              image_height,
                                              out_channel_dim,
                                              self.z_dim,
                              len(self.dataset.classes))

    # Define the network and compute the loss
    d_loss, g_loss = self.loss(input_real, input_z,
                              labels, out_channel_dim)

    # Enumerate the trainable_variables, split into G and D parts
    d_vars = [v for v in tf.trainable_variables() \
                if v.name.startswith('discriminator')]
    g_vars = [v for v in tf.trainable_variables() \
                if v.name.startswith('generator')]
    self.g_vars = g_vars

    # Optimize firt the discriminator, then the generatvor
    with tf.control_dependencies(\
                tf.get_collection(tf.GraphKeys.UPDATE_OPS)):
        d_train_opt = tf.train.AdamOptimizer(
                                      self.learning_rate,
                self.beta1).minimize(d_loss, var_list=d_vars)
        g_train_opt = tf.train.AdamOptimizer(
                                      self.learning_rate,
```

```
        self.beta1).minimize(g_loss, var_list=g_vars)

    return input_real, input_z, labels, learn_rate,
            d_loss, g_loss, d_train_opt, g_train_opt
```

At last, we have the complete training phase. In the training, there are two parts that require attention:

- How the optimization is done in two steps:
  1. Running the discriminator optimization
  2. Working on the generator's one

- How the random input and the real images are preprocessed by mixing them with labels in a way that creates further image layers containing the one-hot encoded information of the class relative to the image's label

In this way, the class is incorporated into the image, both in input and in output, conditioning the generator to take this information into account also, since it is penalized if it doesn't produce realistic images, that is, images with the right label attached. Let's say that our generator produces the image of a cat, but gives it the label of a dog. In this case, it will be penalized by the discriminator because the discriminator will notice how the generator cat is different from the real cats because of the different labels:

```
def train(self, save_every_n=1000):
    losses = []
    step = 0
    epoch_count = self.epochs
    batch_size = self.batch_size
    z_dim = self.z_dim
    learning_rate = self.learning_rate
    get_batches = self.dataset.get_batches
    classes = len(self.dataset.classes)
    data_image_mode = self.dataset.image_mode

    cases, image_width, image_height,\
    out_channel_dim = self.dataset.shape
    input_real, input_z, labels, learn_rate, d_loss,\
    g_loss, d_train_opt, g_train_opt = self.optimization()

    # Allowing saving the trained GAN
    saver = tf.train.Saver(var_list=self.g_vars)

    # Preparing mask for plotting progression
    rows, cols = min(5, classes), 5
    target = np.array([self.dataset.one_hot[i] \
            for j in range(cols) for i in range(rows)])
```

```
    with tf.Session() as sess:
        sess.run(tf.global_variables_initializer())
        for epoch_i in range(epoch_count):
            for batch_images, batch_labels \
                    in get_batches(batch_size):
                # Counting the steps
                step += 1
                # Defining Z
                batch_z = np.random.uniform(-1, 1, size=\
                                    (len(batch_images), z_dim))
                batch_z = np.concatenate((batch_z,\
                                        batch_labels), axis=1)
                # Reshaping labels for generator
                batch_labels = batch_labels.reshape(batch_size, 1, 1,
classes)
                batch_labels = batch_labels * np.ones((batch_size,
image_width, image_height, classes))
                # Sampling random noise for G
                batch_images = batch_images * 2
                # Running optimizers
                _ = sess.run(d_train_opt, feed_dict={input_real:
batch_images, input_z: batch_z,
                                                    labels:
batch_labels, learn_rate: learning_rate})
                _ = sess.run(g_train_opt, feed_dict={input_z: batch_z,
input_real: batch_images,
                                                    labels:
batch_labels, learn_rate: learning_rate})

                # Cyclic reporting on fitting and generator output
                if step % (save_every_n//10) == 0:
                    train_loss_d = sess.run(d_loss,
                                            {input_z: batch_z,
input_real: batch_images, labels: batch_labels})
                    train_loss_g = g_loss.eval({input_z: batch_z, labels:
batch_labels})
                    print("Epoch %i/%i step %i..." % (epoch_i + 1,
epoch_count, step),
                                "Discriminator Loss: %0.3f..." %
train_loss_d,
                                "Generator Loss: %0.3f" % train_loss_g)
                if step % save_every_n == 0:
                    rows = min(5, classes)
                    cols = 5
                    target = np.array([self.dataset.one_hot[i] for j in
range(cols) for i in range(rows)])
                    self.show_generator_output(sess, rows * cols, input_z,
target, out_channel_dim, data_image_mode)
```

```
                    saver.save(sess,
'./'+self.generator_name+'/generator.ckpt')

            # At the end of each epoch, get the losses and print them out
            try:
                train_loss_d = sess.run(d_loss, {input_z: batch_z,
input_real: batch_images, labels: batch_labels})
                train_loss_g = g_loss.eval({input_z: batch_z, labels:
batch_labels})
                print("Epoch %i/%i step %i..." % (epoch_i + 1, epoch_count,
step),
                      "Discriminator Loss: %0.3f..." % train_loss_d,
                      "Generator Loss: %0.3f" % train_loss_g)
            except:
                train_loss_d, train_loss_g = -1, -1

            # Saving losses to be reported after training
            losses.append([train_loss_d, train_loss_g])

        # Final generator output
        self.show_generator_output(sess, rows * cols, input_z, target,
out_channel_dim, data_image_mode)
        saver.save(sess, './' + self.generator_name + '/generator.ckpt')

    return np.array(losses)
```

During the training, the network is constantly saved on disk. When it is necessary to generate new images, you don't need to retrain, but just upload the network and specify the label you want the GAN to produce images for:

```
def generate_new(self, target_class=-1, rows=5, cols=5, plot=True):
    """
    Generating a new sample
    """
    # Fixing minimum rows and cols values
    rows, cols = max(1, rows), max(1, cols)
    n_images = rows * cols

    # Checking if we already have a TensorFlow graph
    if not self.trained:
        # Operate a complete restore of the TensorFlow graph
        tf.reset_default_graph()
        self._session = tf.Session()
        self._classes = len(self.dataset.classes)
        self._input_z = tf.placeholder(tf.float32, (None, self.z_dim +
self._classes), name='input_z')
        out_channel_dim = self.dataset.shape[3]
```

```
            # Restoring the generator graph
            self._generator = self.generator(self._input_z,
out_channel_dim)
            g_vars = [v for v in tf.trainable_variables() if
v.name.startswith('generator')]
            saver = tf.train.Saver(var_list=g_vars)
            print('Restoring generator graph')
            saver.restore(self._session,
tf.train.latest_checkpoint(self.generator_name))
            # Setting trained flag as True
            self.trained = True

        # Continuing the session
        sess = self._session
        # Building an array of examples examples
        target = np.zeros((n_images, self._classes))
        for j in range(cols):
            for i in range(rows):
                if target_class == -1:
                    target[j * cols + i, j] = 1.0
                else:
                    target[j * cols + i] =
self.dataset.one_hot[target_class].tolist()
        # Generating the random input
        z_dim = self._input_z.get_shape().as_list()[-1]
        example_z = np.random.uniform(-1, 1,
                    size=[n_images, z_dim - target.shape[1]])
        example_z = np.concatenate((example_z, target), axis=1)
        # Generating the images
        sample = sess.run(
            self._generator,
            feed_dict={self._input_z: example_z})
        # Plotting
        if plot:
            if rows * cols==1:
                if sample.shape[3] <= 1:
                    images_grid = sample[0,:,:,0]
                else:
                    images_grid = sample[0]
            else:
                images_grid = self.images_grid(sample, cols)
            plt.imshow(images_grid, cmap=self.cmap)
            plt.show()
        # Returning the sample for later usage
        # (and not closing the session)
        return sample
```

The class is completed by the `fit` method, which accepts both the learning rate parameter and the beta1 (an Adam optimizer parameter, adapting the parameter learning rates based on the average first moment, that is, the mean), and plots the resulting losses from the discriminator and the generator after the training is completed:

```
def fit(self, learning_rate=0.0002, beta1=0.35):
    """
    Fit procedure, starting training and result storage
    """
    # Setting training parameters
    self.learning_rate = learning_rate
    self.beta1 = beta1
    # Training generator and discriminator
    with tf.Graph().as_default():
        train_loss = self.train()
    # Plotting training fitting
    plt.plot(train_loss[:, 0], label='Discriminator')
    plt.plot(train_loss[:, 1], label='Generator')
    plt.title("Training fitting")
    plt.legend()
```

Putting CGAN to work on some examples

Now that the CGAN class is completed, let's go through some examples in order to provide you with fresh ideas on how to use this project. First of all, we will have to get everything ready for both downloading the necessary data and training our GAN. We start by importing the routine libraries:

```
import numpy as np
import urllib.request
import tarfile
import os
import zipfile
import gzip
import os
from glob import glob
from tqdm import tqdm
```

We then proceed by loading in the dataset and CGAN classes that we previously prepared:

```
from cGAN import Dataset, CGAN
```

The class `TqdmUpTo` is just a `tqdm` wrapper that enables the use of the progress display also for downloads. The class has been taken directly from the project's page at `https://github.com/tqdm/tqdm`:

```
class TqdmUpTo(tqdm):
    """
    Provides `update_to(n)` which uses `tqdm.update(delta_n)`.
    Inspired by https://github.com/pypa/twine/pull/242
    https://github.com/pypa/twine/commit/42e55e06
    """

    def update_to(self, b=1, bsize=1, tsize=None):
        """
        Total size (in tqdm units).
        If [default: None] remains unchanged.
        """
        if tsize is not None:
            self.total = tsize
        # will also set self.n = b * bsize
        self.update(b * bsize - self.n)
```

Finally, if we are using a Jupyter notebook (warmly suggested for this roadshow), you have to enable the inline plotting of images:

```
%matplotlib inline
```

We are now ready to proceed with the first example.

MNIST

The `MNIST` database of handwritten digits was provided by Yann LeCun when he was at Courant Institute, NYU, and by Corinna Cortes (Google Labs) and Christopher J.C. Burges (Microsoft Research). It is considered the standard for learning from real-world image data with minimal effort in preprocessing and formatting. The database consists of handwritten digits, offering a training set of 60,000 examples and a test set of 10,000. It is actually a subset of a larger set available from NIST. All the digits have been size-normalized and centered in a fixed-size image:

```
http://yann.lecun.com/exdb/mnist/
```

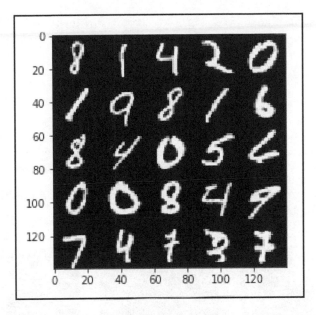

Figure 5: A sample of the original MNIST helps to understand the quality of the images to be reproduced by the CGAN.

As a first step, we upload the dataset from the Internet and store it locally:

```
labels_filename = 'train-labels-idx1-ubyte.gz'
images_filename = 'train-images-idx3-ubyte.gz'

url = "http://yann.lecun.com/exdb/mnist/"
with TqdmUpTo() as t: # all optional kwargs
    urllib.request.urlretrieve(url+images_filename,
                               'MNIST_'+images_filename,
                               reporthook=t.update_to, data=None)
with TqdmUpTo() as t: # all optional kwargs
    urllib.request.urlretrieve(url+labels_filename,
                               'MNIST_'+labels_filename,
                               reporthook=t.update_to, data=None)
```

In order to learn this set of handwritten numbers, we apply a batch of 32 images, a learning rate of 0.0002, a $beta1$ of 0.35, a z_dim of 96, and 15 epochs for training:

```
labels_path = './MNIST_train-labels-idx1-ubyte.gz'
images_path = './MNIST_train-images-idx3-ubyte.gz'

with gzip.open(labels_path, 'rb') as lbpath:
        labels = np.frombuffer(lbpath.read(),
                               dtype=np.uint8, offset=8)
with gzip.open(images_path, 'rb') as imgpath:
```

```
        images = np.frombuffer(imgpath.read(), dtype=np.uint8,
        offset=16).reshape(len(labels), 28, 28, 1)
batch_size = 32
z_dim = 96
epochs = 16

dataset = Dataset(images, labels, channels=1)
gan = CGAN(dataset, epochs, batch_size, z_dim, generator_name='mnist')

gan.show_original_images(25)
gan.fit(learning_rate = 0.0002, beta1 = 0.35)
```

The following image represents a sample of the numbers generated by the GAN at the second epoch and at the last one:

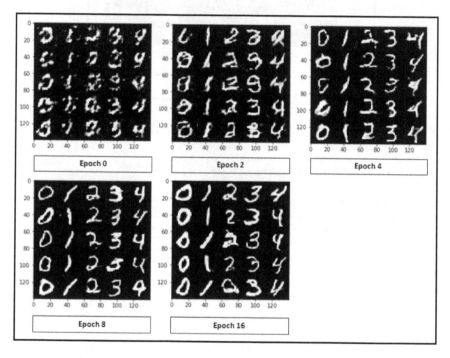

Figure 6: The GAN's results as they appear epoch after epoch

After 16 epochs, the numbers appear to be well shaped and ready to be used. We then extract a sample of all the classes arranged by row.

Evaluating the performances of a GAN is still most often the matter of visual inspecting some of its results by a human judge, trying to figure out if the image could be a fake (like a discriminator) from its overall aspect or by precisely revealing details. GANs lack an objective function to help to evaluate and compare them, though there are some computational techniques that could be used as a metric such as the *log-likelihood*, as described by *THEIS, Lucas; OORD, Aäron van den; BETHGE, Matthias. A note on the evaluation of generative models. arXiv preprint arXiv:1511.01844, 2015*: `https://arxiv.org/abs/1511.01844`.

We will keep our evaluation simple and empirical and thus we will use a sample of images generated by the trained GAN in order to evaluate the performances of the network and we also try to inspect the training loss for both the generator and the discriminator in order to spot any particular trend:

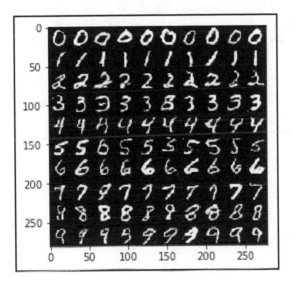

Figure 7: A sample of the final results after training on MNIST reveals it is an accessible task for a GAN network

Observing the training fit chart, represented in the figure the following, we notice how the generator reached the lowest error when the training was complete. The discriminator, after a previous peak, is struggling to get back to its previous performance values, pointing out a possible generator's breakthrough. We can expect that even more training epochs could improve the performance of this GAN network, but as you progress in the quality the output, it may take exponentially more time. In general, a good indicator of convergence of a GAN is having a downward trend of both the discriminator and generator, which is something that could be inferred by fitting a linear regression line to both loss vectors:

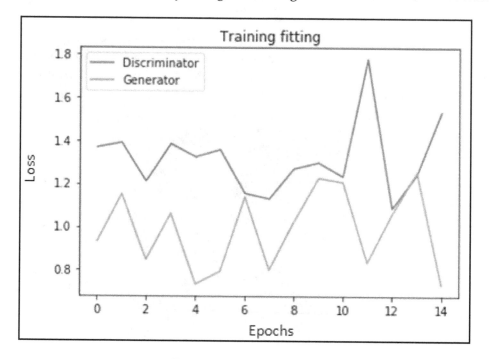

Figure 8: The training fit along the 16 epochs

Training an amazing GAN network may take a very long time and a lot of computational resources. By reading this recent article appeared in the New York Times, https://www.nytimes.com/interactive/2018/01/02/technology/ai-generated-photos.html, you can find a chart from NVIDIA showing the progress in time for the training of a progressive GAN learning from photos of celebrities. Whereas it can take a few days to get a decent result, for an astonishing one you need at least a fortnight. In the same way, even with our examples, the more training epochs you put in, the better the results.

Zalando MNIST

Fashion `MNIST` is a dataset of Zalando's article images, composed of a training set of 60,000 examples and a test set of 10,000 examples. As with `MNIST`, each example is a 28x28 grayscale image, associated with a label from 10 classes. It was intended by authors from Zalando Research (`https://github.com/zalandoresearch/fashion-mnist/graphs/contributors`) as a replacement for the original MNIST dataset in order to better benchmark machine learning algorithms since it is more challenging to learn and much more representative of deep learning in real-world tasks (`https://twitter.com/fchollet/status/852594987527045120`).

`https://github.com/zalandoresearch/fashion-mnist`

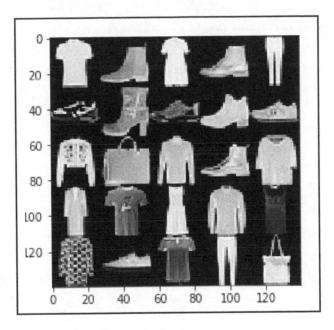

Figure 9: A sample of the original Zalando dataset

We download the images and their labels separately:

```
url = "http://fashion-mnist.s3-website.eu-central-\
        1.amazonaws.com/train-images-idx3-ubyte.gz"
filename = "train-images-idx3-ubyte.gz"
with TqdmUpTo() as t: # all optional kwargs
    urllib.request.urlretrieve(url, filename,
                            reporthook=t.update_to, data=None)
```

```
url = "http://fashion-mnist.s3-website.eu-central-\
      1.amazonaws.com/train-labels-idx1-ubyte.gz"
filename = "train-labels-idx1-ubyte.gz"
_ = urllib.request.urlretrieve(url, filename)
```

In order to learn this set of images, we apply a batch of 32 images, a learning rate of 0.0002, a beta1 of 0.35, a z_dim of 96, and 10 epochs for training:

```
labels_path = './train-labels-idx1-ubyte.gz'
images_path = './train-images-idx3-ubyte.gz'
label_names = ['t_shirt_top', 'trouser', 'pullover',
               'dress', 'coat', 'sandal', 'shirt',
               'sneaker', 'bag', 'ankle_boots']

with gzip.open(labels_path, 'rb') as lbpath:
        labels = np.frombuffer(lbpath.read(),
                                dtype=np.uint8,
                                offset=8)
with gzip.open(images_path, 'rb') as imgpath:
        images = np.frombuffer(imgpath.read(), dtype=np.uint8,
            offset=16).reshape(len(labels), 28, 28, 1)
batch_size = 32
z_dim = 96
epochs = 64

dataset = Dataset(images, labels, channels=1)
gan = CGAN(dataset, epochs, batch_size, z_dim, generator_name='zalando')

gan.show_original_images(25)
gan.fit(learning_rate = 0.0002, beta1 = 0.35)
```

The training takes a long time to go through all the epochs, but the quality appears to soon stabilize, though some problems take more epochs to disappear (for instance holes in shirts):

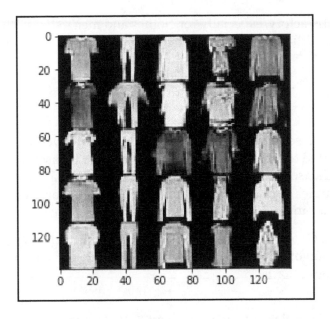

Figure 10: The evolution of the CGAN's training through epochs

Here is the result after 64 epochs:

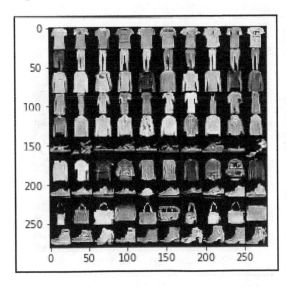

Figure 11: An overview of the results achieved after 64 epochs on Zalando dataset

The result is fully satisfactory, especially for clothes and men's shoes. Women's shoes, however, seem more difficult to be learned because smaller and more detailed than the other images.

EMNIST

The EMNIST dataset is a set of handwritten character digits derived from the NIST Special Database and converted to a 28 x 28 pixel image format and dataset structure that directly matches the MNIST dataset. We will be using EMNIST Balanced, a set of characters with an equal number of samples per class, which consists of 131,600 characters spread over 47 balanced classes. You can find all the references to the dataset in:

 Cohen, G., Afshar, S., Tapson, J., & van Schaik, A. (2017). EMNIST: an extension of MNIST to handwritten letters. Retrieved from http://arxiv. org/abs/1702.05373.

You can also explore complete information about EMNIST by browsing the official page of the dataset: https://www.nist.gov/itl/iad/image-group/emnist-dataset. Here is an extraction of the kind of characters that can be found in the EMNIST Balanced:

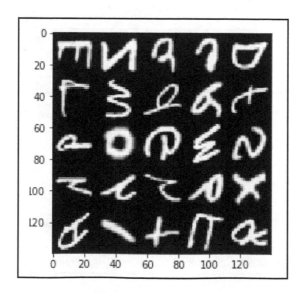

Figure 11: A sample of the original EMNIST dataset

```
url = "http://biometrics.nist.gov/cs_links/EMNIST/gzip.zip"
filename = "gzip.zip"
with TqdmUpTo() as t: # all optional kwargs
    urllib.request.urlretrieve(url, filename,
                               reporthook=t.update_to,
                               data=None)
```

After downloading from the NIST website, we unzip the downloaded package:

```
zip_ref = zipfile.ZipFile(filename, 'r')
zip_ref.extractall('.')
zip_ref.close()
```

We remove the unused ZIP file after checking that the unzipping was successful:

```
if os.path.isfile(filename):
    os.remove(filename)
```

In order to learn this set of handwritten numbers, we apply a batch of 32 images, a learning rate of 0.0002, a beta1 of 0.35, a z_dim of 96, and 10 epochs for training:

```
labels_path = './gzip/emnist-balanced-train-labels-idx1-ubyte.gz'
images_path = './gzip/emnist-balanced-train-images-idx3-ubyte.gz'
label_names = []

with gzip.open(labels_path, 'rb') as lbpath:
        labels = np.frombuffer(lbpath.read(), dtype=np.uint8,
            offset=8)
with gzip.open(images_path, 'rb') as imgpath:
        images = np.frombuffer(imgpath.read(), dtype=np.uint8,
                    offset=16).reshape(len(labels), 28, 28, 1)
batch_size = 32
z_dim = 96
epochs = 32

dataset = Dataset(images, labels, channels=1)
gan = CGAN(dataset, epochs, batch_size, z_dim,
           generator_name='emnist')

gan.show_original_images(25)
gan.fit(learning_rate = 0.0002, beta1 = 0.35)
```

Here is a sample of some handwritten letters when completing the training after 32 epochs:

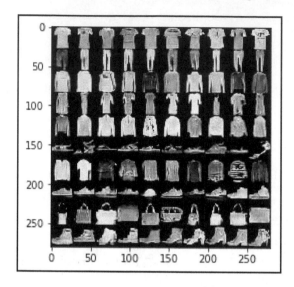

Figure 12: An overview of the results obtained training a CGAN on the EMNIST dataset

As for MNIST, a GAN can learn in a reasonable time to replicate handwritten letters in an accurate and credible way.

Reusing the trained CGANs

After training a CGAN, you may find useful to use the produced images in other applications. The method `generate_new` can be used to extract single images as well as a set of images (in order to check the quality of results for a specific image class). It operates on a previously trained CGan class, so all you have to do is just to pickle it in order first to save it, then to restore it again when needed.

When the training is complete, you can save your CGan class using `pickle`, as shown by these commands:

```
import pickle
pickle.dump(gan, open('mnist.pkl', 'wb'))
```

In this case, we have saved the CGAN trained on the MNIST dataset.

After you have restarted the Python session and memory is clean of any variable, you can just `import` again all the classes and restore the pickled CGan:

```
from CGan import Dataset, CGan
import pickle
gan = pickle.load(open('mnist.pkl', 'rb'))
```

When done, you set the target class you would like to be generated by the CGan (in the example we ask for the number 8 to be printed) and you can ask for a single example, a grid 5 x 5 of examples or a larger 10 x 10 grid:

```
nclass = 8
_ = gan.generate_new(target_class=nclass,
                     rows=1, cols=1, plot=True)
_ = gan.generate_new(target_class=nclass,
                     rows=5, cols=5, plot=True)
images = gan.generate_new(target_class=nclass,
                          rows=10, cols=10, plot=True)
print(images.shape)
```

 If you just want to obtain an overview of all the classes, just set the parameter target_class to -1.

After having set out target class to be represented, the generate_new is called three times and the last one the returned values are stored into the images variable, which is sized (100, 28, 28, 1) and contains a Numpy array of the produced images that can be reused for our purposes. Each time you call the method, a grid of results is plotted as shown in the following figure:

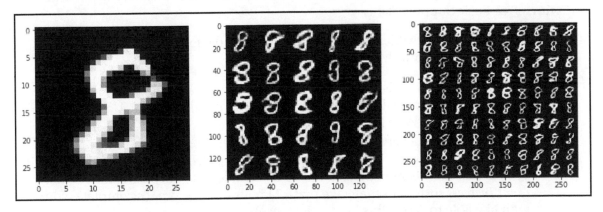

Figure 13: The plotted grid is a composition of the produced images, that is an image itself. From left to right, the plot of a request for a 1 x 1, 5 x 5, 10 x 10 grid of results. The real images are returned by the method and can be reused.

> If you don't need `generate_new` to plot the results, you simply set the `plot` parameter to False: `images = gan.generate_new(target_class=nclass, rows=10, cols=10, plot=False)`.

Resorting to Amazon Web Service

As previously noticed, it is warmly suggested you use a GPU in order to train the examples proposed in this chapter. Managing to obtain results in a reasonable time using just a CPU is indeed impossible, and also using a GPU may turn into quite long hours waiting for the computer to complete the training. A solution, requiring the payment of a fee, could be to resort to Amazon Elastic Compute Cloud, also known as Amazon EC2 (`https://aws.amazon.com/it/ec2/`), part of the **Amazon Web Services** (**AWS**). On EC2 you can launch virtual servers that you can control from your computer using the Internet connection. You can require servers with powerful GPUs on EC2 and make your life with TensorFlow projects much easier.

Amazon EC2 is not the only cloud service around. We have suggested you this service because it is the one we used in order to test the code in this book. Actually, there are alternatives, such as Google Cloud Compute (`cloud.google.com`), Microsoft Azure (azure.microsoft.com) and many others.

Running the chapter's code on EC2 requires having an account in AWS. If you don't have one, the first step is to register at `aws.amazon.com`, complete all the necessary forms and start with a free Basic Support Plan.

After you are registered on AWS, you just sign in and visit the EC2 page (`https://aws.amazon.com/ec2`). There you will:

1. Select a region which is both cheap and near to you which allows the kind of GPU instances we need, from EU (Ireland), Asia Pacific (Tokyo), US East (N. Virginia) and US West (Oregon).
2. Upgrade your EC2 Service Limit report at: `https://console.aws.amazon.com/ec2/v2/home?#Limits`. You will need to access a **p3.2xlarge** instance. Therefore if your actual limit is zero, that should be taken at least to one, using the *Request Limit Increase* form (this may take up to 24 hours, but before it's complete, you won't be able to access this kind of instance).
3. Get some AWS credits (providing your credit card, for instance).

After setting your region and having enough credit and request limit increase, you can start a **p3.2xlarge** server (a GPU compute server for deep learning applications) set up with an OS already containing all the software you need (thanks to an AMI, an image prepared by Amazon):

1. Get to the EC2 Management Console, and click on the **Launch Instance** button.

2. Click on AWS Marketplace, and search for **Deep Learning AMI with Source Code v2.0 (ami-bcce6ac4)** AMI. This AMI has everything pre-installed: CUDA, cuDNN (`https://developer.nvidia.com/cudnn`), Tensorflow.

3. Select the *GPU* compute **p3.2xlarge** instance. This instance has a powerful NVIDIA Tesla V100 GPU.

4. Configure a security group (which you may call **Jupyter**) by adding **Custom TCP Rule**, with TCP protocol, on `port 8888`, accessible from anywhere. This will allow you to run a Jupyter server on the machine and see the interface from any computer connected to the Internet.

5. Create an **Authentication Key Pair**. You can call it `deeplearning_jupyter.pem` for instance. Save it on your computer in a directory you can easily access.

6. Launch the instance. Remember that you will be paying since this moment unless you **stop** it from the AWS menu—you still will incur in some costs, but minor ones and you will have the instance available for you, with all your data—or simply **terminate** it and don't pay any more for it.

After everything is launched, you can access the server from your computer using ssh.

- Take notice of the IP of the machine. Let's say it is xx.xx.xxx.xxx, as an example.
- From a shell pointing to the directory where you .pem file is, type:
  ```
  ssh -i deeplearning_jupyter.pem ubuntu@ xx.xx.xxx.xxx
  ```
- When you have accessed the server machine, configure its Jupyter server by typing these commands:
  ```
  jupyter notebook --generate-config
  sed -ie "s/#c.NotebookApp.ip = 'localhost'/#c.NotebookApp.ip =
  '*'/g" ~/.jupyter/jupyter_notebook_config.py
  ```

- Operate on the server by copying the code (for instance by git cloning the code repository) and installing any library you may require. For instance, you could install these packages for this specific project:
```
sudo pip3 install tqdm
sudo pip3 install conda
```
- Launch the Jupyter server by running the command:
```
jupyter notebook --ip=0.0.0.0 --no-browser
```

- At this point, the server will run and your ssh shell will prompt you the logs from Jupyter. Among the logs, take note of the token (it is something like a sequence of numbers and letters).
- Open your browser and write in the address bar:
```
http:// xx.xx.xxx.xxx:8888/
```

When required type the token and you are ready to use the Jupiter notebook as you were on your local machine, but it is actually operating on the server. At this point, you will have a powerful server with GPU for running all your experiments with GANs.

Acknowledgements

In concluding this chapter, we would like to thank Udacity and Mat Leonard for their DCGAN tutorial, licensed under MIT (`https://github.com/udacity/deep-learning/blob/master/LICENSE`) which provided a good starting point and a benchmark for this project.

Summary

In this chapter, we have discussed at length the topic of Generative Adversarial Networks, how they work, and how they can be trained and used for different purposes. As a project, we have created a conditional GAN, one that can generate different types of images, based on your input and we learned how to process some example datasets and train them in order to have a pickable class capable of creating new images on demand.

Stock Price Prediction with LSTM

5

In this chapter, you'll be introduced to how to predict a timeseries composed of real values. Specifically, we will predict the stock price of a large company listed on the NYSE stock exchange, given its historical performance.

In this chapter we will look at:

- How to collect the historical stock price information
- How to format the dataset for a timeseries prediction task
- How to use regression to predict the future prices of a stock
- Long short-term memory (LSTM) 101
- How LSTM will boost the predictive performance
- How to visualize the performance on the Tensorboard

Each of these bullet points is a section in this chapter. Moreover, to make the chapter visually and intuitively easier to understand, we will first apply each technique on a simpler signal: a cosine. A cosine is more deterministic than a stock price and will help with the understanding and the potentiality of the algorithm.

 Note: we would like to point out that this project is just an experiment that works on the simple data we have available. Please don't use the code or the same model in a real-world scenario, since it may not perform at the same level. Remember: your capital is at risk, and there are no guarantees you'll always gain more.

Input datasets – cosine and stock price

As we claimed before, we will use two mono-dimensional signals as timeseries for our experiment. The first is a cosine wave with some added uniform noise.

This is the function to generate the cosine signal, given (as parameters) the number of points, the frequency of the signal, and the absolute intensity of the uniform generator for the noise. Also, in the body of the function, we're making sure to set the random seed, so we can make our experiments replicable:

```
def fetch_cosine_values(seq_len, frequency=0.01, noise=0.1):
    np.random.seed(101)
    x = np.arange(0.0, seq_len, 1.0)
    return np.cos(2 * np.pi * frequency * x) + np.random.uniform(low=-
noise, high=noise, size=seq_len)
```

To print 10 points, one full oscillation of the cosine (therefore `frequency` is `0.1`) with 0.1 magnitude noise, run:

```
print(fetch_cosine_values(10, frequency=0.1))
```

The output is:

```
[ 1.00327973 0.82315051 0.21471184 -0.37471266 -0.7719616 -0.93322063
 -0.84762375 -0.23029438 0.35332577 0.74700479]
```

In our analysis, we will pretend this is a stock price, where each point of the timeseries is a mono-dimensional feature representing the price of the stock itself for that day.

The second signal, instead, comes from the real financial world. Financial data can be expensive and hard to extract, that's why in this experiment we use the Python library `quandl` to obtain such information. The library has been chosen since it's easy to use, cheap (XX free queries per day), and great for this exercise, where we want to predict only the closing price of the stock. If you're into automatic trading, you should look for more information, in the premium version of the library, or in some other libraries or data sources.

Quandl is an API, and the Python library is a wrapper over the APIs. To see what's returned, run the following command in your prompt:

```
$> curl "https://www.quandl.com/api/v3/datasets/WIKI/FB/data.csv"
Date,Open,High,Low,Close,Volume,Ex-Dividend,Split Ratio,Adj. Open,Adj.
High,Adj. Low,Adj. Close,Adj. Volume
2017-08-18,166.84,168.67,166.21,167.41,14933261.0,0.0,1.0,166.84,168.67,166
.21,167.41,14933261.0
```

```
2017-08-17,169.34,169.86,166.85,166.91,16791591.0,0.0,1.0,169.34,169.86,166
.85,166.91,16791591.0
2017-08-16,171.25,171.38,169.24,170.0,15580549.0,0.0,1.0,171.25,171.38,169.
24,170.0,15580549.0
2017-08-15,171.49,171.5,170.01,171.0,8621787.0,0.0,1.0,171.49,171.5,170.01,
171.0,8621787.0
...
```

The format is a CSV, and each line contains the date, the opening price, the highest and the lowest of the day, the closing, the adjusted, and some volumes. The lines are sorted from the most recent to the least. The column we're interested in is the Adj. Close, that is, the closing price after adjustments.

 The adjusted closing price is a stock closing price after it has been amended to include any dividend, split, or merge.

Keep in mind that many online services show the unadjusted price or the opening price, therefore the numbers may not match.

Now, let's build a Python function to extract the adjusted price using the Python APIs. The full documentation of the APIs is available at https://docs.quandl.com/v1.0/docs, but we will just use the quandl.get function. Note that the default sorting is ascending, that is, from the oldest price to the newest one.

The function we're looking for should be able to cache calls and specify an initial and final timestamp to get the historical data beyond the symbol. Here's the code to do so:

```
def date_obj_to_str(date_obj):
    return date_obj.strftime('%Y-%m-%d')


def save_pickle(something, path):
    if not os.path.exists(os.path.dirname(path)):
        os.makedirs(os.path.dirname(path))
    with open(path, 'wb') as fh:
        pickle.dump(something, fh, pickle.DEFAULT_PROTOCOL)


def load_pickle(path):
    with open(path, 'rb') as fh:
        return pickle.load(fh)


def fetch_stock_price(symbol,
                      from_date,
                      to_date,
                      cache_path="./tmp/prices/"):
```

```
assert(from_date <= to_date)
filename = "{}_{}_{}.pk".format(symbol, str(from_date), str(to_date))
price_filepath = os.path.join(cache_path, filename)
try:
    prices = load_pickle(price_filepath)
    print("loaded from", price_filepath)
except IOError:
    historic = quandl.get("WIKI/" + symbol,
        start_date=date_obj_to_str(from_date),
        end_date=date_obj_to_str(to_date))
    prices = historic["Adj. Close"].tolist()
    save_pickle(prices, price_filepath)
    print("saved into", price_filepath)
return prices
```

The returned object of the function `fetch_stock_price` is a mono-dimensional array, containing the stock price for the requested symbol, ordered from the `from_date` to the `to_date`. Caching is done within the function, that is, if there's a cache miss, then the quandl API is called. The `date_obj_to_str` function is just a helper function, to convert `datetime.date` to the correct string format needed for the API.

Let's print the adjusted price of the Google stock price (whose symbol is GOOG) for January 2017:

```
import datetime
print(fetch_stock_price("GOOG",
    datetime.date(2017, 1, 1),
    datetime.date(2017, 1, 31)))
```

The output is:

```
[786.14, 786.9, 794.02, 806.15, 806.65, 804.79, 807.91, 806.36, 807.88,
804.61, 806.07, 802.175, 805.02, 819.31, 823.87, 835.67, 832.15, 823.31,
802.32, 796.79]
```

To have all the preceding functions available for all the scripts, we suggest you put them in a Python file, for example, in the code distributed within this book, they are in the `tools.py` file.

Format the dataset

Classic machine-learning algorithms are fed with multiple observations, where each of them has a pre-defined size (that is, the feature size). While working with timeseries, we don't have a pre-defined length: we want to create something that works for both 10 days look-back, but also for three years look-back. How is this possible?

It's very simple, instead of varying the number of features, we will change the number of observations, maintaining a constant feature size. Each observation represents a temporal window of the timeseries, and by sliding the window of one position on the right we create another observation. In code:

```
def format_dataset(values, temporal_features):
    feat_splits = [values[i:i + temporal_features] for i in
range(len(values) - temporal_features)]
    feats = np.vstack(feat_splits)
    labels = np.array(values[temporal_features:])
    return feats, labels
```

Given the timeseries, and the feature size, the function creates a sliding window which sweeps the timeseries, producing features and labels (that is, the value following the end of the sliding window, at each iteration). Finally, all the observations are piled up vertically, as well as the labels. The outcome is an observation with a defined number of columns, and a label vector.

We suggest putting this function in the `tools.py` file, so it can be accessed later.

Graphically, here's the outcome of the operation. Starting with the cosine signal, let's first plot a couple of oscillations of it, in another Python script (in the example, it's named `1_visualization_data.py`):

```
import datetime
import matplotlib.pyplot as plt
import numpy as np
import seaborn
from tools import fetch_cosine_values, fetch_stock_price, format_dataset
np.set_printoptions(precision=2)

cos_values = fetch_cosine_values(20, frequency=0.1)
seaborn.tsplot(cos_values)
plt.xlabel("Days since start of the experiment")
plt.ylabel("Value of the cosine function")
plt.title("Cosine time series over time")
plt.show()
```

The code is very simple; after a few imports, we plot a 20-point cosine timeseries with period 10 (that is frequency 0.01):

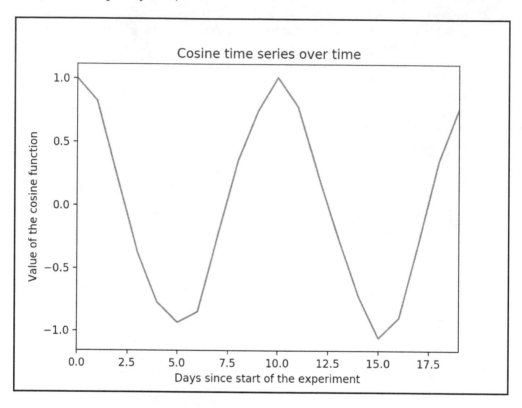

Let's now format the timeseries to be ingested by the machine learning algorithm, creating an observation matrix with five columns:

```
features_size = 5
minibatch_cos_X, minibatch_cos_y = format_dataset(cos_values,
features_size)
print("minibatch_cos_X.shape=", minibatch_cos_X.shape)
print("minibatch_cos_y.shape=", minibatch_cos_y.shape)
```

Starting from a timeseries with 20 points, the output will be an observation matrix of size *15x5*, while the label vector will be 15 elements long. Of course, by changing the feature size, the number of rows will also change.

Let's now visualize the operation, to make it simpler to understand. For example, let's plot the first five observations of the observation matrix. Let's also print the label of each feature (in red):

```
samples_to_plot = 5
f, axarr = plt.subplots(samples_to_plot, sharex=True)
for i in range(samples_to_plot):
    feats = minibatch_cos_X[i, :]
    label = minibatch_cos_y[i]
    print("Observation {}: X={} y={}".format(i, feats, label))
    plt.subplot(samples_to_plot, 1, i+1)
    axarr[i].plot(range(i, features_size + i), feats, '--o')
    axarr[i].plot([features_size + i], label, 'rx')
    axarr[i].set_ylim([-1.1, 1.1])
plt.xlabel("Days since start of the experiment")
axarr[2].set_ylabel("Value of the cosine function")
axarr[0].set_title("Visualization of some observations: Features (blue) and
Labels (red)")
plt.show()
```

And here's the plot:

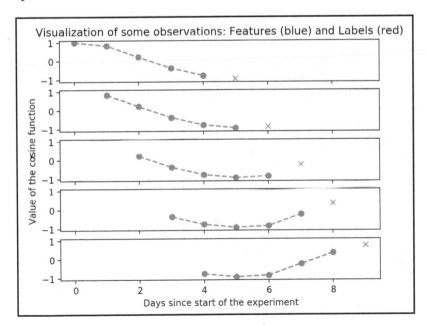

As you can see, the timeseries became an observation vector, each of them with size five.

So far, we haven't shown what the stock prices look like, therefore let's print them here as a timeseries. We selected (cherry-picked) some of the best-known companies in the United States; feel free to add your favorites to see the trend in the last year. In this plot, we'll just limit ourselves to two years: 2015 and 2016. We will also use the very same data in this chapter, therefore the next runs will have the timeseries cached:

```
symbols = ["MSFT", "KO", "AAL", "MMM", "AXP", "GE", "GM", "JPM", "UPS"]
ax = plt.subplot(1,1,1)
for sym in symbols:
    prices = fetch_stock_price(
    sym, datetime.date(2015, 1, 1), datetime.date(2016, 12, 31))
    ax.plot(range(len(prices)), prices, label=sym)

handles, labels = ax.get_legend_handles_labels()
ax.legend(handles, labels)
plt.xlabel("Trading days since 2015-1-1")
plt.ylabel("Stock price [$]")
plt.title("Prices of some American stocks in trading days of 2015 and
2016")
plt.show()
```

And this is the plot of the prices:

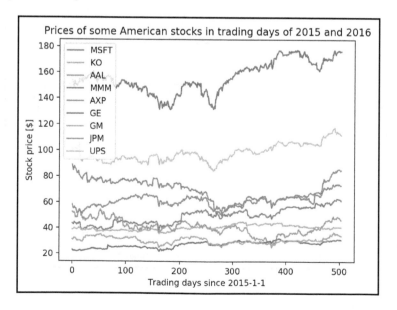

Each of the lines is a timeseries, and as we did for the cosine signal, in this chapter it will be transformed into an observation matrix (with the `format_dataset` function).

Are you excited? The data is ready, now let's move on to the interesting data science part of the project.

Using regression to predict the future prices of a stock

Given the observation matrix and a real value label, we are initially tempted to approach the problem as a regression problem. In this case, the regression is very simple: from a numerical vector, we want to predict a numerical value. That's not ideal. Treating the problem as a regression problem, we force the algorithm to think that each feature is independent, while instead, they're correlated, since they're windows of the same timeseries. Let's start anyway with this simple assumption (each feature is independent), and we will show in the next chapter how performance can be increased by exploiting the temporal correlation.

In order to evaluate the model, we now create a function that, given the observation matrix, the true labels, and the predicted ones, will output the metrics (in terms of **mean square error** (MSE) and **mean absolute error** (MAE) of the predictions. It will also plot the training, testing, and predicted timeseries one onto another, to visually check the performance. In order to compare the results, we also include the metrics in case we don't do use any model, but we simply predict the day-after value as the value of the present day (in the stock market, this means that we will predict the price for tomorrow as the price the stock has today).

Before that, we need a helping function to reshape matrices to mono-dimensional (1D) arrays. Please keep this function in the `tools.py` file, since it will be used by multiple scripts:

```
def matrix_to_array(m):
    return np.asarray(m).reshape(-1)
```

Now, time for the evaluation function. We decided to put this function into the `evaluate_ts.py` file, so many other scripts can access it:

```
import numpy as np
from matplotlib import pylab as plt
from tools import matrix_to_array
```

```
def evaluate_ts(features, y_true, y_pred):
    print("Evaluation of the predictions:")
    print("MSE:", np.mean(np.square(y_true - y_pred)))
    print("mae:", np.mean(np.abs(y_true - y_pred)))

    print("Benchmark: if prediction == last feature")
    print("MSE:", np.mean(np.square(features[:, -1] - y_true)))
    print("mae:", np.mean(np.abs(features[:, -1] - y_true)))

    plt.plot(matrix_to_array(y_true), 'b')
    plt.plot(matrix_to_array(y_pred), 'r--')
    plt.xlabel("Days")
    plt.ylabel("Predicted and true values")
    plt.title("Predicted (Red) VS Real (Blue)")
    plt.show()

    error = np.abs(matrix_to_array(y_pred) - matrix_to_array(y_true))
    plt.plot(error, 'r')
    fit = np.polyfit(range(len(error)), error, deg=1)
    plt.plot(fit[0] * range(len(error)) + fit[1], '--')
    plt.xlabel("Days")
    plt.ylabel("Prediction error L1 norm")
    plt.title("Prediction error (absolute) and trendline")
    plt.show()
```

Now, time to move to the modeling phase.

As previously, we start first with the cosine signal and then we move to the stock price prediction.

We also suggest you put the following code in another file, for example, in `2_regression_cosine.py` (you can find the code in the code bundle under this name).

Let's start with some imports and with the seed for `numpy` and `tensorflow`:

```
import matplotlib.pyplot as plt
import numpy as np
import tensorflow as tf
from evaluate_ts import evaluate_ts
from tensorflow.contrib import rnn
from tools import fetch_cosine_values, format_dataset

tf.reset_default_graph()
tf.set_random_seed(101)
```

Then, it's time to create the cosine signal and to transform it into an observation matrix. In this example, we will use 20 as feature size, since it's roughly the equivalent number of working days in a month. The regression problem has now shaped this way: given the 20 values of the cosine in the past, forecast the next day value.

As training and testing, we will use datasets of 250 observation each, to have the equivalent of one year of data (one year contains just under 250 working days). In this example, we will generate just one cosine signal, and then it will be broken into two pieces: the first half will contain the train data, and the second half the testing. Feel free to change them, and observe how the performance changes when these parameters are changed:

```
feat_dimension = 20
train_size = 250
test_size = 250
```

1. Now, in this part of the script, we will define some parameters for Tensorflow. More specifically: the learning rate, the type of optimizer to use, and the number of epoch (that is, how many times the training dataset goes into the learner during the training operation). These values are not the best, feel free to change them to predict some better ones:

```
learning_rate = 0.01
optimizer = tf.train.AdamOptimizer
n_epochs = 10
```

2. Finally, it's time to prepare the observation matrices, for training and testing. Keep in mind that to speed up the Tensorflow analysis, we will use float32 (4 bytes long) in our analysis:

```
cos_values = fetch_cosine_values(train_size + test_size + feat_dimension)
minibatch_cos_X, minibatch_cos_y = format_dataset(cos_values,
feat_dimension)
train_X = minibatch_cos_X[:train_size, :].astype(np.float32)
train_y = minibatch_cos_y[:train_size].reshape((-1, 1)).astype(np.float32)
test_X = minibatch_cos_X[train_size:, :].astype(np.float32)
test_y = minibatch_cos_y[train_size:].reshape((-1, 1)).astype(np.float32)
```

Given the datasets, let's now define the placeholders for the observation matrix and the labels. Since we're building a generic script, we just set the number of features, and not the number of observations:

```
X_tf = tf.placeholder("float", shape=(None, feat_dimension), name="X")
y_tf = tf.placeholder("float", shape=(None, 1), name="y")
```

Here's the core of our project: the regression algorithm implemented in Tensorflow.

1. We opted for the most classic way of implementing it, that is, the multiplication between the observation matrix with a weights array plus the bias. What's coming out (and the returned value of this function) is the array containing the predictions for all the observations contained in x:

```
def regression_ANN(x, weights, biases):
    return tf.add(biases, tf.matmul(x, weights))
```

2. Now, let's define the trainable parameters of the regressor, which are the tensorflow variables. The weights are a vector with as many values as the feature size, while the bias is just a scalar.

 Note that we initialized the weights using a truncated normal distribution, to have values close to zero, but not too extreme (as a plain normal distribution could output); for the bias we instead set it to zero.

Again, feel free to change the initializations, to see the changes in performance:

```
weights = tf.Variable(tf.truncated_normal([feat_dimension, 1], mean=0.0,
stddev=1.0), name="weights")
biases = tf.Variable(tf.zeros([1, 1]), name="bias")
```

3. The last thing we need to define in the tensorflow graphs are how the predictions are calculated (in our case, it's simply the output of the function which defines the model), the cost (in the example we use the MSE), and the training operator (we want to minimize the MSE, using the optimizer with the learning rate set previously):

```
y_pred = regression_ANN(X_tf, weights, biases)
cost = tf.reduce_mean(tf.square(y_tf - y_pred))
train_op = optimizer(learning_rate).minimize(cost)
```

We're now ready to open a tensorflow session, and train the model.

4. We will first initialize the variables, then, in a loop, we will feed the `training` dataset into the `tensorflow` graph (using the placeholders). At each iteration, we will print the training MSE:

```
with tf.Session() as sess:
    sess.run(tf.global_variables_initializer())
    # For each epoch, the whole training set is feeded into the tensorflow
graph

    for i in range(n_epochs):
        train_cost, _ = sess.run([cost, train_op], feed_dict={X_tf: train_X,
y_tf: train_y})
        print("Training iteration", i, "MSE", train_cost)

    # After the training, let's check the performance on the test set
    test_cost, y_pr = sess.run([cost, y_pred], feed_dict={X_tf: test_X,
y_tf: test_y})
    print("Test dataset:", test_cost)

    # Evaluate the results
    evaluate_ts(test_X, test_y, y_pr)

    # How does the predicted look like?
    plt.plot(range(len(cos_values)), cos_values, 'b')
    plt.plot(range(len(cos_values)-test_size, len(cos_values)), y_pr, 'r--')
    plt.xlabel("Days")
    plt.ylabel("Predicted and true values")
    plt.title("Predicted (Red) VS Real (Blue)")
    plt.show()
```

After the training, we evaluated the MSE on the testing dataset, and finally, we printed and plotted the performance of the model.

With the default values we provided in the scripts, performances are worse than the non-modeling performance. With some tuning, the results improve. For example, by setting the learning rate equal to 0.1 and the number of training epoch to *1000*, the output of the script will be similar to this:

```
Training iteration 0 MSE 4.39424
Training iteration 1 MSE 1.34261
Training iteration 2 MSE 1.28591
Training iteration 3 MSE 1.84253
Training iteration 4 MSE 1.66169
Training iteration 5 MSE 0.993168
...
...
Training iteration 998 MSE 0.00363447
```

```
Training iteration 999 MSE 0.00363426
Test dataset: 0.00454513
Evaluation of the predictions:
MSE: 0.00454513
mae: 0.0568501
Benchmark: if prediction == last feature
MSE: 0.964302
mae: 0.793475
```

Training performance and testing performance are very similar (therefore we're not overfitting the model), and both the MSE and the MAE are better than a no-modeling prediction.

That's how the error looks for each timepoint. It seems that it's contained between +/-0.15, and doesn't have any trend over time. Remember that the noise we artificially introduced with the cosine had a magnitude of +/- 0.1 with a uniform distribution:

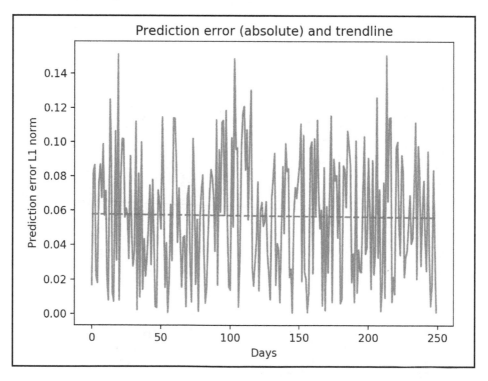

Finally, the last graph shows both the training timeseries overlapped with the predicted one. Not bad for a simple linear regression, right?

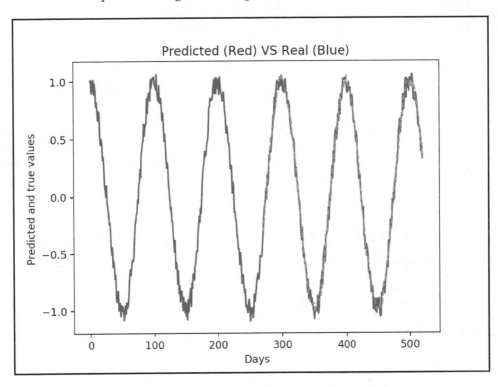

Let's now apply the same model on a stock price. We suggest you copy the content of the current file to a new one, named `3_regression_stock_price.py`. Here we will change only the data importing bit, leaving everything else as it is.

Let's use the Microsoft stock price in this example, whose symbol is `"MSFT"`. It's simple to load the prices for this symbol for 2015/16 and format them as an observation matrix. Here's the code, also containing the casting to float32 and the train/test split. In this example, we have one year of training data (2015) which will be used to predict the stock price for the whole of 2016:

```
symbol = "MSFT"
feat_dimension = 20
train_size = 252
test_size = 252 - feat_dimension

# Settings for tensorflow
learning_rate = 0.05
```

```
optimizer = tf.train.AdamOptimizer
n_epochs = 1000

# Fetch the values, and prepare the train/test split
stock_values = fetch_stock_price(symbol, datetime.date(2015, 1, 1),
datetime.date(2016, 12, 31))
minibatch_cos_X, minibatch_cos_y = format_dataset(stock_values,
feat_dimension)
train_X = minibatch_cos_X[:train_size, :].astype(np.float32)
train_y = minibatch_cos_y[:train_size].reshape((-1, 1)).astype(np.float32)
test_X = minibatch_cos_X[train_size:, :].astype(np.float32)
test_y = minibatch_cos_y[train_size:].reshape((-1, 1)).astype(np.float32)
```

In this script, we found that the best performances have been obtained with the following settings:

```
learning_rate = 0.5
n_epochs = 20000
optimizer = tf.train.AdamOptimizer
```

The output of the script should look like this:

```
Training iteration 0 MSE 15136.7
Training iteration 1 MSE 106385.0
Training iteration 2 MSE 14307.3
Training iteration 3 MSE 15565.6
...
...
Training iteration 19998 MSE 0.577189
Training iteration 19999 MSE 0.57704
Test dataset: 0.539493
Evaluation of the predictions:
MSE: 0.539493
mae: 0.518984
Benchmark: if prediction == last feature
MSE: 33.7714
mae: 4.6968
```

Even in this case, we're not overfitting, and the simple regressor performs better than no model at all (we all would bet that). At the beginning, the cost is really high, but iteration after iteration, it gets very close to zero. Also, the mae score is easy to interpret in this case, they are dollars! With a learner, we would have predicted on average half a dollar closer to the real price the day after; without any learner, nine times more.

Let's now visually evaluate the performance of the model, impressive isn't it?

This is the predicted value:

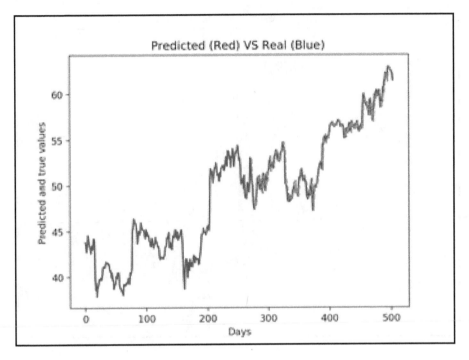

That's the absolute error, with the trend line (dotted):

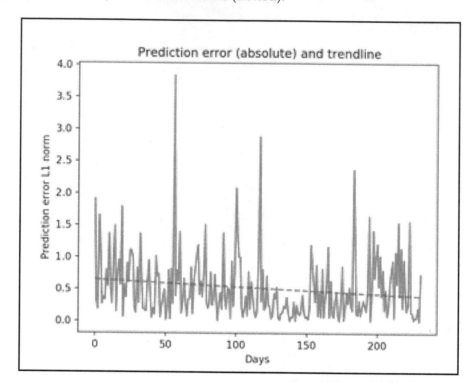

And finally, the real and predicted value in the train set:

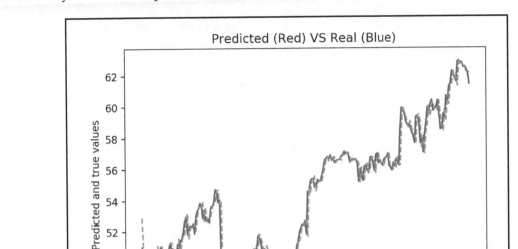

Remember that those are the performances of a simple regression algorithm, without exploiting the temporal correlation between features. How can we exploit it to perform better?

Long short-term memory – LSTM 101

Long Short-Term Memory (**LSTM**), models are a special case of RNNs, Recurrent Neural Networks. A full, rigorous description of them is out of the scope of this book; in this section, we will just provide the essence of them.

You can have a look at the following books published by Packt:
`https://www.packtpub.com/big-data-and-business-intelligence/neur`
`al-network-programming-tensorflow`
Also, you can have a look at this: `https://www.packtpub.com/big-data-`
`and-business-intelligence/neural-networks-r`

Simply speaking, RNN works on sequences: they accept multidimensional signals as input, and they produce a multidimensional output signal. In the following figure, there's an example of an RNN able to cope with a timeseries of five-time steps (one input for each time step). The inputs are in the bottom part of the RNN, with the outputs in the top. Remember that each input/output is an N-dimensional feature:

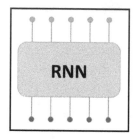

Inside, an RNN has multiple stages; each stage is connected to its input/output and to the output of the previous stage. Thanks to this configuration, each output is not just a function of the input of its own stage, but depends also on the output of the previous stage (which, again, is a function of its input and the previous output). This configuration ensures that each input influences all the following outputs, or, from the other side, an output is a function of all the previous and current stages inputs.

 Note that not all the outputs are always used. Think about a sentiment analysis task, in that case, given a sentence (the timeseries input signals), we just want to get one class (positive/negative); therefore only the last output is considered as output, all the others exist, but they're not used. Keep in mind that we just use the last one because it's the only one with the full visibility of the sentence.

LSTM models are an evolution of RNNs: with long RNNs, the training phase may lead to very tiny or huge gradients back-propagated throughout the network, which leads the weights to zero or to infinity: that's a problem usually expressed as a vanishing/exploding gradient. To mitigate this problem, LSTMs have two outputs for each stage: one is the actual output of the model, and the other one, named memory, is the internal state of the stage.

Both outputs are fed into the following stage, lowering the chances of having vanishing or exploding gradients. Of course, this comes with a price: the complexity (numbers of weights to tune) and the memory footprint of the model are larger, that's why we strongly suggest using GPU devices when training RNNs, the speed up in terms of time is impressive!

Unlike regression, RNNs need a three dimensional signal as input. Tensorflow specifies the format as:

- Samples
- Time steps
- Features

In the preceding example, the sentiment analysis, the training tensor will have the sentences on the *x*-axis, the words composing the sentence on the *y*-axis, and the bag of words with the dictionary on the *z*-axis. For example, for classifying a 1 M corpora in English (with about 20,000 different words), whose sentences are long, up to 50 words, the tensor dimension is 1 M x 50 x 20 K.

Stock price prediction with LSTM

Thanks to LSTM, we can exploit the temporal redundancy contained in our signals. From the previous section, we learned that the observation matrix should be reformatted into a 3D tensor, with three axes:

1. The first containing the samples.
2. The second containing the timeseries.
3. The third containing the input features.

Since we're dealing with just a mono-dimensional signal, the input tensor for the LSTM should have the size (None, `time_dimension`, 1), where `time_dimension` is the length of the time window. Let's code now, starting with the cosine signal. We suggest you name the file `4_rnn_cosine.py`.

1. First of all, some imports:

```
import matplotlib.pyplot as plt
import numpy as np
import tensorflow as tf
from evaluate_ts import evaluate_ts
from tensorflow.contrib import rnn
from tools import fetch_cosine_values, format_dataset
tf.reset_default_graph()
tf.set_random_seed(101)
```

2. Then, we set the window size to chunk the signal. This operation is similar to the observation matrix creation.

```
time_dimension = 20
train_size = 250
test_size = 250
```

3. Then, some settings for Tensorflow. At this stage, let's start with default values:

```
learning_rate = 0.01
optimizer = tf.train.AdagradOptimizer
n_epochs = 100
n_embeddings = 64
```

4. Now, it's time to fetch the noisy cosine, and reshape it to have a 3D tensor shape (None, time_dimension, 1). This is done here:

```
cos_values = fetch_cosine_values(train_size + test_size + time_dimension)
minibatch_cos_X, minibatch_cos_y = format_dataset(cos_values,
time_dimension)
train_X = minibatch_cos_X[:train_size, :].astype(np.float32)
train_y = minibatch_cos_y[:train_size].reshape((-1, 1)).astype(np.float32)
test_X = minibatch_cos_X[train_size:, :].astype(np.float32)
test_y = minibatch_cos_y[train_size:].reshape((-1, 1)).astype(np.float32)
train_X_ts = train_X[:, :, np.newaxis]
test_X_ts = test_X[:, :, np.newaxis]
```

5. Exactly as in the previous script, let's define the placeholders for Tensorflow:

```
X_tf = tf.placeholder("float", shape=(None, time_dimension, 1), name="X")
y_tf = tf.placeholder("float", shape=(None, 1), name="y")
```

6. Here, let's define the model. We will use an LSTM with a variable number of embeddings. Also, as described in the previous chapter, we will consider just the last output of the cells through a linear regression (fully connected layer) to get the prediction:

```
def RNN(x, weights, biases):
    x_ = tf.unstack(x, time_dimension, 1)
    lstm_cell = rnn.BasicLSTMCell(n_embeddings)
    outputs, _ = rnn.static_rnn(lstm_cell, x_, dtype=tf.float32)
    return tf.add(biases, tf.matmul(outputs[-1], weights))
```

7. Let's set the `trainable` variables (`weights`) as before, the `cost` function and the training operator:

```
weights = tf.Variable(tf.truncated_normal([n_embeddings, 1], mean=0.0,
stddev=1.0), name="weights")
biases = tf.Variable(tf.zeros([1]), name="bias")
y_pred = RNN(X_tf, weights, biases)
cost = tf.reduce_mean(tf.square(y_tf - y_pred))
train_op = optimizer(learning_rate).minimize(cost)

# Exactly as before, this is the main loop.
with tf.Session() as sess:
    sess.run(tf.global_variables_initializer())

    # For each epoch, the whole training set is feeded into the tensorflow
graph
    for i in range(n_epochs):
        train_cost, _ = sess.run([cost, train_op], feed_dict={X_tf:
train_X_ts, y_tf: train_y})
        if i%100 == 0:
            print("Training iteration", i, "MSE", train_cost)

    # After the training, let's check the performance on the test set
    test_cost, y_pr = sess.run([cost, y_pred], feed_dict={X_tf: test_X_ts,
y_tf: test_y})
    print("Test dataset:", test_cost)

    # Evaluate the results
    evaluate_ts(test_X, test_y, y_pr)

    # How does the predicted look like?
    plt.plot(range(len(cos_values)), cos_values, 'b')
    plt.plot(range(len(cos_values)-test_size, len(cos_values)), y_pr, 'r--
')
    plt.xlabel("Days")
    plt.ylabel("Predicted and true values")
    plt.title("Predicted (Red) VS Real (Blue)")
    plt.show()
```

The output, after a hyperparameter optimization, is the following:

```
Training iteration 0 MSE 0.0603129
Training iteration 100 MSE 0.0054377
Training iteration 200 MSE 0.00502512
Training iteration 300 MSE 0.00483701
...
Training iteration 9700 MSE 0.0032881
```

```
Training iteration 9800 MSE 0.00327899
Training iteration 9900 MSE 0.00327195
Test dataset: 0.00416444
Evaluation of the predictions:
MSE: 0.00416444
mae: 0.0545878
```

Performances are pretty similar to the ones we obtained with the simple linear regression. Let's see if we can get better performance using a less predictable signal as the stock price. We'll use the same timeseries we used in the previous chapter, to compare the performance.

Modifying the previous program, let's plug in the stock price timeseries instead of the cosine. Modify some lines to load the stock price data:

```
stock_values = fetch_stock_price(symbol, datetime.date(2015, 1, 1),
datetime.date(2016, 12, 31))
minibatch_cos_X, minibatch_cos_y = format_dataset(stock_values,
time_dimension)
train_X = minibatch_cos_X[:train_size, :].astype(np.float32)
train_y = minibatch_cos_y[:train_size].reshape((-1, 1)).astype(np.float32)
test_X = minibatch_cos_X[train_size:, :].astype(np.float32)
test_y = minibatch_cos_y[train_size:].reshape((-1, 1)).astype(np.float32)
train_X_ts = train_X[:, :, np.newaxis]
test_X_ts = test_X[:, :, np.newaxis]
```

Since the dynamic of this signal is wider, we'll also need to modify the distribution used to extract the initial weights. We suggest you set it to:

```
weights = tf.Variable(tf.truncated_normal([n_embeddings, 1], mean=0.0,
stddev=10.0), name="weights")
```

After a few tests, we found we hit the maximum performance with these parameters:

```
learning_rate = 0.1
n_epochs = 5000
n_embeddings = 256
```

The output, using these parameters is:

```
Training iteration 200 MSE 2.39028
Training iteration 300 MSE 1.39495
Training iteration 400 MSE 1.00994
...
Training iteration 4800 MSE 0.593951
Training iteration 4900 MSE 0.593773
Test dataset: 0.497867
Evaluation of the predictions:
MSE: 0.497867
mae: 0.494975
```

This is 8% better than the previous model (test MSE). Remember, it comes with a price! More parameters to train also means the training time is much longer than the previous example (on a laptop, a few minutes, using the GPU).

Finally, let's check the Tensorboard. In order to write the logs, we should add the following code:

1. At the beginning of the files, after the imports:

```
import os
tf_logdir = "./logs/tf/stock_price_lstm"
os.makedirs(tf_logdir, exist_ok=1)
```

2. Also, the whole body of the RNN function should be inside the named-scope LSTM, that is:

```
def RNN(x, weights, biases):
    with tf.name_scope("LSTM"):
        x_ = tf.unstack(x, time_dimension, 1)
        lstm_cell = rnn.BasicLSTMCell(n_embeddings)
        outputs, _ = rnn.static_rnn(lstm_cell, x_, dtype=tf.float32)
        return tf.add(biases, tf.matmul(outputs[-1], weights))
```

3. Similarly, the `cost` function should be wrapped in a Tensorflow scope. Also, we will add the `mae` computation within the `tensorflow` graph:

```
y_pred = RNN(X_tf, weights, biases)
with tf.name_scope("cost"):
    cost = tf.reduce_mean(tf.square(y_tf - y_pred))
    train_op = optimizer(learning_rate).minimize(cost)
    tf.summary.scalar("MSE", cost)
        with tf.name_scope("mae"):
        mae_cost = tf.reduce_mean(tf.abs(y_tf - y_pred))
        tf.summary.scalar("mae", mae_cost)
```

4. Finally, the main function should look like this:

```
with tf.Session() as sess:
    writer = tf.summary.FileWriter(tf_logdir, sess.graph)
    merged = tf.summary.merge_all()
    sess.run(tf.global_variables_initializer())

    # For each epoch, the whole training set is feeded into the tensorflow
graph
    for i in range(n_epochs):
        summary, train_cost, _ = sess.run([merged, cost, train_op],
feed_dict={X_tf:
                                                train_X_ts, y_tf:
train_y})
        writer.add_summary(summary, i)
        if i%100 == 0:
            print("Training iteration", i, "MSE", train_cost)
    # After the training, let's check the performance on the test set
    test_cost, y_pr = sess.run([cost, y_pred], feed_dict={X_tf: test_X_ts,
y_tf:
            test_y})
    print("Test dataset:", test_cost)
```

This way, we separate the scopes of each block, and write a summary report for the trained variables.

Now, let's launch `tensorboard`:

```
$> tensorboard --logdir=./logs/tf/stock_price_lstm
```

After opening the browser at `localhost:6006`, from the first tab, we can observe the behavior of the MSE and MAE:

The trend looks very nice, it goes down until it reaches a plateau. Also, let's check the `tensorflow` graph (in the tab **GRAPH**). Here we can see how things are connected together, and how operators are influenced by each other. You can still zoom in to see exactly how LSTMs are built in Tensorflow:

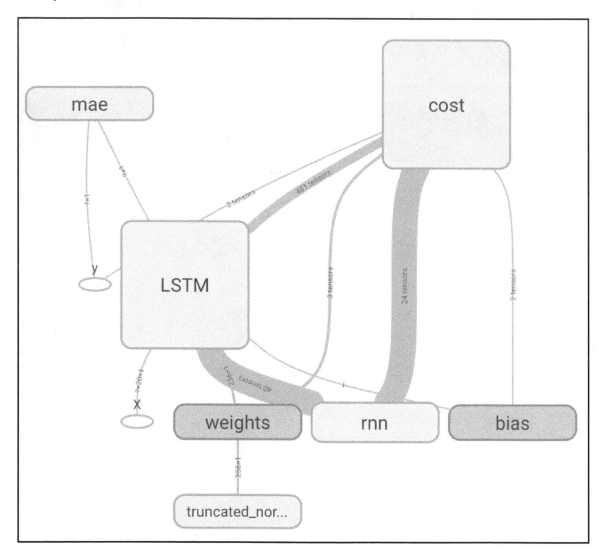

And that's the end of the project.

Possible follow - up questions

- Replace the LSTM with an RNN, and then with a GRU. Who's the best performer?
- Instead of predicting the closing price, try predicting also the high/low the day after. To do so, you can use the same features while training the model (or you can just use the closing price as input).
- Optimize the model for other stocks: is it better to have a generic model working for all the stocks or one specific for each stock?
- Tune the retraining. In the example, we predicted a full year with the model. Can you notice any improvement if you train the model once a month/week/day?
- If you have some financial experience, try building a simple trading simulator and feed it with the predictions. Starting the simulation with $100, will you gain or lose money after a year?

Summary

In this chapter we've shown how to perform a prediction of a timeseries: specifically, we observed how well RNN performs with real datasets as the stock prices. In the next chapter, we will see another application of the RNN, for example, how to perform an automatic machine translation for translating a sentence in another language.

6
Create and Train Machine Translation Systems

The objective of this project is to train an **artificial intelligence** (**AI**) model to be able to translate between two languages. Specifically, we will see an automatic translator which reads German and produces English sentences; although, the model and the code developed in this chapter is generic enough for any language pair.

The project explored in this chapter has four important sections, as follows:

- A walkthrough of the architecture
- Preprocessing the corpora
- Training the machine translator
- Testing and translating

Each of them will describe one key component of the project, and, at the end, you'll have a clear picture of what's going on.

A walkthrough of the architecture

A machine translation system receives as input an arbitrary string in one language and produces, as output, a string with the same meaning but in another language. Google Translate is one example (but also many other main IT companies have their own). There, users are able to translate to and from more than 100 languages. Using the webpage is easy: on the left just put the sentence you want to translate (for example, **Hello World**), select its language (in the example, it's English), and select the language you want it to be translated to.

Here's an example where we translate the sentence **Hello World** to French:

Is it easy? At a glance, we may think it's a simple dictionary substitution. Words are chunked, the translation is looked up on the specific English-to-French dictionary, and each word is substituted with its translation. Unfortunately, that's not the case. In the example, the English sentence has two words, while the French one has three. More generically, think about phrasal verbs (turn up, turn off, turn on, turn down), Saxon genitive, grammatical gender, tenses, conditional sentences... they don't always have a direct translation, and the correct one should follow the context of the sentence.

That's why, for doing machine translation, we need some artificial intelligence tools. Specifically, as for many other **natural language processing (NLP)** tasks, we'll be using **recurrent neural networks** (**RNNs**). We introduced RNNs in the previous chapter, and the main feature they have is that they work on sequences: given an input sequence, they produce an output sequence. The objective of this chapter is to create the correct training pipeline for having a sentence as the input sequence, and its translation as the output one. Remember also the *no free lunch theorem*: this process isn't easy, and more solutions can be created with the same result. Here, in this chapter, we will propose a simple but powerful one.

First of all, we start with the corpora: it's maybe the hardest thing to find, since it should contain a high fidelity translation of many sentences from a language to another one. Fortunately, NLTK, a well-known package of Python for NLP, contains the corpora Comtrans. **Comtrans** is the acronym of **combination approach to machine translation**, and contains an aligned corpora for three languages: German, French, and English.

In this project, we will use these corpora for a few reasons, as follows:

1. It's easy to download and import in Python.
2. No preprocessing is needed to read it from disk / from the internet. NLTK already handles that part.
3. It's small enough to be used on many laptops (a few dozen thousands sentences).
4. It's freely available on the internet.

For more information about the Comtrans project, go to `http://www.fask.uni-mainz.de/user/rapp/comtrans/`.

More specifically, we will try to create a machine translation system to translate German to English. We picked these two languages at random among the ones available in the Comtrans corpora: feel free to flip them, or use the French corpora instead. The pipeline of our project is generic enough to handle any combination.

Let's now investigate how the corpora is organized by typing some commands:

```
from nltk.corpus import comtrans
print(comtrans.aligned_sents('alignment-de-en.txt')[0])
```

The output is as follows:

```
<AlignedSent: 'Wiederaufnahme der S...' -> 'Resumption of the se...'>
```

The pairs of sentences are available using the function `aligned_sents`. The filename contains the from and to language. In this case, as for the following part of the project, we will translate German (*de*) to English (*en*). The returned object is an instance of the class `nltk.translate.api.AlignedSent`. By looking at the documentation, the first language is accessible with the attribute `words`, while the second language is accessible with the attribute `mots`. So, to extract the German sentence and its English translation separately, we should run:

```
print(comtrans.aligned_sents()[0].words)
print(comtrans.aligned_sents()[0].mots)
```

The preceding code outputs:

```
['Wiederaufnahme', 'der', 'Sitzungsperiode']
['Resumption', 'of', 'the', 'session']
```

How nice! The sentences are already tokenized, and they look as sequences. In fact, they will be the input and (hopefully) the output of the RNN which will provide the service of machine translation from German to English for our project.

Furthermore, if you want to understand the dynamics of the language, Comtrans makes available the alignment of the words in the translation:

```
print(comtrans.aligned_sents()[0].alignment)
```

The preceding code outputs:

```
0-0 1-1 1-2 2-3
```

The first word in German is translated to the first word in English *(Wiederaufnahme* to *Resumption),* the second to the second *(der* to both *of* and *the),* and the third (at index 1) is translated with the fourth *(Sitzungsperiode* to *session).*

Preprocessing of the corpora

The first step is to retrieve the corpora. We've already seen how to do this, but let's now formalize it in a function. To make it generic enough, let's enclose these functions in a file named `corpora_tools.py`.

1. Let's do some imports that we will use later on:

```
import pickle
import re
from collections import Counter
from nltk.corpus import comtrans
```

2. Now, let's create the function to retrieve the corpora:

```
def retrieve_corpora(translated_sentences_l1_l2='alignment-de-en.txt'):
    print("Retrieving corpora: {}".format(translated_sentences_l1_l2))
    als = comtrans.aligned_sents(translated_sentences_l1_l2)
    sentences_l1 = [sent.words for sent in als]
    sentences_l2 = [sent.mots for sent in als]
    return sentences_l1, sentences_l2
```

This function has one argument; the file containing the aligned sentences from the NLTK Comtrans corpora. It returns two lists of sentences (actually, they're a list of tokens), one for the source language (in our case, German), the other in the destination language (in our case, English).

3. On a separate Python REPL, we can test this function:

```
sen_l1, sen_l2 = retrieve_corpora()
print("# A sentence in the two languages DE & EN")
print("DE:", sen_l1[0])
print("EN:", sen_l2[0])
print("# Corpora length (i.e. number of sentences)")
print(len(sen_l1))
assert len(sen_l1) == len(sen_l2)
```

4. The preceding code creates the following output:

```
Retrieving corpora: alignment-de-en.txt
# A sentence in the two languages DE & EN
DE: ['Wiederaufnahme', 'der', 'Sitzungsperiode']
EN: ['Resumption', 'of', 'the', 'session']
# Corpora length (i.e. number of sentences)
33334
```

We also printed the number of sentences in each corpora (33,000) and asserted that the number of sentences in the source and the destination languages is the same.

5. In the following step, we want to clean up the tokens. Specifically, we want to tokenize punctuation and lowercase the tokens. To do so, we can create a new function in `corpora_tools.py`. We will use the `regex` module to perform the further splitting tokenization:

```
def clean_sentence(sentence):
    regex_splitter = re.compile("([!?.,:;$\"')( ])")
    clean_words = [re.split(regex_splitter, word.lower()) for word in
sentence]
    return [w for words in clean_words for w in words if words if w]
```

6. Again, in the REPL, let's test the function:

```
clean_sen_l1 = [clean_sentence(s) for s in sen_l1]
clean_sen_l2 = [clean_sentence(s) for s in sen_l2]
print("# Same sentence as before, but chunked and cleaned")
print("DE:", clean_sen_l1[0])
print("EN:", clean_sen_l2[0])
```

The preceding code outputs the same sentence as before, but chunked and cleaned:

```
DE: ['wiederaufnahme', 'der', 'sitzungsperiode']
EN: ['resumption', 'of', 'the', 'session']
```

Nice!

The next step for this project is filtering the sentences that are too long to be processed. Since our goal is to perform the processing on a local machine, we should limit ourselves to sentences up to N tokens. In this case, we set $N=20$, in order to be able to train the learner within 24 hours. If you have a powerful machine, feel free to increase that limit. To make the function generic enough, there's also a lower bound with a default value set to 0, such as an empty token set.

1. The logic of the function is very easy: if the number of tokens for a sentence or its translation is greater than N, then the sentence (in both languages) is removed:

```
def filter_sentence_length(sentences_l1, sentences_l2, min_len=0,
max_len=20):
    filtered_sentences_l1 = []
    filtered_sentences_l2 = []
    for i in range(len(sentences_l1)):
        if min_len <= len(sentences_l1[i]) <= max_len and \
                min_len <= len(sentences_l2[i]) <= max_len:
            filtered_sentences_l1.append(sentences_l1[i])
            filtered_sentences_l2.append(sentences_l2[i])
    return filtered_sentences_l1, filtered_sentences_l2
```

2. Again, let's see in the REPL how many sentences survived this filter. Remember, we started with more than 33,000:

```
filt_clean_sen_l1, filt_clean_sen_l2 = filter_sentence_length(clean_sen_l1,
        clean_sen_l2)
print("# Filtered Corpora length (i.e. number of sentences)")
print(len(filt_clean_sen_l1))
assert len(filt_clean_sen_l1) == len(filt_clean_sen_l2)
```

The preceding code prints the following output:

```
# Filtered Corpora length (i.e. number of sentences)
14788
```

Almost 15,000 sentences survived, that is, half of the corpora.

Now, we finally move from text to numbers (which AI mainly uses). To do so, we shall create a dictionary of the words for each language. The dictionary should be big enough to contain most of the words, though we can discard some if the language has words with low occourrence. This is a common practice even in the tf-idf (term frequency within a document, multiplied by the inverse of the document frequency, i.e. in how many documents that token appears), where very rare words are discarded to speed up the computation, and make the solution more scalable and generic. We need here four special symbols in both dictionaries:

1. One symbol for padding (we'll see later why we need it)
2. One symbol for dividing the two sentences
3. One symbol to indicate where the sentence stops
4. One symbol to indicate unknown words (like the very rare ones)

For doing so, let's create a new file named `data_utils.py` containing the following lines of code:

```
_PAD = "_PAD"
_GO = "_GO"
_EOS = "_EOS"
_UNK = "_UNK"
_START_VOCAB = [_PAD, _GO, _EOS, _UNK]
PAD_ID = 0
GO_ID = 1
EOS_ID = 2
UNK_ID = 3
OP_DICT_IDS = [PAD_ID, GO_ID, EOS_ID, UNK_ID]
```

Then, back to the `corpora_tools.py` file, let's add the following function:

```
import data_utils

def create_indexed_dictionary(sentences, dict_size=10000,
storage_path=None):
    count_words = Counter()
    dict_words = {}
    opt_dict_size = len(data_utils.OP_DICT_IDS)
    for sen in sentences:
```

```
        for word in sen:
            count_words[word] += 1
    dict_words[data_utils._PAD] = data_utils.PAD_ID
    dict_words[data_utils._GO] = data_utils.GO_ID
    dict_words[data_utils._EOS] = data_utils.EOS_ID
    dict_words[data_utils._UNK] = data_utils.UNK_ID

    for idx, item in enumerate(count_words.most_common(dict_size)):
        dict_words[item[0]] = idx + opt_dict_size
    if storage_path:
        pickle.dump(dict_words, open(storage_path, "wb"))
    return dict_words
```

This function takes as arguments the number of entries in the dictionary and the path of where to store the dictionary. Remember, the dictionary is created while training the algorithms: during the testing phase it's loaded, and the association token/symbol should be the same one as used in the training. If the number of unique tokens is greater than the value set, only the most popular ones are selected. At the end, the dictionary contains the association between a token and its ID for each language.

After building the dictionary, we should look up the tokens and substitute them with their token ID.

For that, we need another function:

```
def sentences_to_indexes(sentences, indexed_dictionary):
    indexed_sentences = []
    not_found_counter = 0
    for sent in sentences:
        idx_sent = []
        for word in sent:
            try:
                idx_sent.append(indexed_dictionary[word])
            except KeyError:
                idx_sent.append(data_utils.UNK_ID)
                not_found_counter += 1
        indexed_sentences.append(idx_sent)
    print('[sentences_to_indexes] Did not find {}
words'.format(not_found_counter))
    return indexed_sentences
```

This step is very simple; the token is substituted with its ID. If the token is not in the dictionary, the ID of the unknown token is used. Let's see in the REPL how our sentences look after these steps:

```
dict_l1 = create_indexed_dictionary(filt_clean_sen_l1, dict_size=15000,
storage_path="/tmp/l1_dict.p")
dict_l2 = create_indexed_dictionary(filt_clean_sen_l2, dict_size=10000,
storage_path="/tmp/l2_dict.p")
idx_sentences_l1 = sentences_to_indexes(filt_clean_sen_l1, dict_l1)
idx_sentences_l2 = sentences_to_indexes(filt_clean_sen_l2, dict_l2)
print("# Same sentences as before, with their dictionary ID")
print("DE:", list(zip(filt_clean_sen_l1[0], idx_sentences_l1[0])))
```

This code prints the token and its ID for both the sentences. What's used in the RNN will be just the second element of each tuple, that is, the integer ID:

```
# Same sentences as before, with their dictionary ID
DE: [('wiederaufnahme', 1616), ('der', 7), ('sitzungsperiode', 618)]
EN: [('resumption', 1779), ('of', 8), ('the', 5), ('session', 549)]
```

Please also note how frequent tokens, such as *the* and *of* in English, and *der* in German, have a low ID. That's because the IDs are sorted by popularity (see the body of the function `create_indexed_dictionary`).

Even though we did the filtering to limit the maximum size of the sentences, we should create a function to extract the maximum size. For the lucky owners of very powerful machines, which didn't do any filtering, that's the moment to see how long the longest sentence in the RNN will be. That's simply the function:

```
def extract_max_length(corpora):
    return max([len(sentence) for sentence in corpora])
```

Let's apply the following to our sentences:

```
max_length_l1 = extract_max_length(idx_sentences_l1)
max_length_l2 = extract_max_length(idx_sentences_l2)
print("# Max sentence sizes:")
print("DE:", max_length_l1)
print("EN:", max_length_l2)
```

As expected, the output is:

```
# Max sentence sizes:
DE: 20
EN: 20
```

The final preprocessing step is padding. We need all the sequences to be the same length, therefore we should pad the shorter ones. Also, we need to insert the correct tokens to instruct the RNN where the string begins and ends.

Basically, this step should:

- Pad the input sequences, for all being 20 symbols long
- Pad the output sequence, to be 20 symbols long
- Insert an _GO at the beginning of the output sequence and an _EOS at the end to position the start and the end of the translation

This is done by this function (insert it in the `corpora_tools.py`):

```python
def prepare_sentences(sentences_l1, sentences_l2, len_l1, len_l2):
    assert len(sentences_l1) == len(sentences_l2)
    data_set = []
    for i in range(len(sentences_l1)):
        padding_l1 = len_l1 - len(sentences_l1[i])
        pad_sentence_l1 = ([data_utils.PAD_ID]*padding_l1) +
sentences_l1[i]
        padding_l2 = len_l2 - len(sentences_l2[i])
        pad_sentence_l2 = [data_utils.GO_ID] + sentences_l2[i] +
[data_utils.EOS_ID] + ([data_utils.PAD_ID] * padding_l2)
        data_set.append([pad_sentence_l1, pad_sentence_l2])
    return data_set
```

To test it, let's prepare the dataset and print the first sentence:

```python
data_set = prepare_sentences(idx_sentences_l1, idx_sentences_l2,
max_length_l1, max_length_l2)
print("# Prepared minibatch with paddings and extra stuff")
print("DE:", data_set[0][0])
print("EN:", data_set[0][1])
print("# The sentence pass from X to Y tokens")
print("DE:", len(idx_sentences_l1[0]), "->", len(data_set[0][0]))
print("EN:", len(idx_sentences_l2[0]), "->", len(data_set[0][1]))
```

The preceding code outputs the following:

```
# Prepared minibatch with paddings and extra stuff
DE: [0, 0, 0, 0, 0, 0, 0, 0, 0, 0, 0, 0, 0, 0, 0, 0, 0, 1616, 7, 618]
EN: [1, 1779, 8, 5, 549, 2, 0, 0, 0, 0, 0, 0, 0, 0, 0, 0, 0, 0, 0, 0, 0, 0]
# The sentence pass from X to Y tokens
DE: 3 -> 20
EN: 4 -> 22
```

As you can see, the input and the output are padded with zeros to have a constant length (in the dictionary, they correspond to _PAD, see `data_utils.py`), and the output contains the markers 1 and 2 just before the start and the end of the sentence. As proven effective in the literature, we're going to pad the input sentences at the start and the output sentences at the end. After this operation, all the input sentences are 20 items long, and the output sentences 22.

Training the machine translator

So far, we've seen the steps to preprocess the corpora, but not the model used. The model is actually already available on the TensorFlow Models repository, freely downloadable from `https://github.com/tensorflow/models/blob/master/tutorials/rnn/translate/seq2seq_model.py`.

The piece of code is licensed with Apache 2.0. We really thank the authors for having open sourced such a great model. Copyright 2015 The TensorFlow Authors. All Rights Reserved. Licensed under the Apache License, Version 2.0 (the License); You may not use this file except in compliance with the License. You may obtain a copy of the License at: `http://www.apache.org/licenses/LICENSE-2.0`
Unless required by applicable law or agreed to in writing, software. Distributed under the License is distributed on an AS IS BASIS, WITHOUT WARRANTIES OR CONDITIONS OF ANY KIND, either express or implied. See the License for the specific language governing permissions and limitations under the License.

We will see the usage of the model throughout this section. First, let's create a new file named `train_translator.py` and put in some imports and some constants. We will save the dictionary in the /tmp/ directory, as well as the model and its checkpoints:

```
import time
import math
import sys
import pickle
import glob
import os
import tensorflow as tf
from seq2seq_model import Seq2SeqModel
from corpora_tools import *

path_l1_dict = "/tmp/l1_dict.p"
path_l2_dict = "/tmp/l2_dict.p"
```

```
model_dir = "/tmp/translate "
model_checkpoints = model_dir + "/translate.ckpt"
```

Now, let's use all the tools created in the previous section within a function that, given a Boolean flag, returns the corpora. More specifically, if the argument is False, it builds the dictionary from scratch (and saves it); otherwise, it uses the dictionary available in the path:

```
def build_dataset(use_stored_dictionary=False):
    sen_l1, sen_l2 = retrieve_corpora()
    clean_sen_l1 = [clean_sentence(s) for s in sen_l1]
    clean_sen_l2 = [clean_sentence(s) for s in sen_l2]
    filt_clean_sen_l1, filt_clean_sen_l2 =
filter_sentence_length(clean_sen_l1, clean_sen_l2)

    if not use_stored_dictionary:
        dict_l1 = create_indexed_dictionary(filt_clean_sen_l1,
    dict_size=15000, storage_path=path_l1_dict)
        dict_l2 = create_indexed_dictionary(filt_clean_sen_l2,
    dict_size=10000, storage_path=path_l2_dict)
    else:
        dict_l1 = pickle.load(open(path_l1_dict, "rb"))
        dict_l2 = pickle.load(open(path_l2_dict, "rb"))

    dict_l1_length = len(dict_l1)
    dict_l2_length = len(dict_l2)

    idx_sentences_l1 = sentences_to_indexes(filt_clean_sen_l1, dict_l1)
    idx_sentences_l2 = sentences_to_indexes(filt_clean_sen_l2, dict_l2)

    max_length_l1 = extract_max_length(idx_sentences_l1)
    max_length_l2 = extract_max_length(idx_sentences_l2)

    data_set = prepare_sentences(idx_sentences_l1, idx_sentences_l2,
max_length_l1, max_length_l2)
    return (filt_clean_sen_l1, filt_clean_sen_l2), \
        data_set, \
        (max_length_l1, max_length_l2), \
        (dict_l1_length, dict_l2_length)
```

This function returns the cleaned sentences, the dataset, the maximum length of the sentences, and the lengths of the dictionaries.

Also, we need to have a function to clean up the model. Every time we run the training routine we need to clean up the model directory, as we haven't provided any garbage information. We can do this with a very simple function:

```
def cleanup_checkpoints(model_dir, model_checkpoints):
    for f in glob.glob(model_checkpoints + "*"):
    os.remove(f)
    try:
        os.mkdir(model_dir)
    except FileExistsError:
        pass
```

Finally, let's create the model in a reusable fashion:

```
def get_seq2seq_model(session, forward_only, dict_lengths,
max_sentence_lengths, model_dir):
    model = Seq2SeqModel(
            source_vocab_size=dict_lengths[0],
            target_vocab_size=dict_lengths[1],
            buckets=[max_sentence_lengths],
            size=256,
            num_layers=2,
            max_gradient_norm=5.0,
            batch_size=64,
            learning_rate=0.5,
            learning_rate_decay_factor=0.99,
            forward_only=forward_only,
            dtype=tf.float16)
    ckpt = tf.train.get_checkpoint_state(model_dir)
    if ckpt and tf.train.checkpoint_exists(ckpt.model_checkpoint_path):
        print("Reading model parameters from
{}".format(ckpt.model_checkpoint_path))
        model.saver.restore(session, ckpt.model_checkpoint_path)
    else:
        print("Created model with fresh parameters.")
        session.run(tf.global_variables_initializer())
    return model
```

This function calls the constructor of the model, passing the following parameters:

- The source vocabulary size (German, in our example)
- The target vocabulary size (English, in our example)
- The buckets (in our example is just one, since we padded all the sequences to a single size)
- The **long short-term memory** (**LSTM**) internal units size

- The number of stacked LSTM layers
- The maximum norm of the gradient (for gradient clipping)
- The mini-batch size (that is, how many observations for each training step)
- The learning rate
- The learning rate decay factor
- The direction of the model
- The type of data (in our example, we will use flat16, that is, float using 2 bytes)

To make the training faster and obtain a model with good performance, we have already set the values in the code; feel free to change them and see how it performs.

The final if/else in the function retrieves the model, from its checkpoint, if the model already exists. In fact, this function will be used in the decoder too to retrieve and model on the test set.

Finally, we have reached the function to train the machine translator. Here it is:

```
def train():
    with tf.Session() as sess:
        model = get_seq2seq_model(sess, False, dict_lengths,
max_sentence_lengths, model_dir)
        # This is the training loop.
        step_time, loss = 0.0, 0.0
        current_step = 0
        bucket = 0
        steps_per_checkpoint = 100
        max_steps = 20000
        while current_step < max_steps:
            start_time = time.time()
            encoder_inputs, decoder_inputs, target_weights =
model.get_batch([data_set], bucket)
            _, step_loss, _ = model.step(sess, encoder_inputs,
decoder_inputs, target_weights, bucket, False)
            step_time += (time.time() - start_time) / steps_per_checkpoint
            loss += step_loss / steps_per_checkpoint
            current_step += 1
            if current_step % steps_per_checkpoint == 0:
                perplexity = math.exp(float(loss)) if loss < 300 else
float("inf")
                print ("global step {} learning rate {} step-time {}
perplexity {}".format(
                    model.global_step.eval(), model.learning_rate.eval(),
step_time, perplexity))
                sess.run(model.learning_rate_decay_op)
                model.saver.save(sess, model_checkpoints,
```

```
global_step=model.global_step)
                    step_time, loss = 0.0, 0.0
                    encoder_inputs, decoder_inputs, target_weights =
model.get_batch([data_set], bucket)
                    _, eval_loss, _ = model.step(sess, encoder_inputs,
decoder_inputs, target_weights, bucket, True)
                    eval_ppx = math.exp(float(eval_loss)) if eval_loss < 300
else float("inf")
                    print(" eval: perplexity {}".format(eval_ppx))
                    sys.stdout.flush()
```

The function starts by creating the model. Also, it sets some constants on the steps per checkpoints and the maximum number of steps. Specifically, in the code, we will save a model every 100 steps and we will perform no more than 20,000 steps. If it still takes too long, feel free to kill the program: every checkpoint contains a trained model, and the decoder will use the most updated one.

At this point, we enter the while loop. For each step, we ask the model to get a minibatch of data (of size 64, as set previously). The method `get_batch` returns the inputs (that is, the source sequence), the outputs (that is, the destination sequence), and the weights of the model. With the method `step`, we run one step of the training. One piece of information returned is the loss for the current minibatch of data. That's all the training!

To report the performance and store the model every 100 steps, we print the average perplexity of the model (the lower, the better) on the 100 previous steps, and we save the checkpoint. The perplexity is a metric connected to the uncertainty of the predictions: the more confident we're about the tokens, the lower will be the perplexity of the output sentence. Also, we reset the counters and we extract the same metric from a single minibatch of the test set (in this case, it's a random minibatch of the dataset), and performances of it are printed too. Then, the training process restarts again.

As an improvement, every 100 steps we also reduce the learning rate by a factor. In this case, we multiply it by 0.99. This helps the convergence and the stability of the training.

We now have to connect all the functions together. In order to create a script that can be called by the command line but is also used by other scripts to import functions, we can create a `main`, as follows:

```
if __name__ == "__main__":
    _, data_set, max_sentence_lengths, dict_lengths = build_dataset(False)
    cleanup_checkpoints(model_dir, model_checkpoints)
    train()
```

In the console, you can now train your machine translator system with a very simple command:

```
$> python train_translator.py
```

On an average laptop, without an NVIDIA GPU, it takes more than a day to reach a perplexity below 10 (12+ hours). This is the output:

```
Retrieving corpora: alignment-de-en.txt
[sentences_to_indexes] Did not find 1097 words
[sentences_to_indexes] Did not find 0 words
Created model with fresh parameters.
global step 100 learning rate 0.5 step-time 4.3573073434829713 perplexity
526.6638556683066
eval: perplexity 159.2240770935855
[...]
global step 10500 learning rate 0.180419921875 step-time
4.35106209993362414 perplexity 2.0458043055629487
eval: perplexity 1.8646006006241982
[...]
```

Test and translate

The code for the translation is in the file `test_translator.py`.

We start with some imports and the location of the pre-trained model:

```
import pickle
import sys
import numpy as np
import tensorflow as tf
import data_utils
from train_translator import (get_seq2seq_model, path_l1_dict,
path_l2_dict,
build_dataset)
model_dir = "/tmp/translate"
```

Now, let's create a function to decode the output sequence generated by the RNN. Mind that the sequence is multidimensional, and each dimension corresponds to the probability of that word, therefore we will pick the most likely one. With the help of the reverse dictionary, we can then figure out what was the actual word. Finally, we will trim the markings (padding, start, end of string) and print the output.

In this example, we will decode the first five sentences in the training set, starting from the raw corpora. Feel free to insert new strings or use different corpora:

```python
def decode():
    with tf.Session() as sess:
        model = get_seq2seq_model(sess, True, dict_lengths,
max_sentence_lengths, model_dir)
        model.batch_size = 1
        bucket = 0
        for idx in range(len(data_set))[:5]:
            print("-------------------")
            print("Source sentence: ", sentences[0][idx])
            print("Source tokens: ", data_set[idx][0])
            print("Ideal tokens out: ", data_set[idx][1])
            print("Ideal sentence out: ", sentences[1][idx])
            encoder_inputs, decoder_inputs, target_weights =
model.get_batch(
                            {bucket: [(data_set[idx][0], [])]}, bucket)
            _, _, output_logits = model.step(sess, encoder_inputs,
decoder_inputs,
                target_weights, bucket, True)
            outputs = [int(np.argmax(logit, axis=1)) for logit in
output_logits]
            if data_utils.EOS_ID in outputs:
                outputs = outputs[1:outputs.index(data_utils.EOS_ID)]
            print("Model output: ", "
".join([tf.compat.as_str(inv_dict_12[output]) for output in outputs]))
            sys.stdout.flush()
```

Here, again, we need a `main` to work with the command line, as follows:

```python
if __name__ == "__main__":
    dict_12 = pickle.load(open(path_12_dict, "rb"))
    inv_dict_12 = {v: k for k, v in dict_12.items()}
    build_dataset(True)
    sentences, data_set, max_sentence_lengths, dict_lengths =
build_dataset(False)
    try:
        print("Reading from", model_dir)
        print("Dictionary lengths", dict_lengths)
        print("Bucket size", max_sentence_lengths)
    except NameError:
        print("One or more variables not in scope. Translation not
possible")
        exit(-1)
    decode()
```

Running the preceding code generates the following output:

```
Reading model parameters from /tmp/translate/translate.ckpt-10500
-------------------
Source sentence: ['wiederaufnahme', 'der', 'sitzungsperiode']
Source tokens: [0, 0, 0, 0, 0, 0, 0, 0, 0, 0, 0, 0, 0, 0, 0, 0, 0, 1616, 7,
618]
Ideal tokens out: [1, 1779, 8, 5, 549, 2, 0, 0, 0, 0, 0, 0, 0, 0, 0, 0, 0,
0, 0, 0, 0, 0]
Ideal sentence out: ['resumption', 'of', 'the', 'session']
Model output: resumption of the session
-------------------
Source sentence: ['ich', 'bitte', 'sie', ',', 'sich', 'zu', 'einer',
'schweigeminute', 'zu', 'erheben', '.']
Source tokens: [0, 0, 0, 0, 0, 0, 0, 0, 0, 13, 266, 22, 5, 29, 14, 78,
3931, 14, 2414, 4]
Ideal tokens out: [1, 651, 932, 6, 159, 6, 19, 11, 1440, 35, 51, 2639, 4,
2, 0, 0, 0, 0, 0, 0, 0, 0]
Ideal sentence out: ['please', 'rise', ',', 'then', ',', 'for', 'this',
'minute', "'", 's', 'silence', '.']
Model output: i ask you to move , on an approach an approach .
-------------------
Source sentence: ['(', 'das', 'parlament', 'erhebt', 'sich', 'zu', 'einer',
'schweigeminute', '.', ')']
Source tokens: [0, 0, 0, 0, 0, 0, 0, 0, 0, 0, 52, 11, 58, 3267, 29, 14, 78,
3931, 4, 51]
Ideal tokens out: [1, 54, 5, 267, 3541, 14, 2095, 12, 1440, 35, 51, 2639,
53, 2, 0, 0, 0, 0, 0, 0, 0, 0]
Ideal sentence out: ['(', 'the', 'house', 'rose', 'and', 'observed', 'a',
'minute', "'", 's', 'silence', ')']
Model output: ( the house ( observed and observed a speaker )
-------------------
Source sentence: ['frau', 'präsidentin', ',', 'zur', 'geschäftsordnung',
'.']
Source tokens: [0, 0, 0, 0, 0, 0, 0, 0, 0, 0, 0, 0, 0, 0, 79, 151, 5, 49,
488, 4]
Ideal tokens out: [1, 212, 44, 6, 22, 12, 91, 8, 218, 4, 2, 0, 0, 0, 0, 0,
0, 0, 0, 0, 0, 0]
Ideal sentence out: ['madam', 'president', ',', 'on', 'a', 'point', 'of',
'order', '.']
Model output: madam president , on a point of order .
-------------------
Source sentence: ['wenn', 'das', 'haus', 'damit', 'einverstanden', 'ist',
',', 'werde', 'ich', 'dem', 'vorschlag', 'von', 'herrn', 'evans', 'folgen',
'.']
Source tokens: [0, 0, 0, 0, 85, 11, 603, 113, 831, 9, 5, 243, 13, 39, 141,
18, 116, 1939, 417, 4]
Ideal tokens out: [1, 87, 5, 267, 2096, 6, 16, 213, 47, 29, 27, 1941, 25,
```

```
1441, 4, 2, 0, 0, 0, 0, 0, 0]
Ideal sentence out: ['if', 'the', 'house', 'agrees', ',', 'i', 'shall',
'do', 'as', 'mr', 'evans', 'has', 'suggested', '.']
Model output: if the house gave this proposal , i would like to hear mr
byrne .
```

As you can see, the output is mainly correct, although there are still some problematic tokens. To mitigate the problem, we'd need a more complex RNN, a longer corpora or a more diverse one.

Home assignments

This model is trained and tested on the same dataset; that's not ideal for data science, but it was needed to have a working project. Try to find a longer corpora and split it into two pieces, one for training and one for testing:

- Change the settings of the model: how does that impact the performance and the training time?
- Analyze the code in seq2seq_model.py. How can you insert the plot of the loss in TensorBoard?
- NLTK also contains the French corpora; can you create a system to translate them both together?

Summary

In this chapter we've seen how to create a machine translation system based on an RNN. We've seen how to organize the corpus, how to train it and how to test it. In the next chapter, we'll see another application where RNN can be used: chatbots.

7
Train and Set up a Chatbot, Able to Discuss Like a Human

This chapter will show you how to train an automatic chatbot that will be able to answer simple and generic questions, and how to create an endpoint over HTTP for providing the answers via an API. More specifically, we will show:

- What's the corpus and how to preprocess the corpus
- How to train a chatbot and how to test it
- How to create an HTTP endpoint to expose the API

Introduction to the project

Chatbots are becoming increasingly used as a way to provide assistance to users. Many companies, including banks, mobile/landline companies and large e-sellers now use chatbots for customer assistance and for helping users in pre-sales. The Q&A page is not enough anymore: each customer is nowadays expecting an answer to his very own question which maybe is not covered or only partially covered in the Q&A. Also, chatbots are a great tool for companies which don't need to provide additional customer service capacity for trivial questions: they really look like a win-win situation!

Chatbots have become very popular tools ever since deep learning became popular. Thanks to deep learning, we're now able to train the bot to provide better and personalized questions, and, in the last implementation, to retain a per-user context.

Cutting it short, there are mainly two types of chatbot: the first is a simple one, which tries to understand the topic, always providing the same answer for all questions about the same topic. For example, on a train website, the questions *Where can I find the timetable of the City_A to City_B service?* and *What's the next train departing from City_A?* will likely get the same answer, that could read *Hi! The timetable on our network is available on this page: <link>*.

Basically, behind the scene, this types of chatbots use classification algorithms to understand the topic (in the example, both questions are about the timetable topic). Given the topic, they always provide the same answer. Usually, they have a list of N topics and N answers; also, if the probability of the classified topic is low (the question is too vague, or it's on a topic not included in the list), they usually ask the user to be more specific and repeat the question, eventually pointing out other ways to do the question (send an email or call the customer service number, for example).

The second type of chatbots is more advanced, smarter, but also more complex. For those, the answers are built using an RNN, in the same way that machine translation is performed (see the previous chapter). Those chatbots are able to provide more personalized answers, and they may provide a more specific reply. In fact, they don't just guess the topic, but with an RNN engine they're able to understand more about the user's questions and provide the best possible answer: in fact, it's very unlikely you'll get the same answers with two different questions using these types if chatbots.

In this chapter, we will try to build a chatbot of the second type using an RNN similarly to what we've done in the previous chapter with the machine translation system. Also, we will show how to put the chatbot behind an HTTP endpoint, in order to use the chatbot as a service from your website, or, more simply, from your command line.

The input corpus

Unfortunately, we haven't found any consumer-oriented dataset that is open source and freely available on the Internet. Therefore, we will train the chatbot with a more generic dataset, not really focused on customer service. Specifically, we will use the Cornell Movie Dialogs Corpus, from the Cornell University. The corpus contains the collection of conversations extracted from raw movie scripts, therefore the chatbot will be able to give answer more to fictional questions than real ones. The Cornell corpus contains more than 200,000 conversational exchanges between 10+ thousands of movie characters, extracted from 617 movies.

The dataset is available here: `https://www.cs.cornell.edu/~cristian/Cornell_Movie-Dialogs_Corpus.html`.
We would like to thank the authors for having released the corpus: that makes experimentation, reproducibility and knowledge sharing easier.

The dataset comes as a `.zip` archive file. After decompressing it, you'll find several files in it:

- `README.txt` contains the description of the dataset, the format of the corpora files, the details on the collection procedure and the author's contact.
- `Chameleons.pdf` is the original paper for which the corpus has been released. Although the goal of the paper is strictly not around chatbots, it studies the language used in dialogues, and it's a good source of information to understanding more
- `movie_conversations.txt` contains all the dialogues structure. For each conversation, it includes the ID of the two characters involved in the discussion, the ID of the movie and the list of sentences IDs (or utterances, to be more precise) in chronological order. For example, the first line of the file is:

u0 +++$+++ u2 +++$+++ m0 +++$+++ ['L194', 'L195', 'L196', 'L197']

That means that user `u0` had a conversation with user `u2` in the movie `m0` and the conversation had 4 utterances: `'L194'`, `'L195'`, `'L196'` and `'L197'`

- `movie_lines.txt` contains the actual text of each utterance ID and the person who produced it. For example, the utterance `L195` is listed here as:

L195 +++$+++ u2 +++$+++ m0 +++$+++ CAMERON +++$+++ Well, I thought we'd start with pronunciation, if that's okay with you.

So, the text of the utterance `L195` is *Well, I thought we'd start with pronunciation, if that's okay with you.* And it was pronounced by the character `u2` whose name is CAMERON in the movie `m0`.

- `movie_titles_metadata.txt` contains information about the movies, including the title, year, IMDB rating, the number of votes in IMDB and the genres. For example, the movie `m0` here is described as:

m0 +++$+++ 10 things i hate about you +++$+++ 1999 +++$+++ 6.90 +++$+++ 62847 +++$+++ ['comedy', 'romance']

So, the title of the movie whose ID is `m0` is *10 things i hate about you*, it's from 1999, it's a comedy with romance and it received almost 63 thousand votes on IMDB with an average score of 6.9 (over 10.0)

- `movie_characters_metadata.txt` contains information about the movie characters, including the name the title of the movie where he/she appears, the gender (if known) and the position in the credits (if known). For example, the character "u2" appears in this file with this description:

  u2 +++$+++ CAMERON +++$+++ m0 +++$+++ 10 things i hate about you +++$+++ m +++$+++ 3

  The character u2 is named *CAMERON*, it appears in the movie m0 whose title is *10 things i hate about you*, his gender is male and he's the third person appearing in the credits.

- `raw_script_urls.txt` contains the source URL where the dialogues of each movie can be retrieved. For example, for the movie m0 that's it:

  m0 +++$+++ 10 things i hate about you +++$+++
  http://www.dailyscript.com/scripts/10Things.html

  As you will have noticed, most files use the token +++$+++ to separate the fields. Beyond that, the format looks pretty straightforward to parse. Please take particular care while parsing the files: their format is not UTF-8 but *ISO-8859-1*.

Creating the training dataset

Let's now create the training set for the chatbot. We'd need all the conversations between the characters in the correct order: fortunately, the corpora contains more than what we actually need. For creating the dataset, we will start by downloading the zip archive, if it's not already on disk. We'll then decompress the archive in a temporary folder (if you're using Windows, that should be `C:\Temp`), and we will read just the `movie_lines.txt` and the `movie_conversations.txt` files, the ones we really need to create a dataset of consecutive utterances.

Let's now go step by step, creating multiple functions, one for each step, in the file `corpora_downloader.py`. The first function we need is to retrieve the file from the Internet, if not available on disk.

```
def download_and_decompress(url, storage_path, storage_dir):
    import os.path
    directory = storage_path + "/" + storage_dir
    zip_file = directory + ".zip"
    a_file = directory + "/cornell movie-dialogs corpus/README.txt"
    if not os.path.isfile(a_file):
```

```
import urllib.request
import zipfile
urllib.request.urlretrieve(url, zip_file)
with zipfile.ZipFile(zip_file, "r") as zfh:
    zfh.extractall(directory)
return
```

This function does exactly that: it checks whether the "README.txt" file is available locally; if not, it downloads the file (thanks for the urlretrieve function in the urllib.request module) and it decompresses the zip (using the zipfile module).

The next step is read the conversation file and extract the list of utterance IDS. As a reminder, its format is: *u0 +++$+++ u2 +++$+++ m0 +++$+++ ['L194', 'L195', 'L196', 'L197'],* therefore what we're looking for is the fourth element of the list after we split it on the token +++$+++ . Also, we'd need to clean up the square brackets and the apostrophes to have a clean list of IDs. For doing that, we shall import the re module, and the function will look like this.

```
import re
def read_conversations(storage_path, storage_dir):
    filename = storage_path + "/" + storage_dir + "/cornell movie-dialogs
corpus/movie_conversations.txt"
    with open(filename, "r", encoding="ISO-8859-1") as fh:
        conversations_chunks = [line.split(" +++$+++ ") for line in fh]
    return [re.sub('[\[\]\']', '', el[3].strip()).split(", ") for el in
conversations_chunks]
```

As previously said, remember to read the file with the right encoding, otherwise, you'll get an error. The output of this function is a list of lists, each of them containing the sequence of utterance IDS in a conversation between characters. Next step is to read and parse the movie_lines.txt file, to extract the actual utterances texts. As a reminder, the file looks like this line:

L195 +++$+++ u2 +++$+++ m0 +++$+++ CAMERON +++$+++ Well, I thought we'd start with pronunciation, if that's okay with you.

Here, what we're looking for are the first and the last chunks.

```
def read_lines(storage_path, storage_dir):
    filename = storage_path + "/" + storage_dir + "/cornell movie-dialogs
corpus/movie_lines.txt"
    with open(filename, "r", encoding="ISO-8859-1") as fh:
        lines_chunks = [line.split(" +++$+++ ") for line in fh]
    return {line[0]: line[-1].strip() for line in lines_chunks}
```

The very last bit is about tokenization and alignment. We'd like to have a set whose observations have two sequential utterances. In this way, we will train the chatbot, given the first utterance, to provide the next one. Hopefully, this will lead to a smart chatbot, able to reply to multiple questions. Here's the function:

```
def get_tokenized_sequencial_sentences(list_of_lines, line_text):
    for line in list_of_lines:
        for i in range(len(line) - 1):
            yield (line_text[line[i]].split(" "),
line_text[line[i+1]].split(" "))
```

Its output is a generator containing a tuple of the two utterances (the one on the right follows temporally the one on the left). Also, utterances are tokenized on the space character.

Finally, we can wrap up everything into a function, which downloads the file and unzip it (if not cached), parse the conversations and the lines, and format the dataset as a generator. As a default, we will store the files in the /tmp directory:

```
def retrieve_cornell_corpora(storage_path="/tmp",
storage_dir="cornell_movie_dialogs_corpus"):
download_and_decompress("http://www.cs.cornell.edu/~cristian/data/cornell_m
ovie_dialogs_corpus.zip",
                        storage_path,
                            storage_dir)
    conversations = read_conversations(storage_path, storage_dir)
    lines = read_lines(storage_path, storage_dir)
    return tuple(zip(*list(get_tokenized_sequencial_sentences(conversations,
lines))))
```

At this point, our training set looks very similar to the training set used in the translation project, in the previous chapter. Actually, it's not just similar, it's the same format with the same goal. We can, therefore, use some pieces of code we've developed in the previous chapter. For example, the corpora_tools.py file can be used here without any change (also, it requires the data_utils.py).

Given that file, we can dig more into the corpora, with a script to check the chatbot input.

To inspect the corpora, we can use the corpora_tools.py we made in the previous chapter, and the file we've previously created. Let's retrieve the Cornell Movie Dialog Corpus, format the corpora and print an example and its length:

```
from corpora_tools import *
from corpora_downloader import retrieve_cornell_corpora
sen_l1, sen_l2 = retrieve_cornell_corpora()
```

```
print ("# Two consecutive sentences in a conversation")
print ("Q:", sen_l1[0])
print ("A:", sen_l2[0])
print ("# Corpora length (i.e. number of sentences)")
print (len(sen_l1))
assert len(sen_l1) == len(sen_l2)
```

This code prints an example of two tokenized consecutive utterances, and the number of examples in the dataset, that is more than 220,000:

```
# Two consecutive sentences in a conversation
Q: ['Can', 'we', 'make', 'this', 'quick?', '', 'Roxanne', 'Korrine', 'and',
'Andrew', 'Barrett', 'are', 'having', 'an', 'incredibly', 'horrendous',
'public', 'break-', 'up', 'on', 'the', 'quad.', '', 'Again.']
A: ['Well,', 'I', 'thought', "we'd", 'start', 'with', 'pronunciation,',
'if', "that's", 'okay', 'with', 'you.']
# Corpora length (i.e. number of sentences)
221616
```

Let's now clean the punctuation in the sentences, lowercase them and limits their size to 20 words maximum (that is examples where at least one of the sentences is longer than 20 words are discarded). This is needed to standardize the tokens:

```
clean_sen_l1 = [clean_sentence(s) for s in sen_l1]
clean_sen_l2 = [clean_sentence(s) for s in sen_l2]
filt_clean_sen_l1, filt_clean_sen_l2 = filter_sentence_length(clean_sen_l1,
clean_sen_l2)
print ("# Filtered Corpora length (i.e. number of sentences)")
print (len(filt_clean_sen_l1))
assert len(filt_clean_sen_l1) == len(filt_clean_sen_l2)
```

This leads us to almost 140,000 examples:

```
# Filtered Corpora length (i.e. number of sentences)
140261
```

Then, let's create the dictionaries for the two sets of sentences. Practically, they should look the same (since the same sentence appears once on the left side, and once in the right side) except there might be some changes introduced by the first and last sentences of a conversation (they appear only once). To make the best out of our corpora, let's build two dictionaries of words and then encode all the words in the corpora with their dictionary indexes:

```
dict_l1 = create_indexed_dictionary(filt_clean_sen_l1, dict_size=15000,
storage_path="/tmp/l1_dict.p")
dict_l2 = create_indexed_dictionary(filt_clean_sen_l2, dict_size=15000,
storage_path="/tmp/l2_dict.p")
```

```
idx_sentences_l1 = sentences_to_indexes(filt_clean_sen_l1, dict_l1)
idx_sentences_l2 = sentences_to_indexes(filt_clean_sen_l2, dict_l2)
print("# Same sentences as before, with their dictionary ID")
print("Q:", list(zip(filt_clean_sen_l1[0], idx_sentences_l1[0])))
print("A:", list(zip(filt_clean_sen_l2[0], idx_sentences_l2[0])))
```

That prints the following output. We also notice that a dictionary of 15 thousand entries doesn't contain all the words and more than 16 thousand (less popular) of them don't fit into it:

```
[sentences_to_indexes] Did not find 16823 words
[sentences_to_indexes] Did not find 16649 words
# Same sentences as before, with their dictionary ID
Q: [('well', 68), (',', 8), ('i', 9), ('thought', 141), ('we', 23), ("'",
5), ('d', 83), ('start', 370), ('with', 46), ('pronunciation', 3), (',',
8), ('if', 78), ('that', 18), ("'", 5), ('s', 12), ('okay', 92), ('with',
46), ('you', 7), ('.', 4)]
A: [('not', 31), ('the', 10), ('hacking', 7309), ('and', 23), ('gagging',
8761), ('and', 23), ('spitting', 6354), ('part', 437), ('.', 4), ('please',
145), ('.', 4)]
```

As the final step, let's add paddings and markings to the sentences:

```
data_set = prepare_sentences(idx_sentences_l1, idx_sentences_l2,
max_length_l1, max_length_l2)
print("# Prepared minibatch with paddings and extra stuff")
print("Q:", data_set[0][0])
print("A:", data_set[0][1])
print("# The sentence pass from X to Y tokens")
print("Q:", len(idx_sentences_l1[0]), "->", len(data_set[0][0]))
print("A:", len(idx_sentences_l2[0]), "->", len(data_set[0][1]))
```

And that, as expected, prints:

```
# Prepared minibatch with paddings and extra stuff
Q: [0, 68, 8, 9, 141, 23, 5, 83, 370, 46, 3, 8, 78, 18, 5, 12, 92, 46, 7,
4]
A: [1, 31, 10, 7309, 23, 8761, 23, 6354, 437, 4, 145, 4, 2, 0, 0, 0, 0, 0,
0, 0, 0, 0]
# The sentence pass from X to Y tokens
Q: 19 -> 20
A: 11 -> 22
```

Training the chatbot

After we're done with the corpora, it's now time to work on the model. This project requires again a sequence to sequence model, therefore we can use an RNN. Even more, we can reuse part of the code from the previous project: we'd just need to change how the dataset is built, and the parameters of the model. We can then copy the training script built in the previous chapter, and modify the build_dataset function, to use the Cornell dataset.

Mind that the dataset used in this chapter is bigger than the one used in the previous, therefore you may need to limit the corpora to a few dozen thousand lines. On a 4 years old laptop with 8GB RAM, we had to select only the first 30 thousand lines, otherwise, the program ran out of memory and kept swapping. As a side effect of having fewer examples, even the dictionaries are smaller, resulting in less than 10 thousands words each.

```
def build_dataset(use_stored_dictionary=False):
    sen_l1, sen_l2 = retrieve_cornell_corpora()
    clean_sen_l1 = [clean_sentence(s) for s in sen_l1][:30000] ### OTHERWISE
IT DOES NOT RUN ON MY LAPTOP
    clean_sen_l2 = [clean_sentence(s) for s in sen_l2][:30000] ### OTHERWISE
IT DOES NOT RUN ON MY LAPTOP
    filt_clean_sen_l1, filt_clean_sen_l2 =
filter_sentence_length(clean_sen_l1, clean_sen_l2, max_len=10)
    if not use_stored_dictionary:
        dict_l1 = create_indexed_dictionary(filt_clean_sen_l1,
dict_size=10000, storage_path=path_l1_dict)
        dict_l2 = create_indexed_dictionary(filt_clean_sen_l2,
dict_size=10000, storage_path=path_l2_dict)
    else:
        dict_l1 = pickle.load(open(path_l1_dict, "rb"))
        dict_l2 = pickle.load(open(path_l2_dict, "rb"))
    dict_l1_length = len(dict_l1)
    dict_l2_length = len(dict_l2)
    idx_sentences_l1 = sentences_to_indexes(filt_clean_sen_l1, dict_l1)
    idx_sentences_l2 = sentences_to_indexes(filt_clean_sen_l2, dict_l2)
    max_length_l1 = extract_max_length(idx_sentences_l1)
    max_length_l2 = extract_max_length(idx_sentences_l2)
    data_set = prepare_sentences(idx_sentences_l1, idx_sentences_l2,
max_length_l1, max_length_l2)
    return (filt_clean_sen_l1, filt_clean_sen_l2), \
            data_set, \
            (max_length_l1, max_length_l2), \
            (dict_l1_length, dict_l2_length)
```

By inserting this function into the train_translator.py file (from the previous chapter) and rename the file as train_chatbot.py, we can run the training of the chatbot.

After a few iterations, you can stop the program and you'll see something similar to this output:

```
[sentences_to_indexes] Did not find 0 words
[sentences_to_indexes] Did not find 0 words
global step 100 learning rate 1.0 step-time 7.708967611789704 perplexity
444.90090078460474
eval: perplexity 57.442316329639176
global step 200 learning rate 0.990234375 step-time 7.700247814655302
perplexity 48.8545568311572
eval: perplexity 42.190180314697045
global step 300 learning rate 0.98046875 step-time 7.69800933599472
perplexity 41.620538109894945
eval: perplexity 31.291903031786116
...
...
...
global step 2400 learning rate 0.79833984375 step-time 7.686293318271639
perplexity 3.7086356605442767
eval: perplexity 2.8348589631663046
global step 2500 learning rate 0.79052734375 step-time 7.689657487869262
perplexity 3.211876894960698
eval: perplexity 2.973809378544393
global step 2600 learning rate 0.78271484375 step-time 7.690396382808681
perplexity 2.878854805600354
eval: perplexity 2.563583924617356
```

Again, if you change the settings, you may end up with a different perplexity. To obtain these results, we set the RNN size to 256 and 2 layers, the batch size of 128 samples, and the learning rate to 1.0.

At this point, the chatbot is ready to be tested. Although you can test the chatbot with the same code as in the `test_translator.py` of the previous chapter, here we would like to do a more elaborate solution, which allows exposing the chatbot as a service with APIs.

Chatbox API

First of all, we need a web framework to expose the API. In this project, we've chosen Bottle, a lightweight simple framework very easy to use.

 To install the package, run `pip install bottle` from the command line. To gather further information and dig into the code, take a look at the project webpage, `https://bottlepy.org`.

Let's now create a function to parse an arbitrary sentence provided by the user as an argument. All the following code should live in the `test_chatbot_aas.py` file. Let's start with some imports and the function to clean, tokenize and prepare the sentence using the dictionary:

```
import pickle
import sys
import numpy as np
import tensorflow as tf
import data_utils
from corpora_tools import clean_sentence, sentences_to_indexes,
prepare_sentences
from train_chatbot import get_seq2seq_model, path_l1_dict, path_l2_dict
model_dir = "/home/abc/chat/chatbot_model"
def prepare_sentence(sentence, dict_l1, max_length):
    sents = [sentence.split(" ")]
    clean_sen_l1 = [clean_sentence(s) for s in sents]
    idx_sentences_l1 = sentences_to_indexes(clean_sen_l1, dict_l1)
    data_set = prepare_sentences(idx_sentences_l1, [[]], max_length,
max_length)
    sentences = (clean_sen_l1, [[]])
    return sentences, data_set
```

The function `prepare_sentence` does the following:

- Tokenizes the input sentence
- Cleans it (lowercase and punctuation cleanup)
- Converts tokens to dictionary IDs
- Add markers and paddings to reach the default length

Next, we will need a function to convert the predicted sequence of numbers to an actual sentence composed of words. This is done by the function `decode`, which runs the prediction given the input sentence and with softmax predicts the most likely output. Finally, it returns the sentence without paddings and markers (a more exhaustive description of the function is provided in the previous chapter):

```
def decode(data_set):
with tf.Session() as sess:
    model = get_seq2seq_model(sess, True, dict_lengths,
max_sentence_lengths, model_dir)
    model.batch_size = 1
    bucket = 0
    encoder_inputs, decoder_inputs, target_weights = model.get_batch(
      {bucket: [(data_set[0][0], [])]}, bucket)
    _, _, output_logits = model.step(sess, encoder_inputs, decoder_inputs,
```

```
                                          target_weights, bucket, True)
    outputs = [int(np.argmax(logit, axis=1)) for logit in output_logits]
    if data_utils.EOS_ID in outputs:
        outputs = outputs[1:outputs.index(data_utils.EOS_ID)]
tf.reset_default_graph()
return " ".join([tf.compat.as_str(inv_dict_l2[output]) for output in
outputs])
```

Finally, the main function, that is, the function to run in the script:

```
if __name__ == "__main__":
    dict_l1 = pickle.load(open(path_l1_dict, "rb"))
    dict_l1_length = len(dict_l1)
    dict_l2 = pickle.load(open(path_l2_dict, "rb"))
    dict_l2_length = len(dict_l2)
    inv_dict_l2 = {v: k for k, v in dict_l2.items()}
    max_lengths = 10
    dict_lengths = (dict_l1_length, dict_l2_length)
    max_sentence_lengths = (max_lengths, max_lengths)
    from bottle import route, run, request
    @route('/api')
    def api():
        in_sentence = request.query.sentence
      _, data_set = prepare_sentence(in_sentence, dict_l1, max_lengths)
        resp = [{"in": in_sentence, "out": decode(data_set)}]
        return dict(data=resp)
    run(host='127.0.0.1', port=8080, reloader=True, debug=True)
```

Initially, it loads the dictionary and prepares the inverse dictionary. Then, it uses the Bottle API to create an HTTP GET endpoint (under the /api URL). The route decorator sets and enriches the function to run when the endpoint is contacted via HTTP GET. In this case, the api() function is run, which first reads the sentence passed as HTTP parameter, then calls the prepare_sentence function, described above, and finally runs the decoding step. What's returned is a dictionary containing both the input sentence provided by the user and the reply of the chatbot.

Finally, the webserver is turned on, on the localhost at port 8080. Isn't very easy to have a chatbot as a service with Bottle?

It's now time to run it and check the outputs. To run it, run from the command line:

```
$> python3 -u test_chatbot_aas.py
```

Then, let's start querying the chatbot with some generic questions, to do so we can use CURL, a simple command line; also all the browsers are ok, just remember that the URL should be encoded, for example, the space character should be replaced with its encoding, that is, %20.

Curl makes things easier, having a simple way to encode the URL request. Here are a couple of examples:

```
$> curl -X GET -G http://127.0.0.1:8080/api --data-urlencode "sentence=how
are you?"
{"data": [{"out": "i ' m here with you .", "in": "where are you?"}]}
$> curl -X GET -G http://127.0.0.1:8080/api --data-urlencode "sentence=are
you here?"
{"data": [{"out": "yes .", "in": "are you here?"}]}
$> curl -X GET -G http://127.0.0.1:8080/api --data-urlencode "sentence=are
you a chatbot?"
{"data": [{"out": "you ' for the stuff to be right .", "in": "are you a
chatbot?"}]}
$> curl -X GET -G http://127.0.0.1:8080/api --data-urlencode "sentence=what
is your name ?"
{"data": [{"out": "we don ' t know .", "in": "what is your name ?"}]}
$> curl -X GET -G http://127.0.0.1:8080/api --data-urlencode "sentence=how
are you?"
{"data": [{"out": "that ' s okay .", "in": "how are you?"}]}
```

> If the system doesn't work with your browser, try encoding the URL, for example:
> ```
> $> curl -X GET
> http://127.0.0.1:8080/api?sentence=how%20are%20you?
> {"data": [{"out": "that ' s okay .", "in": "how are
> you?"}]}.
> ```

Replies are quite funny; always remember that we trained the chatbox on movies, therefore the type of replies follow that style.

To turn off the webserver, use *Ctrl + C*.

Home assignments

Following are the home assignments:

- Can you create a simple webpage which queries the chatbot via JS?
- Many other training sets are available on the Internet; try to see the differences of answers between the models. Which one is the best for a customer service bot?
- Can you modify the model, to be trained as a service, that is, by passing the sentences via HTTP GET/POST?

Summary

In this chapter, we've implemented a chatbot, able to respond to questions through an HTTP endpoint and a GET API. It's another great example of what we can do with RNN. In the next chapter, we're moving to a different topic: how to create a recommender system using Tensorflow.

Detecting Duplicate Quora Questions

8

Quora (www.quora.com) is a community-driven question and answer website where users, either anonymously or publicly, ask and answer questions. In January 2017, Quora first released a public dataset consisting of question pairs, either duplicate or not. A duplicate pair of questions is semantically similar; in other words, two questions being duplicated means that they carry the same meaning, although they use a different set of words to express the exact same intent. For Quora, it is paramount to have a single question page for each distinct question, in order to offer a better service to users consulting its repository of answers, so they won't have to look for any more sources before finding all they need to know. Moderators can be helpful in avoiding duplicated content on the site, but that won't easily scale, given the increasing number of questions answered each day and a growing historical repository. In this case, an automation project based on **Natural Language Processing (NLP)** and deep learning could be the right solution for the task.

This chapter will deal with understanding how to build a project based on TensorFlow that explicates the semantic similarity between sentences using the Quora dataset. The chapter is based on the work of Abhishek Thakur (https://www.linkedin.com/pulse/duplicate-quora-question-abhishek-thakur/), who originally developed a solution based on the Keras package. The presented techniques can also easily be applied to other problems that deal with semantic similarity. In this project, we will cover the following:

- Feature engineering on text data
- TF-IDF and SVD
- Word2vec and GloVe based features
- Traditional machine learning models such as logistic regression and gradient boosting using xgboost
- Deep learning models including LSTM, GRU, and 1D-CNN

By the end of the chapter, you will be able to train your own deep learning model on similar problems. To start with, let's have a quick look at the Quora dataset.

Presenting the dataset

The data, made available for non-commercial purposes (`https://www.quora.com/about/tos`) in a Kaggle competition (`https://www.kaggle.com/c/quora-question-pairs`) and on Quora's blog (`https://data.quora.com/First-Quora-Dataset-Release-Question-Pairs`), consists of 404,351 question pairs with 255,045 negative samples (non-duplicates) and 149,306 positive samples (duplicates). There are approximately 40% positive samples, a slight imbalance that won't need particular corrections. Actually, as reported on the Quora blog, given their original sampling strategy, the number of duplicated examples in the dataset was much higher than the non-duplicated ones. In order to set up a more balanced dataset, the negative examples were upsampled by using pairs of related questions, that is, questions about the same topic that are actually not similar.

Before starting work on this project, you can simply directly download the data, which is about 55 MB, from its Amazon S3 repository at this link: `http://qim.ec.quoracdn.net/quora_duplicate_questions.tsv` into our working directory.

After loading it, we can start diving directly into the data by picking some example rows and examining them. The following diagram shows an actual snapshot of the few first rows from the dataset:

	id	qid1	qid2	question1	question2	is_duplicate
0	0	1	2	What is the step by step guide to invest in sh...	What is the step by step guide to invest in sh...	0
1	1	3	4	What is the story of Kohinoor (Koh-i-Noor) Dia...	What would happen if the Indian government sto...	0
2	2	5	6	How can I increase the speed of my internet co...	How can Internet speed be increased by hacking...	0
3	3	7	8	Why am I mentally very lonely? How can I solve...	Find the remainder when [math]23^{24}[/math] i...	0
4	4	9	10	Which one dissolve in water quikly sugar, salt...	Which fish would survive in salt water?	0

First few rows of the Quora dataset

Exploring further into the data, we can find some examples of question pairs that mean the same thing, that is, duplicates, as follows:

How does Quora quickly mark questions as needing improvement?	Why does Quora mark my questions as needing improvement/clarification before I have time to give it details? Literally within seconds…
Why did Trump win the Presidency?	How did Donald Trump win the 2016 Presidential Election?
What practical applications might evolve from the discovery of the Higgs Boson?	What are some practical benefits of the discovery of the Higgs Boson?

At first sight, duplicated questions have quite a few words in common, but they could be very different in length.

On the other hand, examples of non-duplicate questions are as follows:

Who should I address my cover letter to if I'm applying to a big company like Mozilla?	**Which car is better from a safety persepctive? swift or grand i10. My first priority is safety?**
Mr. Robot (TV series): Is Mr. Robot a good representation of real-life hacking and hacking culture? Is the depiction of hacker societies realistic?	What mistakes are made when depicting hacking in Mr. Robot compared to real-life cyber security breaches or just a regular use of technologies?
How can I start an online shopping (e-commerce) website?	Which web technology is best suited for building a big e-commerce website?

Some questions from these examples are clearly not duplicated and have few words in common, but some others are more difficult to detect as unrelated. For instance, the second pair in the example might turn being appealing to some and leave even a human judge uncertain. The two questions might mean different things: *why* versus *how,* or they could be intended as the same from a superficial examination. Looking deeper, we may even find more doubtful examples and even some clear data mistakes; we surely have some anomalies in the dataset (as the Quota post on the dataset warned) but, given that the data is derived from a real-world problem, we can't do anything but deal with this kind of imperfection and strive to find a robust solution that works.

At this point, our exploration becomes more quantitative than qualitative and some statistics on the question pairs are provided here:

Average number of characters in question1	**59.57**
Minimum number of characters in question1	1
Maximum number of characters in question1	623
Average number of characters in question2	60.14
Minimum number of characters in question2	1
Maximum number of characters in question2	1169

Question 1 and question 2 are roughly the same average characters, though we have more extremes in question 2. There also must be some trash in the data, since we cannot figure out a question made up of a single character.

We can even get a completely different vision of our data by plotting it into a word cloud and highlighting the most common words present in the dataset:

Figure 1: A word cloud made up of the most frequent words to be found in the Quora dataset

The presence of word sequences such as **Hillary Clinton** and **Donald Trump** reminds us that the data was gathered at a certain historical moment, and that many questions we can find inside it are clearly ephemeral, reasonable only at the very time the dataset was collected. Other topics, such as **programming language**, **World War**, or **earn money** could be longer lasting, both in terms of interest and in the validity of the answers provided.

After exploring the data a bit, it is now time to decide what target metric we will strive to optimize in our project. Throughout the chapter, we will be using accuracy as a metric to evaluate the performance of our models. Accuracy as a measure is simply focused on the effectiveness of the prediction, and it may miss some important differences between alternative models, such as discrimination power (is the model more able to detect duplicates or not?) or the exactness of probability scores (how much margin is there between being a duplicate and not being one?). We chose accuracy based on the fact that this metric was the one decided on by Quora's engineering team to create a benchmark for this dataset (as stated in this blog post of theirs: `https://engineering.quora.com/Semantic-Question-Matching-with-Deep-Learning`). Using accuracy as the metric makes it easier for us to evaluate and compare our models with the one from Quora's engineering team, and also several other research papers. In addition, in a real-world application, our work may simply be evaluated on the basis of how many times it is just right or wrong, regardless of other considerations.

We can now proceed furthermore in our projects with some very basic feature engineering to start with.

Starting with basic feature engineering

Before starting to code, we have to load the dataset in Python and also provide Python with all the necessary packages for our project. We will need to have these packages installed on our system (the latest versions should suffice, no need for any specific package version):

- Numpy
- pandas
- fuzzywuzzy
- python-Levenshtein
- scikit-learn
- gensim
- pyemd
- NLTK

As we will be using each one of these packages in the project, we will provide specific instructions and tips to install them.

For all dataset operations, we will be using pandas (and Numpy will come in handy, too). To install `numpy` and `pandas`:

```
pip install numpy
pip install pandas
```

The dataset can be loaded into memory easily by using pandas and a specialized data structure, the pandas dataframe (we expect the dataset to be in the same directory as your script or Jupyter notebook):

```
import pandas as pd
import numpy as np

data = pd.read_csv('quora_duplicate_questions.tsv', sep='\t')
data = data.drop(['id', 'qid1', 'qid2'], axis=1)
```

We will be using the pandas dataframe denoted by `data` throughout this chapter, and also when we work with our TensorFlow model and provide input to it.

We can now start by creating some very basic features. These basic features include length-based features and string-based features:

1. Length of question1
2. Length of question2
3. Difference between the two lengths
4. Character length of question1 without spaces
5. Character length of question2 without spaces
6. Number of words in question1
7. Number of words in question2
8. Number of common words in question1 and question2

These features are dealt with one-liners transforming the original input using the pandas package in Python and its method `apply`:

```
# length based features
data['len_q1'] = data.question1.apply(lambda x: len(str(x)))
data['len_q2'] = data.question2.apply(lambda x: len(str(x)))

# difference in lengths of two questions
data['diff_len'] = data.len_q1 - data.len_q2
```

```
# character length based features
data['len_char_q1'] = data.question1.apply(lambda x:
                    len(''.join(set(str(x).replace(' ', '')))))
data['len_char_q2'] = data.question2.apply(lambda x:
                    len(''.join(set(str(x).replace(' ', '')))))

# word length based features
data['len_word_q1'] = data.question1.apply(lambda x:
                                len(str(x).split()))
data['len_word_q2'] = data.question2.apply(lambda x:
                                len(str(x).split()))

# common words in the two questions
data['common_words'] = data.apply(lambda x:
                        len(set(str(x['question1'])
                        .lower().split())
                        .intersection(set(str(x['question2'])
                        .lower().split()))), axis=1)
```

For future reference, we will mark this set of features as feature set-1 or `fs_1`:

```
fs_1 = ['len_q1', 'len_q2', 'diff_len', 'len_char_q1',
        'len_char_q2', 'len_word_q1', 'len_word_q2',
        'common_words']
```

This simple approach will help you to easily recall and combine a different set of features in the machine learning models we are going to build, turning comparing different models run by different feature sets into a piece of cake.

Creating fuzzy features

The next set of features are based on fuzzy string matching. Fuzzy string matching is also known as approximate string matching and is the process of finding strings that approximately match a given pattern. The closeness of a match is defined by the number of primitive operations necessary to convert the string into an exact match. These primitive operations include insertion (to insert a character at a given position), deletion (to delete a particular character), and substitution (to replace a character with a new one).

Fuzzy string matching is typically used for spell checking, plagiarism detection, DNA sequence matching, spam filtering, and so on and it is part of the larger family of edit distances, distances based on the idea that a string can be transformed into another one. It is frequently used in natural language processing and other applications in order to ascertain the grade of difference between two strings of characters.

It is also known as Levenshtein distance, from the name of the Russian scientist, Vladimir Levenshtein, who introduced it in 1965.

These features were created using the `fuzzywuzzy` package available for Python (`https://pypi.python.org/pypi/fuzzywuzzy`). This package uses Levenshtein distance to calculate the differences in two sequences, which in our case are the pair of questions.

The `fuzzywuzzy` package can be installed using pip3:

```
pip install fuzzywuzzy
```

As an important dependency, `fuzzywuzzy` requires the `Python-Levenshtein` package (`https://github.com/ztane/python-Levenshtein/`), which is a blazingly fast implementation of this classic algorithm, powered by compiled C code. To make the calculations much faster using `fuzzywuzzy`, we also need to install the `Python-Levenshtein` package:

```
pip install python-Levenshtein
```

The `fuzzywuzzy` package offers many different types of ratio, but we will be using only the following:

1. QRatio
2. WRatio
3. Partial ratio
4. Partial token set ratio
5. Partial token sort ratio
6. Token set ratio
7. Token sort ratio

Examples of `fuzzywuzzy` features on Quora data:

```
from fuzzywuzzy import fuzz

fuzz.QRatio("Why did Trump win the Presidency?",
"How did Donald Trump win the 2016 Presidential Election")
```

This code snippet will result in the value of 67 being returned:

```
fuzz.QRatio("How can I start an online shopping (e-commerce) website?",
"Which web technology is best suitable for building a big E-Commerce
website?")
```

In this comparison, the returned value will be 60. Given these examples, we notice that although the values of QRatio are close to each other, the value for the similar question pair from the dataset is higher than the pair with no similarity. Let's take a look at another feature from fuzzywuzzy for these same pairs of questions:

```
fuzz.partial_ratio("Why did Trump win the Presidency?",
"How did Donald Trump win the 2016 Presidential Election")
```

In this case, the returned value is 73:

```
fuzz.partial_ratio("How can I start an online shopping (e-commerce)
website?", "Which web technology is best suitable for building a big E-
Commerce website?")
```

Now the returned value is 57.

Using the partial_ratio method, we can observe how the difference in scores for these two pairs of questions increases notably, allowing an easier discrimination between being a duplicate pair or not. We assume that these features might add value to our models.

By using pandas and the fuzzywuzzy package in Python, we can again apply these features as simple one-liners:

```
data['fuzz_qratio'] = data.apply(lambda x: fuzz.QRatio(
    str(x['question1']), str(x['question2'])), axis=1)

data['fuzz_WRatio'] = data.apply(lambda x: fuzz.WRatio(
    str(x['question1']), str(x['question2'])), axis=1)

data['fuzz_partial_ratio'] = data.apply(lambda x:
                fuzz.partial_ratio(str(x['question1']),
                str(x['question2'])), axis=1)

data['fuzz_partial_token_set_ratio'] = data.apply(lambda x:
        fuzz.partial_token_set_ratio(str(x['question1']),
        str(x['question2'])), axis=1)

data['fuzz_partial_token_sort_ratio'] = data.apply(lambda x:
        fuzz.partial_token_sort_ratio(str(x['question1']),
        str(x['question2'])), axis=1)

data['fuzz_token_set_ratio'] = data.apply(lambda x:
                fuzz.token_set_ratio(str(x['question1']),
                str(x['question2'])), axis=1)
```

```
data['fuzz_token_sort_ratio'] = data.apply(lambda x:
                fuzz.token_sort_ratio(str(x['question1']),
                str(x['question2']))), axis=1)
```

This set of features are henceforth denoted as feature set-2 or `fs_2`:

```
fs_2 = ['fuzz_qratio', 'fuzz_WRatio', 'fuzz_partial_ratio',
        'fuzz_partial_token_set_ratio', 'fuzz_partial_token_sort_ratio',
        'fuzz_token_set_ratio', 'fuzz_token_sort_ratio']
```

Again, we will store our work and save it for later use when modeling.

Resorting to TF-IDF and SVD features

The next few sets of features are based on TF-IDF and SVD. **Term Frequency-Inverse Document Frequency (TF-IDF)**. Is one of the algorithms at the foundation of information retrieval. Here, the algorithm is explained using a formula:

$$TF(t) = C(t)/N$$

$$IDF(t) = log(ND/ND_t)$$

You can understand the formula using this notation: $C(t)$ is the number of times a term t appears in a document, N is the total number of terms in the document, this results in the **Term Frequency (TF)**. ND is the total number of documents and ND_t is the number of documents containing the term t, this provides the **Inverse Document Frequency (IDF)**. TF-IDF for a term t is a multiplication of Term Frequency and Inverse Document Frequency for the given term t:

$$TFIDF(t) = TF(t) * IDF(t)$$

Without any prior knowledge, other than about the documents themselves, such a score will highlight all the terms that could easily discriminate a document from the others, down-weighting the common words that won't tell you much, such as the common parts of speech (such as articles, for instance).

 If you need a more hands-on explanation of TFIDF, this great online tutorial will help you try coding the algorithm yourself and testing it on some text data: https://stevenloria.com/tf-idf/

For convenience and speed of execution, we resorted to the `scikit-learn` implementation of TFIDF. If you don't already have `scikit-learn` installed, you can install it using pip:

```
pip install -U scikit-learn
```

We create TFIDF features for both question1 and question2 separately (in order to type less, we just deep copy the question1 `TfidfVectorizer`):

```
from sklearn.feature_extraction.text import TfidfVectorizer
from copy import deepcopy

tfv_q1 = TfidfVectorizer(min_df=3,
                         max_features=None,
                         strip_accents='unicode',
                         analyzer='word',
                         token_pattern=r'\w{1,}',
                         ngram_range=(1, 2),
                         use_idf=1,
                         smooth_idf=1,
                         sublinear_tf=1,
                         stop_words='english')

tfv_q2 = deepcopy(tfv_q1)
```

It must be noted that the parameters shown here have been selected after quite a lot of experiments. These parameters generally work pretty well with all other problems concerning natural language processing, specifically text classification. One might need to change the stop word list to the language in question.

We can now obtain the TFIDF matrices for question1 and question2 separately:

```
q1_tfidf = tfv_q1.fit_transform(data.question1.fillna(""))
q2_tfidf = tfv_q2.fit_transform(data.question2.fillna(""))
```

> In our TFIDF processing, we computed the TFIDF matrices based on all the data available (we used the `fit_transform` method). This is quite a common approach in Kaggle competitions because it helps to score higher on the leaderboard. However, if you are working in a real setting, you may want to exclude a part of the data as a training or validation set in order to be sure that your TFIDF processing helps your model to generalize to a new, unseen dataset.

After we have the TFIDF features, we move to SVD features. SVD is a feature decomposition method and it stands for singular value decomposition. It is largely used in NLP because of a technique called Latent Semantic Analysis (LSA).

A detailed discussion of SVD and LSA is beyond the scope of this chapter, but you can get an idea of their workings by trying these two approachable and clear online tutorials: `https://alyssaq.github.io/2015/singular-value-decomposition-visualisation/` and `https://technowiki.wordpress.com/2011/08/27/latent-semantic-analysis-lsa-tutorial/`

To create the SVD features, we again use `scikit-learn` implementation. This implementation is a variation of traditional SVD and is known as `TruncatedSVD`.

 A `TruncatedSVD` is an approximate SVD method that can provide you with reliable yet computationally fast SVD matrix decomposition. You can find more hints about how this technique works and it can be applied by consulting this web page: `http://langvillea.people.cofc.edu/DISSECTION-LAB/Emmie'sLSI-SVDModule/p5module.html`

```
from sklearn.decomposition import TruncatedSVD
svd_q1 = TruncatedSVD(n_components=180)
svd_q2 = TruncatedSVD(n_components=180)
```

We chose 180 components for SVD decomposition and these features are calculated on a TF-IDF matrix:

```
question1_vectors = svd_q1.fit_transform(q1_tfidf)
question2_vectors = svd_q2.fit_transform(q2_tfidf)
```

Feature set-3 is derived from a combination of these TF-IDF and SVD features. For example, we can have only the TF-IDF features for the two questions separately going into the model, or we can have the TF-IDF of the two questions combined with an SVD on top of them, and then the model kicks in, and so on. These features are explained as follows.

Feature set-3(1) or `fs3_1` is created using two different TF-IDFs for the two questions, which are then stacked together horizontally and passed to a machine learning model:

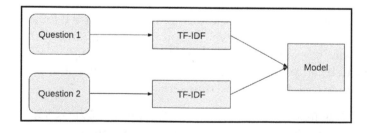

This can be coded as:

```
from scipy import sparse

# obtain features by stacking the sparse matrices together
fs3_1 = sparse.hstack((q1_tfidf, q2_tfidf))
```

Feature set-3(2), or `fs3_2`, is created by combining the two questions and using a single TF-IDF:

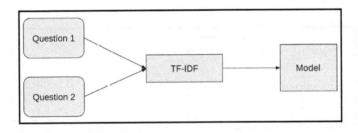

```
tfv = TfidfVectorizer(min_df=3,
                      max_features=None,
                      strip_accents='unicode',
                      analyzer='word',
                      token_pattern=r'\w{1,}',
                      ngram_range=(1, 2),
                      use_idf=1,
                      smooth_idf=1,
                      sublinear_tf=1,
                      stop_words='english')

# combine questions and calculate tf-idf
q1q2 = data.question1.fillna("")
q1q2 += " " + data.question2.fillna("")
fs3_2 = tfv.fit_transform(q1q2)
```

The next subset of features in this feature set, feature set-3(3) or `fs3_3`, consists of separate TF-IDFs and SVDs for both questions:

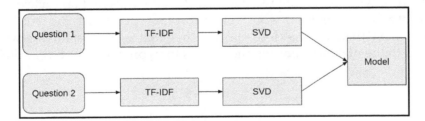

This can be coded as follows:

```
# obtain features by stacking the matrices together
fs3_3 = np.hstack((question1_vectors, question2_vectors))
```

We can similarly create a couple more combinations using TF-IDF and SVD, and call them `fs3-4` and `fs3-5`, respectively. These are depicted in the following diagrams, but the code is left as an exercise for the reader.

Feature set-3(4) or `fs3-4`:

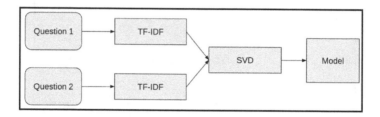

Feature set-3(5) or `fs3-5`:

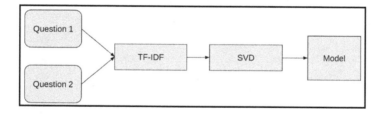

After the basic feature set and some TF-IDF and SVD features, we can now move to more complicated features before diving into the machine learning and deep learning models.

Mapping with Word2vec embeddings

Very broadly, Word2vec models are two-layer neural networks that take a text corpus as input and output a vector for every word in that corpus. After fitting, the words with similar meaning have their vectors close to each other, that is, the distance between them is small compared to the distance between the vectors for words that have very different meanings.

Nowadays, Word2vec has become a standard in natural language processing problems and often it provides very useful insights into information retrieval tasks. For this particular problem, we will be using the Google news vectors. This is a pretrained Word2vec model trained on the Google News corpus.

Every word, when represented by its Word2vec vector, gets a position in space, as depicted in the following diagram:

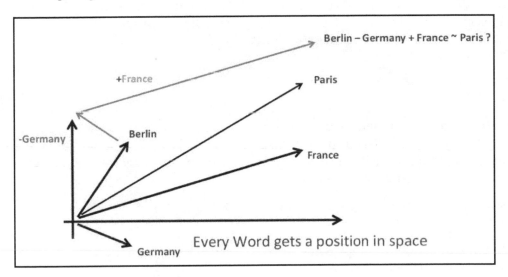

All the words in this example, such as Germany, Berlin, France, and Paris, can be represented by a 300-dimensional vector, if we are using the pretrained vectors from the Google news corpus. When we use Word2vec representations for these words and we subtract the vector of Germany from the vector of Berlin and add the vector of France to it, we will get a vector that is very similar to the vector of Paris. The Word2vec model thus carries the meaning of words in the vectors. The information carried by these vectors constitutes a very useful feature for our task.

For a user-friendly, yet more in-depth, explanation and description of possible applications of Word2vec, we suggest reading `https://www.distilled.net/resources/a-beginners-guide-to-Word2vec-aka-whats-the-opposite-of-canada/,` or if you need a more mathematically defined explanation, we recommend reading this paper: `http://www.1-4-5.net/~dmm/ml/how_does_Word2vec_work.pdf`

To load the Word2vec features, we will be using Gensim. If you don't have Gensim, you can install it easily using pip. At this time, it is suggested you also install the pyemd package, which will be used by the WMD distance function, a function that will help us to relate two Word2vec vectors:

```
pip install gensim
pip install pyemd
```

To load the Word2vec model, we download the `GoogleNews-vectors-negative300.bin.gz` binary and use Gensim's `load_Word2vec_format` function to load it into memory. You can easily download the binary from an Amazon AWS repository using the `wget` command from a shell:

```
wget -c "https://s3.amazonaws.com/dl4j-distribution/GoogleNews-vectors-negative300.bin.gz"
```

After downloading and decompressing the file, you can use it with the Gensim `KeyedVectors` functions:

```
import gensim

model = gensim.models.KeyedVectors.load_word2vec_format(
        'GoogleNews-vectors-negative300.bin.gz', binary=True)
```

Now, we can easily get the vector of a word by calling model[word]. However, a problem arises when we are dealing with sentences instead of individual words. In our case, we need vectors for all of question1 and question2 in order to come up with some kind of comparison. For this, we can use the following code snippet. The snippet basically adds the vectors for all words in a sentence that are available in the Google news vectors and gives a normalized vector at the end. We can call this sentence to vector, or Sent2Vec.

Make sure that you have **Natural Language Tool Kit** (**NLTK**) installed before running the preceding function:

```
$ pip install nltk
```

It is also suggested that you download the `punkt` and `stopwords` packages, as they are part of NLTK:

```
import nltk
nltk.download('punkt')
nltk.download('stopwords')
```

If NLTK is now available, you just have to run the following snippet and define the `sent2vec` function:

```
from nltk.corpus import stopwords
from nltk import word_tokenize

stop_words = set(stopwords.words('english'))

def sent2vec(s, model):
    M = []
    words = word_tokenize(str(s).lower())
    for word in words:
        #It shouldn't be a stopword
        if word not in stop_words:
            #nor contain numbers
            if word.isalpha():
                #and be part of word2vec
                if word in model:
                    M.append(model[word])
    M = np.array(M)
    if len(M) > 0:
        v = M.sum(axis=0)
        return v / np.sqrt((v ** 2).sum())
    else:
        return np.zeros(300)
```

When the phrase is null, we arbitrarily decide to give back a standard vector of zero values.

To calculate the similarity between the questions, another feature that we created was word mover's distance. Word mover's distance uses Word2vec embeddings and works on a principle similar to that of earth mover's distance to give a distance between two text documents. Simply put, word mover's distance provides the minimum distance needed to move all the words from one document to an other document.

The WMD has been introduced by this paper: *KUSNER, Matt, et al. From word embeddings to document distances. In: International Conference on Machine Learning. 2015. p. 957-966* which can be found at `http://proceedings.mlr.press/v37/kusnerb15.pdf`. For a hands-on tutorial on the distance, you can also refer to this tutorial based on the Gensim implementation of the distance: `https://markroxor.github.io/gensim/static/notebooks/WMD_tutorial.html`

Final **Word2vec** (**w2v**) features also include other distances, more usual ones such as the Euclidean or cosine distance. We complete the sequence of features with some measurement of the distribution of the two document vectors:

1. Word mover distance
2. Normalized word mover distance
3. Cosine distance between vectors of question1 and question2
4. Manhattan distance between vectors of question1 and question2
5. Jaccard similarity between vectors of question1 and question2
6. Canberra distance between vectors of question1 and question2
7. Euclidean distance between vectors of question1 and question2
8. Minkowski distance between vectors of question1 and question2
9. Braycurtis distance between vectors of question1 and question2
10. The skew of the vector for question1
11. The skew of the vector for question2
12. The kurtosis of the vector for question1
13. The kurtosis of the vector for question2

All the Word2vec features are denoted by **fs4**.

A separate set of w2v features consists in the matrices of Word2vec vectors themselves:

1. Word2vec vector for question1
2. Word2vec vector for question2

These will be represented by **fs5**:

```
w2v_q1 = np.array([sent2vec(q, model)
                    for q in data.question1])
w2v_q2 = np.array([sent2vec(q, model)
                    for q in data.question2])
```

In order to easily implement all the different distance measures between the vectors of the Word2vec embeddings of the Quora questions, we use the implementations found in the `scipy.spatial.distance` module:

```
from scipy.spatial.distance import cosine, cityblock,
         jaccard, canberra, euclidean, minkowski, braycurtis

data['cosine_distance'] = [cosine(x,y)
                         for (x,y) in zip(w2v_q1, w2v_q2)]
data['cityblock_distance'] = [cityblock(x,y)
                         for (x,y) in zip(w2v_q1, w2v_q2)]
data['jaccard_distance'] = [jaccard(x,y)
                         for (x,y) in zip(w2v_q1, w2v_q2)]
data['canberra_distance'] = [canberra(x,y)
                         for (x,y) in zip(w2v_q1, w2v_q2)]
data['euclidean_distance'] = [euclidean(x,y)
                         for (x,y) in zip(w2v_q1, w2v_q2)]
data['minkowski_distance'] = [minkowski(x,y,3)
                         for (x,y) in zip(w2v_q1, w2v_q2)]
data['braycurtis_distance'] = [braycurtis(x,y)
                         for (x,y) in zip(w2v_q1, w2v_q2)]
```

All the features names related to distances are gathered under the list `fs4_1`:

```
fs4_1 = ['cosine_distance', 'cityblock_distance',
         'jaccard_distance', 'canberra_distance',
         'euclidean_distance', 'minkowski_distance',
         'braycurtis_distance']
```

The Word2vec matrices for the two questions are instead horizontally stacked and stored away in the `w2v` variable for later usage:

```
w2v = np.hstack((w2v_q1, w2v_q2))
```

The Word Mover's Distance is implemented using a function that returns the distance between two questions, after having transformed them into lowercase and after removing any stopwords. Moreover, we also calculate a normalized version of the distance, after transforming all the Word2vec vectors into L2-normalized vectors (each vector is transformed to the unit norm, that is, if we squared each element in the vector and summed all of them, the result would be equal to one) using the `init_sims` method:

```
def wmd(s1, s2, model):
    s1 = str(s1).lower().split()
    s2 = str(s2).lower().split()
    stop_words = stopwords.words('english')
    s1 = [w for w in s1 if w not in stop_words]
```

```
    s2 = [w for w in s2 if w not in stop_words]
    return model.wmdistance(s1, s2)

data['wmd'] = data.apply(lambda x: wmd(x['question1'],
                        x['question2'], model), axis=1)
model.init_sims(replace=True)
data['norm_wmd'] = data.apply(lambda x: wmd(x['question1'],
                        x['question2'], model), axis=1)
fs4_2 = ['wmd', 'norm_wmd']
```

After these last computations, we now have most of the important features that are needed to create some basic machine learning models, which will serve as a benchmark for our deep learning models. The following table displays a snapshot of the available features:

question1	What is the story of Kohinoor (Koh-i-Noor) Dia...
question2	What would happen if the Indian government sto...
is_duplicate	0
len_q1	51
len_q2	88
diff_len	-37
len_char_q1	21
len_char_q2	29
len_word_q1	8
len_word_q2	13
common_words	4
fuzz_qratio	66
fuzz_WRatio	86
fuzz_partial_ratio	73
fuzz_partial_token_set_ratio	100
fuzz_partial_token_sort_ratio	75
fuzz_token_set_ratio	86
fuzz_token_sort_ratio	63
wmd	3.77235
norm_wmd	1.3688
cosine_distance	0.512164
cityblock_distance	14.1951
jaccard_distance	1
canberra_distance	177.588
euclidean_distance	1.01209
minkowski_distance	0.45591
braycurtis_distance	0.592655
skew_q1vec	0.00873466
skew_q2vec	0.0947038
kur_q1vec	0.28401
kur_q2vec	-0.034444

Let's train some machine learning models on these and other Word2vec based features.

Testing machine learning models

Before proceeding, depending on your system, you may need to clean up the memory a bit and free space for machine learning models from previously used data structures. This is done using `gc.collect`, after deleting any past variables not required anymore, and then checking the available memory by exact reporting from the `psutil.virtualmemory` function:

```
import gc
```

```
import psutil
del([tfv_q1, tfv_q2, tfv, q1q2,
     question1_vectors, question2_vectors, svd_q1,
     svd_q2, q1_tfidf, q2_tfidf])
del([w2v_q1, w2v_q2])
del([model])
gc.collect()
psutil.virtual_memory()
```

At this point, we simply recap the different features created up to now, and their meaning in terms of generated features:

- `fs_1`: List of basic features
- `fs_2`: List of fuzzy features
- `fs3_1`: Sparse data matrix of TFIDF for separated questions
- `fs3_2`: Sparse data matrix of TFIDF for combined questions
- `fs3_3`: Sparse data matrix of SVD
- `fs3_4`: List of SVD statistics
- `fs4_1`: List of w2vec distances
- `fs4_2`: List of wmd distances
- `w2v`: A matrix of transformed phrase's Word2vec vectors by means of the `Sent2Vec` function

We evaluate two basic and very popular models in machine learning, namely logistic regression and gradient boosting using the `xgboost` package in Python. The following table provides the performance of the logistic regression and `xgboost` algorithms on different sets of features created earlier, as obtained during the Kaggle competition:

Feature set	Logistic regression accuracy	xgboost accuracy
Basic features (fs1)	0.658	0.721
Basic features + fuzzy features (fs1 + fs2)	0.660	0.738
Basic features + fuzzy features + w2v features (fs1 + fs2 + fs4)	0.676	0.766
W2v vector features (fs5)	*	0.78

Basic features + fuzzy features + w2v features + w2v vector features (fs1 + fs2 + fs4 + fs5)	*	**0.814**
TFIDF-SVD features (`fs3-1`)	0.777	0.749
TFIDF-SVD features (`fs3-2`)	0.804	0.748
TFIDF-SVD features (`fs3-3`)	0.706	0.763
TFIDF-SVD features (`fs3-4`)	0.700	0.753
TFIDF-SVD features (`fs3-5`)	0.714	0.759

* = These models were not trained due to high memory requirements.

We can treat the performances achieved as benchmarks or baseline numbers before starting with deep learning models, but we won't limit ourselves to that and we will be trying to replicate some of them.

We are going to start by importing all the necessary packages. As for as the logistic regression, we will be using the scikit-learn implementation.

The xgboost is a scalable, portable, and distributed gradient boosting library (a tree ensemble machine learning algorithm). Initially created by Tianqi Chen from Washington University, it has been enriched with a Python wrapper by Bing Xu, and an R interface by Tong He (you can read the story behind xgboost directly from its principal creator at `homes.cs.washington.edu/~tqchen/2016/03/10/story-and-lessons-behind-the-evolution-of-xgboost.html`). The xgboost is available for Python, R, Java, Scala, Julia, and C++, and it can work both on a single machine (leveraging multithreading) and in Hadoop and Spark clusters.

> Detailed instruction for installing xgboost on your system can be found on this page: `github.com/dmlc/xgboost/blob/master/doc/build.md`
>
> The installation of xgboost on both Linux and macOS is quite straightforward, whereas it is a little bit trickier for Windows users.

> For this reason, we provide specific installation steps for having xgboost working on Windows:
>
> 1. First, download and install Git for Windows (`git-for-windows.github.io`)
> 2. Then, you need a MINGW compiler present on your system. You can download it from `www.mingw.org` according to the characteristics of your system

3. From the command line, execute:

```
$> git clone --recursive https://github.com/dmlc/
xgboost
$> cd xgboost
$> git submodule init
$> git submodule update
```

4. Then, always from the command line, you copy the configuration for 64-byte systems to be the default one:

```
$> copy make\mingw64.mk config.mk
```

Alternatively, you just copy the plain 32-byte version:

```
$> copy make\mingw.mk config.mk
```

5. After copying the configuration file, you can run the compiler, setting it to use four threads in order to speed up the compiling process:

```
$> mingw32-make -j4
```

6. In MinGW, the `make` command comes with the name `mingw32-make`; if you are using a different compiler, the previous command may not work, but you can simply try:

```
$> make -j4
```

7. Finally, if the compiler completed its work without errors, you can install the package in Python with:

```
$> cd python-package
$> python setup.py install
```

If xgboost has also been properly installed on your system, you can proceed with importing both machine learning algorithms:

```
from sklearn import linear_model
from sklearn.preprocessing import StandardScaler
import xgboost as xgb
```

Since we will be using a logistic regression solver that is sensitive to the scale of the features (it is the `sag` solver from `https://github.com/EpistasisLab/tpot/issues/292`, which requires a linear computational time in respect to the size of the data), we will start by standardizing the data using the `scaler` function in scikit-learn:

```
scaler = StandardScaler()
y = data.is_duplicate.values
y = y.astype('float32').reshape(-1, 1)
X = data[fs_1+fs_2+fs3_4+fs4_1+fs4_2]
X = X.replace([np.inf, -np.inf], np.nan).fillna(0).values
X = scaler.fit_transform(X)
```

```
X = np.hstack((X, fs3_3))
```

We also select the data for the training by first filtering the fs_1, fs_2, fs3_4, fs4_1, and fs4_2 set of variables, and then stacking the fs3_3 sparse SVD data matrix. We also provide a random split, separating 1/10 of the data for validation purposes (in order to effectively assess the quality of the created model):

```
np.random.seed(42)
n_all, _ = y.shape
idx = np.arange(n_all)
np.random.shuffle(idx)
n_split = n_all // 10
idx_val = idx[:n_split]
idx_train = idx[n_split:]
x_train = X[idx_train]
y_train = np.ravel(y[idx_train])
x_val = X[idx_val]
y_val = np.ravel(y[idx_val])
```

As a first model, we try logistic regression, setting the regularization l2 parameter C to 0.1 (modest regularization). Once the model is ready, we test its efficacy on the validation set (x_val for the training matrix, y_val for the correct answers). The results are assessed on accuracy, that is the proportion of exact guesses on the validation set:

```
logres = linear_model.LogisticRegression(C=0.1,
                              solver='sag', max_iter=1000)
logres.fit(x_train, y_train)
lr_preds = logres.predict(x_val)
log_res_accuracy = np.sum(lr_preds == y_val) / len(y_val)
print("Logistic regr accuracy: %0.3f" % log_res_accuracy)
```

After a while (the solver has a maximum of 1,000 iterations before giving up converging the results), the resulting accuracy on the validation set will be 0.743, which will be our starting baseline.

Now, we try to predict using the xgboost algorithm. Being a gradient boosting algorithm, this learning algorithm has more variance (ability to fit complex predictive functions, but also to overfit) than a simple logistic regression afflicted by greater bias (in the end, it is a summation of coefficients) and so we expect much better results. We fix the max depth of its decision trees to 4 (a shallow number, which should prevent overfitting) and we use an eta of 0.02 (it will need to grow many trees because the learning is a bit slow). We also set up a watchlist, keeping an eye on the validation set for an early stop if the expected error on the validation doesn't decrease for over 50 steps.

TIP

It is not best practice to stop early on the same set (the validation set in our case) we use for reporting the final results. In a real-world setting, ideally, we should set up a validation set for tuning operations, such as early stopping, and a test set for reporting the expected results when generalizing to new data.

After setting all this, we run the algorithm. This time, we will have to wait for longer than we when running the logistic regression:

```
params = dict()
params['objective'] = 'binary:logistic'
params['eval_metric'] = ['logloss', 'error']
params['eta'] = 0.02
params['max_depth'] = 4
d_train = xgb.DMatrix(x_train, label=y_train)
d_valid = xgb.DMatrix(x_val, label=y_val)
watchlist = [(d_train, 'train'), (d_valid, 'valid')]
bst = xgb.train(params, d_train, 5000, watchlist,
                early_stopping_rounds=50, verbose_eval=100)
xgb_preds = (bst.predict(d_valid) >= 0.5).astype(int)
xgb_accuracy = np.sum(xgb_preds == y_val) / len(y_val)
print("Xgb accuracy: %0.3f" % xgb_accuracy)
```

The final result reported by xgboost is 0.803 accuracy on the validation set.

Building a TensorFlow model

The deep learning models in this chapter are built using TensorFlow, based on the original script written by Abhishek Thakur using Keras (you can read the original code at https://github.com/abhishekkrthakur/is_that_a_duplicate_quora_question). Keras is a Python library that provides an easy interface to TensorFlow. Tensorflow has official support for Keras, and the models trained using Keras can easily be converted to TensorFlow models. Keras enables the very fast prototyping and testing of deep learning models. In our project, we rewrote the solution entirely in TensorFlow from scratch anyway.

To start, let's import the necessary libraries, in particular TensorFlow, and let's check its version by printing it:

```
import zipfile
from tqdm import tqdm_notebook as tqdm
import tensorflow as tf
print("TensorFlow version %s" % tf.__version__)
```

At this point, we simply load the data into the `df` pandas dataframe or we load it from disk. We replace the missing values with an empty string and we set the `y` variable containing the target answer encoded as 1 (duplicated) or 0 (not duplicated):

```
try:
    df = data[['question1', 'question2', 'is_duplicate']]
except:
    df = pd.read_csv('data/quora_duplicate_questions.tsv',
                                                sep='\t')
    df = df.drop(['id', 'qid1', 'qid2'], axis=1)
df = df.fillna('')
y = df.is_duplicate.values
y = y.astype('float32').reshape(-1, 1)
```

We can now dive into deep neural network models for this dataset.

Processing before deep neural networks

Before feeding data into any neural network, we must first tokenize the data and then convert the data to sequences. For this purpose, we use the Keras `Tokenizer` provided with TensorFlow, setting it using a maximum number of words limit of 200,000 and a maximum sequence length of 40. Any sentence with more than 40 words is consequently cut off to its first 40 words:

```
Tokenizer = tf.keras.preprocessing.text.Tokenizer pad_sequences =
tf.keras.preprocessing.sequence.pad_sequences

tk = Tokenizer(num_words=200000) max_len = 40
```

After setting the `Tokenizer`, `tk`, this is fitted on the concatenated list of the first and second questions, thus learning all the possible word terms present in the learning corpus:

```
tk.fit_on_texts(list(df.question1) + list(df.question2))
x1 = tk.texts_to_sequences(df.question1)
x1 = pad_sequences(x1, maxlen=max_len)
x2 = tk.texts_to_sequences(df.question2)
x2 = pad_sequences(x2, maxlen=max_len)
word_index = tk.word_index
```

In order to keep track of the work of the tokenizer, `word_index` is a dictionary containing all the tokenized words paired with an index assigned to them.

Using the GloVe embeddings, we must load them into memory, as previously seen when discussing how to get the Word2vec embeddings.

The GloVe embeddings can be easily recovered using this command from a shell:

```
wget http://nlp.stanford.edu/data/glove.840B.300d.zip
```

The GloVe embeddings are similar to Word2vec in the sense that they encode words into a complex multidimensional space based on their co-occurrence. However, as explained by the paper http://clic.cimec.unitn.it/marco/publications/acl2014/baroni-etal-countpredict-acl2014.pdf —*BARONI, Marco; DINU, Georgiana; KRUSZEWSKI, Germán. Don't count, predict! A systematic comparison of context-counting vs. context-predicting semantic vectors. In: Proceedings of the 52nd Annual Meeting of the Association for Computational Linguistics (Volume 1: Long Papers). 2014. p. 238-247.*

GloVe is not derived from a neural network optimization that strives to predict a word from its context, as Word2vec is. Instead, GloVe is generated starting from a co-occurrence count matrix (where we count how many times a word in a row co-occurs with the words in the columns) that underwent a dimensionality reduction (a factorization just like SVD, as we mentioned before when preparing our data).

Why are we now using GloVe instead of Word2vec? In practice, the main difference between the two simply boils down to the empirical fact that GloVe embeddings work better on some problems, whereas Word2vec embeddings perform better on others. In our case, after experimenting, we found GloVe embeddings working better with deep learning algorithms. You can read more information about GloVe and its uses from its official page at Stanford University: https://nlp.stanford.edu/projects/glove/

Having got a hold of the GloVe embeddings, we can now proceed to create an `embedding_matrix` by filling the rows of the `embedding_matrix` array with the embedding vectors (sized at 300 elements each) extracted from the GloVe file.

The following code reads the glove embeddings file and stores them into our embedding matrix, which in the end will consist of all the tokenized words in the dataset with their respective vectors:

```
embedding_matrix = np.zeros((len(word_index) + 1, 300), dtype='float32')

glove_zip = zipfile.ZipFile('data/glove.840B.300d.zip')
glove_file = glove_zip.filelist[0]

f_in = glove_zip.open(glove_file)
for line in tqdm(f_in):
    values = line.split(b' ')
    word = values[0].decode()
```

```
if word not in word_index:
    continue
i = word_index[word]
coefs = np.asarray(values[1:], dtype='float32')
embedding_matrix[i, :] = coefs

f_in.close()
glove_zip.close()
```

Starting from an empty `embedding_matrix`, each row vector is placed on the precise row number of the matrix that is expected to represent its corresponding wording. Such correspondence between words and rows has previously been defined by the encoding process completed by the tokenizer and is now available for consultation in the `word_index` dictionary.

After the `embedding_matrix` has completed loading the embeddings, it is time to start building some deep learning models.

Deep neural networks building blocks

In this section, we are going to present the key functions that will allow our deep learning project to work. Starting from batch feeding (providing chunks of data to learn to the deep neural network) we will prepare the building blocks of a complex LSTM architecture.

 The LSTM architecture is presented in a hands-on and detailed way in `Chapter 7`, *Stock Price Prediction with LSTM*, inside the *Long short-term memory – LSTM 101* section

The first function we start working with is the `prepare_batches` one. This function takes the question sequences and based on a step value (the batch size), returns a list of lists, where the internal lists are the sequence batches to be learned:

```
def prepare_batches(seq, step):
    n = len(seq)
    res = []
    for i in range(0, n, step):
        res.append(seq[i:i+step])
    return res
```

The dense function will create a dense layer of neurons based on the provided size and activate and initialize them with random normally distributed numbers that have a mean of zero, and as a standard deviation, the square root of 2 divided by the number of input features.

A proper initialization helps back-propagating the input derivative deep inside the network. In fact:

- If you initialize the weights in a network too small, then the derivative shrinks as it passes through each layer until it's too faint to trigger the activation functions.
- If the weights in a network are initialized too large, then the derivative simply grows (the so-called exploding gradient problem) as it traverses through each layer, the network won't converge to a proper solution and it will break because of handling numbers that are too large.

The initialization procedure makes sure the weights are just right by setting a reasonable starting point where the derivative can propagate through many layers. There are quite a few initialization procedures for deep learning networks, such as Xavier by Glorot and Bengio (Xavier is Glorot's first name), and the one proposed by He, Rang, Zhen, and Sun, and built on the Glorot and Bengio one, which is commonly referred to as He.

Weight initialization is quite a technical aspect of building a neural network architecture, yet a relevant one. If you want to know more about it, you can start by consulting this post, which also delves into more mathematical explanations of the topic: `http://deepdish.io/2015/02/24/network-initialization/`

In this project, we opted for the He initialization, since it works quite well for rectified units. Rectified units, or ReLu, are the powerhouse of deep learning because they allow signals to propagate and avoid the exploding or vanishing gradient problems, yet neurons activated by the ReLU, from a practical point of view, are actually most of the time just firing a zero value. Keeping the variance large enough in order to have a constant variance of the input and output gradient passing through the layer really helps this kind of activation to work best, as explained in this paper: *HE, Kaiming, et al. Delving deep into rectifiers: Surpassing human-level performance on imagenet classification. In: Proceedings of the IEEE international conference on computer vision.* 2015. p. 1026-1034 which can be found and read at `https://arxiv.org/abs/1502.01852`:

```
def dense(X, size, activation=None):
    he_std = np.sqrt(2 / int(X.shape[1]))
    out = tf.layers.dense(X, units=size,
            activation=activation,
            kernel_initializer=\
```

```
                        tf.random_normal_initializer(stddev=he_std))
        return out
```

Next, we work on another kind of layer, the time distributed dense layer.

This kind of layer is used on recurrent neural networks in order to keep a one-to-one relationship between the input and the output. An RNN (with a certain number of cells providing channel outputs), fed by a standard dense layer, receives matrices whose dimensions are rows (examples) by columns (sequences) and it produces as output a matrix whose dimensions are rows by the number of channels (cells). If you feed it using the time distributed dense layer, its output will instead be dimensionality shaped as rows by columns by channels. In fact, it happens that a dense neural network is applied to timestamp (each column).

A time distributed dense layer is commonly used when you have, for instance, a sequence of inputs and you want to label each one of them, taking into account the sequence that arrived. This is a common scenario for tagging tasks, such as multilabel classification or Part-Of-Speech tagging. In our project, we will be using it just after the GloVe embedding in order to process how each GloVe vector changes by passing from a word to another in the question sequence.

As an example, let's say you have a sequence of two cases (a couple of question examples), and each one has three sequences (some words), each of which is made of four elements (their embeddings). If we have such a dataset passed through the time distributed dense layer with five hidden units, we will obtain a tensor of size (2, 3, 5). In fact, passing through the time distributed layer, each example retains the sequences, but the embeddings are replaced by the result of the five hidden units. Passing them through a reduction on the 1 axis, we will simply have a tensor of size (2,5), that is a result vector for each since example.

If you want to replicate the previous example:

```
print("Tensor's shape:", X.shape)
tensor = tf.convert_to_tensor(X, dtype=tf.float32)
dense_size = 5
i = time_distributed_dense(tensor, dense_size)
print("Shape of time distributed output:", i)
j = tf.reduce_sum(i, axis=1)
print("Shape of reduced output:", j)
```

The concept of a time distributed dense layer could be a bit trickier to grasp than others and there is much discussion online about it. You can also read this thread from the Keras issues to get more insight into the topic: `https://github.com/keras-team/keras/issues/1029`

```
def time_distributed_dense(X, dense_size):
    shape = X.shape.as_list()
    assert len(shape) == 3
    _, w, d = shape
    X_reshaped = tf.reshape(X, [-1, d])
    H = dense(X_reshaped, dense_size,
                          tf.nn.relu)
    return tf.reshape(H, [-1, w, dense_size])
```

The `conv1d` and `maxpool1d_global` functions are in the end wrappers of the TensorFlow functions `tf.layers.conv1d` (`https://www.tensorflow.org/api_docs/python/tf/layers/conv1d`), which is a convolution layer, and `tf.reduce_max` (`https://www.tensorflow.org/api_docs/python/tf/reduce_max`), which computes the maximum value of elements across the dimensions of an input tensor. In natural language processing, this kind of pooling (called global max pooling) is more frequently used than the standard max pooling that is commonly found in deep learning applications for computer vision. As explained by a Q&A on cross-validated (`https://stats.stackexchange.com/a/257325/49130`) global max pooling simply takes the maximum value of an input vector, whereas standard max pooling returns a new vector made of the maximum values found in different pools of the input vector given a certain pool size:

```
def conv1d(inputs, num_filters, filter_size, padding='same'):
    he_std = np.sqrt(2 / (filter_size * num_filters))
    out = tf.layers.conv1d(
        inputs=inputs, filters=num_filters, padding=padding,
        kernel_size=filter_size,
        activation=tf.nn.relu,
        kernel_initializer=tf.random_normal_initializer(
                                          stddev=he_std))

    return out

def maxpool1d_global(X):
    out = tf.reduce_max(X, axis=1)
    return out
```

Our core `lstm` function is initialized by a different scope at every run due to a random integer number generator, initialized by He initialization (as seen before), and it is a wrapper of the TensorFlow `tf.contrib.rnn.BasicLSTMCell` for the layer of Basic LSTM recurrent network cells (`https://www.tensorflow.org/api_docs/python/tf/contrib/rnn/BasicLSTMCell`) and `tf.contrib.rnn.static_rnn` for creating a recurrent neural network specified by the layer of cells (`https://www.tensorflow.org/versions/r1.1/api_docs/python/tf/contrib/rnn/static_rnn`).

 The implementation of the Basic LSTM recurrent network cells is based on the paper *ZAREMBA, Wojciech; SUTSKEVER, Ilya; VINYALS, Oriol. Recurrent neural network regularization. arXiv preprint arXiv:1409.2329, 2014* found at `https://arxiv.org/abs/1409.2329`.

```python
def lstm(X, size_hidden, size_out):
    with tf.variable_scope('lstm_%d'
                           % np.random.randint(0, 100)):
        he_std = np.sqrt(2 / (size_hidden * size_out))
        W = tf.Variable(tf.random_normal([size_hidden, size_out],
                                         stddev=he_std))
        b = tf.Variable(tf.zeros([size_out]))
        size_time = int(X.shape[1])
        X = tf.unstack(X, size_time, axis=1)
        lstm_cell = tf.contrib.rnn.BasicLSTMCell(size_hidden,
                                                 forget_bias=1.0)
        outputs, states = tf.contrib.rnn.static_rnn(lstm_cell, X,
                                                    dtype='float32')
        out = tf.matmul(outputs[-1], W) + b
        return out
```

At this stage of our project, we have gathered all the building blocks necessary to define the architecture of the neural network that will be learning to distinguish duplicated questions.

Designing the learning architecture

We start defining our architecture by fixing some parameters such as the number of features considered by the GloVe embeddings, the number and length of filters, the length of maxpools, and the learning rate:

```python
max_features = 200000
filter_length = 5
nb_filter = 64
pool_length = 4
learning_rate = 0.001
```

Managing to grasp the different semantic meanings of less or more different phrases in order to spot possible duplicated questions is indeed a hard task that requires a complex architecture. For this purpose, after various experimentation, we create a deeper model consisting of LSTM, time-distributed dense layers, and 1d-cnn. Such a model has six heads, which are merged into one by concatenation. After concatenation, the architecture is completed by five dense layers and an output layer with sigmoid activation.

The full model is shown in the following diagram:

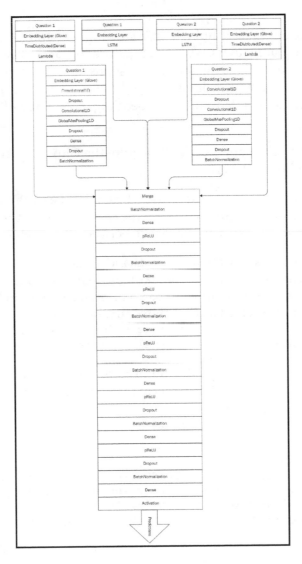

The first head consists of an embedding layer initialized by GloVe embeddings, followed by a time-distributed dense layer. The second head consists of 1D convolutional layers on top of embeddings initialized by the GloVe model, and the third head is an LSTM model on the embeddings learned from scratch. The other three heads follow the same pattern for the other question in the pair of questions.

We start defining the six models and concatenating them. In the end, the models are merged by concatenation, that is, the vectors from the six models are stacked together horizontally.

Even if the following code chunk is quite long, following it is straightforward. Everything starts at the three input placeholders, `place_q1`, `place_q2`, and `place_y`, which feed all six models with the first questions, the second questions, and the target response respectively. The questions are embedded using GloVe (`q1_glove_lookup` and `q2_glove_lookup`) and a random uniform embedding. Both embeddings have 300 dimensions.

The first two models, `model_1` and `model_2`, acquire the GloVe embeddings and they apply a time distributed dense layer.

The following two models, `model_3` and `model_4`, acquire the GloVe embeddings and process them by a series of convolutions, dropouts, and maxpools. The final output vector is batch normalized in order to keep stable variance between the produced batches.

If you want to know about the nuts and bolts of batch normalization, this Quora answer by Abhishek Shivkumar clearly provides all the key points you need to know about what batch normalization is and why it is effective in neural network architecture: https://www.quora.com/In-layman%E2%80%99s-terms-what-is-batch-normalisation-what-does-it-do-and-why-does-it-work-so-well/answer/Abhishek-Shivkumar

Finally, `model_5` and `model_6` acquire the uniform random embedding and process it with an LSTM. The results of all six models are concatenated together and batch normalized:

```
graph = tf.Graph()
graph.seed = 1

with graph.as_default():
    place_q1 = tf.placeholder(tf.int32, shape=(None, max_len))
    place_q2 = tf.placeholder(tf.int32, shape=(None, max_len))
    place_y = tf.placeholder(tf.float32, shape=(None, 1))
    place_training = tf.placeholder(tf.bool, shape=())

    glove = tf.Variable(embedding_matrix, trainable=False)
```

```
q1_glove_lookup = tf.nn.embedding_lookup(glove, place_q1)
q2_glove_lookup = tf.nn.embedding_lookup(glove, place_q2)

emb_size = len(word_index) + 1
emb_dim = 300
emb_std = np.sqrt(2 / emb_dim)
emb = tf.Variable(tf.random_uniform([emb_size, emb_dim],
                                    -emb_std, emb_std))
q1_emb_lookup = tf.nn.embedding_lookup(emb, place_q1)
q2_emb_lookup = tf.nn.embedding_lookup(emb, place_q2)
model1 = q1_glove_lookup
model1 = time_distributed_dense(model1, 300)
model1 = tf.reduce_sum(model1, axis=1)

model2 = q2_glove_lookup
model2 = time_distributed_dense(model2, 300)
model2 = tf.reduce_sum(model2, axis=1)

model3 = q1_glove_lookup
model3 = conv1d(model3, nb_filter, filter_length,
                                    padding='valid')
model3 = tf.layers.dropout(model3, rate=0.2,
training=place_training)
model3 = conv1d(model3, nb_filter, filter_length,
padding='valid')
model3 = maxpool1d_global(model3)
model3 = tf.layers.dropout(model3, rate=0.2,
training=place_training)
model3 = dense(model3, 300)
model3 = tf.layers.dropout(model3, rate=0.2,
training=place_training)
model3 = tf.layers.batch_normalization(model3,
training=place_training)

model4 = q2_glove_lookup
model4 = conv1d(model4, nb_filter, filter_length,
padding='valid')
model4 = tf.layers.dropout(model4, rate=0.2,
training=place_training)
model4 = conv1d(model4, nb_filter, filter_length,
padding='valid')
model4 = maxpool1d_global(model4)
model4 = tf.layers.dropout(model4, rate=0.2,
training=place_training)
model4 = dense(model4, 300)
model4 = tf.layers.dropout(model4, rate=0.2,
training=place_training)
model4 = tf.layers.batch_normalization(model4,
```

```
training=place_training)

    model5 = q1_emb_lookup
    model5 = tf.layers.dropout(model5, rate=0.2,
training=place_training)
    model5 = lstm(model5, size_hidden=300, size_out=300)

    model6 = q2_emb_lookup
    model6 = tf.layers.dropout(model6, rate=0.2,
training=place_training)
    model6 = lstm(model6, size_hidden=300, size_out=300)

    merged = tf.concat([model1, model2, model3, model4, model5,
model6], axis=1)

    merged = tf.layers.batch_normalization(merged,
training=place_training)
```

We then complete the architecture by adding five dense layers with dropout and batch normalization. Then, there is an output layer with sigmoid activation. The model is optimized using an AdamOptimizer based on log-loss:

```
    for i in range(5):
        merged = dense(merged, 300, activation=tf.nn.relu)
        merged = tf.layers.dropout(merged, rate=0.2,
training=place_training)
        merged = tf.layers.batch_normalization(merged,
training=place_training)

    merged = dense(merged, 1, activation=tf.nn.sigmoid)
    loss = tf.losses.log_loss(place_y, merged)
    prediction = tf.round(merged)
    accuracy = tf.reduce_mean(tf.cast(tf.equal(place_y,
prediction), 'float32'))
    opt = tf.train.AdamOptimizer(learning_rate=learning_rate)

    # for batchnorm
    extra_update_ops = tf.get_collection(tf.GraphKeys.UPDATE_OPS)
    with tf.control_dependencies(extra_update_ops):
        step = opt.minimize(loss)

    init = tf.global_variables_initializer()

session = tf.Session(config=None, graph=graph)
session.run(init)
```

After defining the architecture, we initialize the sessions and we are ready for learning. As a good practice, we split the available data into a training part (9/10) and a testing one (1/10). Fixing a random seed allows replicability of the results:

```
np.random.seed(1)

n_all, _ = y.shape
idx = np.arange(n_all)
np.random.shuffle(idx)

n_split = n_all // 10
idx_val = idx[:n_split]
idx_train = idx[n_split:]

x1_train = x1[idx_train]
x2_train = x2[idx_train]
y_train = y[idx_train]

x1_val = x1[idx_val]
x2_val = x2[idx_val]
y_val = y[idx_val]
```

If you run the following code snippet, the training will start and you will notice that the model accuracy increases with the increase in the number of epochs. However, the model will take a lot of time to train, depending on the number of batches you decide to iterate through. On an NVIDIA Titan X, the model takes over 300 seconds per epoch. As a good balance between obtained accuracy and training time, we opt for running 10 epochs:

```
val_idx = np.arange(y_val.shape[0])
val_batches = prepare_batches(val_idx, 5000)

no_epochs = 10

# see https://github.com/tqdm/tqdm/issues/481
tqdm.monitor_interval = 0

for i in range(no_epochs):
    np.random.seed(i)
    train_idx_shuffle = np.arange(y_train.shape[0])
    np.random.shuffle(train_idx_shuffle)
    batches = prepare_batches(train_idx_shuffle, 384)
    progress = tqdm(total=len(batches))
    for idx in batches:
        feed_dict = {
            place_q1: x1_train[idx],
            place_q2: x2_train[idx],
            place_y: y_train[idx],
```

```
            place_training: True,
        }
        _, acc, l = session.run([step, accuracy, loss],
   feed_dict)
        progress.update(1)
        progress.set_description('%.3f / %.3f' % (acc, l))


    y_pred = np.zeros_like(y_val)
    for idx in val_batches:
        feed_dict = {
            place_q1: x1_val[idx],
            place_q2: x2_val[idx],
            place_y: y_val[idx],
            place_training: False,
        }
        y_pred[idx, :] = session.run(prediction, feed_dict)

    print('batch %02d, accuracy: %0.3f' % (i,
                                np.mean(y_val == y_pred)))
```

Trained for 10 epochs, the model produces an accuracy of 82.5%. This is much higher than the benchmarks we had before. Of course, the model could be improved further by using better preprocessing and tokenization. More epochs (up to 200) could also help raise the accuracy a bit more. Stemming and lemmatization may also definitely help to get near the state-of-the-art accuracy of 88% reported by Quora on its blog.

Having completed the training, we can use the in-memory session to test some question evaluations. We try with two questions about the duplicated questions on Quora, but the procedure works with any pair of questions you would like to test the algorithm on.

 As with many machine learning algorithms, this one depends on the distribution that it has learned. Questions completely different from the ones it has been trained on could prove difficult for the algorithm to guess.

```
def convert_text(txt, tokenizer, padder):
    x = tokenizer.texts_to_sequences(txt)
    x = padder(x, maxlen=max_len)
    return x

def evaluate_questions(a, b, tokenizer, padder, pred):
    feed_dict = {
            place_q1: convert_text([a], tk, pad_sequences),
            place_q2: convert_text([b], tk, pad_sequences),
            place_y: np.zeros((1,1)),
```

```
            place_training: False,
        }
    return session.run(pred, feed_dict)
isduplicated = lambda a, b: evaluate_questions(a, b, tk, pad_sequences,
prediction)

a = "Why are there so many duplicated questions on Quora?"
b = "Why do people ask similar questions on Quora multiple times?"

print("Answer: %0.2f" % isduplicated(a, b))
```

After running the code, the answer should reveal that the questions are duplicated (answer: 1.0).

Summary

In this chapter, we built a very deep neural network with the help of TensorFlow in order to detect duplicated questions from the Quora dataset. The project allowed us to discuss, revise, and practice plenty of different topics previously seen in other chapters: TF-IDF, SVD, classic machine learning algorithms, Word2vec and GloVe embeddings, and LSTM models.

In the end, we obtained a model whose achieved accuracy is about 82.5%, a figure that is higher than traditional machine learning approaches and is also near other state-of-the-art deep learning solutions, as reported by the Quora blog.

It should also be noted that the models and approaches discussed in this chapter can easily be applied to any semantic matching problem.

Building a TensorFlow Recommender System

9

A recommender system is an algorithm that makes personalized suggestions to users based on their past interactions with the software. The most famous example is the "customers who bought X also bought Y" type of recommendation on Amazon and other e-commerce websites.

In the past few years, recommender systems have gained a lot of importance: it has become clear for the online businesses that the better the recommendations they give on their websites, the more money they make. This is why today almost every website has a block with personalized recommendations.

In this chapter, we will see how we can use TensorFlow to build our own recommender system.

In particular, we will cover the following topics:

- Basics of recommender systems
- Matrix Factorization for recommender systems
- Bayesian Personalized Ranking
- Advanced recommender systems based on Recurrent Neural Nets

By the end of this chapter, you will know how to prepare data for training a recommender system, how to build your own models with TensorFlow, and how to perform a simple evaluation of the quality of these models.

Recommender systems

The task of a **recommender system** is to take a list of all possible items and rank them according to preferences of particular users. This ranked list is referred to as a personalized ranking, or, more often, as a **recommendation**.

For example, a shopping website may have a section with recommendations where users can see items that they may find relevant and could decide to buy. Websites selling tickets to concerts may recommend interesting shows, and an online music player may suggest songs that the user is likely to enjoy. Or a website with online courses, such as Coursera.org, may recommend a course similar to ones the user has already finished:

Course recommendation on website

The recommendations are typically based on historical data: the past transaction history, visits, and clicks that the users have made. So, a recommender system is a system that takes this historical data and uses machine learning to extract patterns in the behavior of the users and based on that comes up with the best recommendations.

Companies are quite interested in making the recommendations as good as possible: this usually makes users engaged by improving their experience. Hence, it brings the revenue up. When we recommend an item that the user otherwise would not notice, and the user buys it, not only do we make the user satisfied, but we also sell an item that we would not otherwise have sold.

This chapter project is about implementing multiple recommender system algorithms using TensorFlow. We will start with classical time-proven algorithms and then go deeper and try a more complex model based on RNN and LSTM. For each model in this chapter, we will first give a short introduction and then we implement this model in TensorFlow.

To illustrate these ideas, we use the Online Retail Dataset from the UCI Machine Learning repository. This dataset can be downloaded from `http://archive.ics.uci.edu/ml/datasets/online+retail`.

The dataset itself is an Excel file with the following features:

- `InvoiceNo`: The invoice number, which is used to uniquely identify each transaction
- `StockCode`: The code of the purchased item
- `Description`: The name of the product
- `Quantity`: The number of times the item is purchased in the transaction
- `UnitPrice`: Price per item
- `CustomerID`: The ID of the customer
- `Country`: The name of the customer's country of the customer

It consists of 25,900 transactions, with each transaction containing around 20 items. This makes approximately 540,000 items in total. The recorded transactions were made by 4,300 users starting from December 2010 up until December 2011.

To download the dataset, we can either use the browser and save the file or use `wget`:

```
wget
http://archive.ics.uci.edu/ml/machine-learning-databases/00352/Online%20Ret
ail.xlsx
```

For this project, we will use the following Python packages:

- `pandas` for reading the data
- `numpy` and `scipy` for numerical data manipulations
- `tensorflow` for creating the models
- `implicit` for the baseline solution
- [optional] `tqdm` for monitoring the progress
- [optional] `numba` for speeding up the computations

If you use Anaconda, then you should already have `numba` installed, but if not, a simple `pip install numba` will get this package for you. To install `implicit`, we again use `pip`:

```
pip install implicit
```

Once the dataset is downloaded and the packages are installed, we are ready to start. In the next section, we will review the Matrix Factorization techniques, then prepare the dataset, and finally implement some of them in TensorFlow.

Matrix factorization for recommender systems

In this section, we will go over traditional techniques for recommending systems. As we will see, these techniques are really easy to implement in TensorFlow, and the resulting code is very flexible and easily allows modifications and improvements.

For this section, we will use the Online Retail Dataset. We first define the problem we want to solve and establish a few baselines. Then we implement the classical Matrix factorization algorithm as well as its modification based on Bayesian Personalized Ranking.

Dataset preparation and baseline

Now we are ready to start building a recommender system.

First, declare the imports:

```
import tensorflow as tf
import pandas as pd
import numpy as np
import scipy.sparse as sp
from tqdm import tqdm
```

Let us read the dataset:

```
df = pd.read_excel('Online Retail.xlsx')
```

Reading `xlsx` files may take a while. To save time when we next want to read the file, we can save the loaded copy into a `pickle` file:

```
import pickle
with open('df_retail.bin', 'wb') as f_out:
    pickle.dump(df, f_out)
```

This file is a lot faster to read, so for loading, we should use the pickled version:

```
with open('df_retail.bin', 'rb') as f_in:
    df = pickle.load(f_in)
```

Once the data is loaded, we can have a look at the data. We can do this by invoking the `head` function:

```
df.head()
```

We then see the following table:

	InvoiceNo	StockCode	Description	Quantity	InvoiceDate	UnitPrice	CustomerID	Country
0	536365	85123A	WHITE HANGING HEART T-LIGHT HOLDER	6	2010-12-01 08:26:00	2.55	17850.0	United Kingdom
1	536365	71053	WHITE METAL LANTERN	6	2010-12-01 08:26:00	3.39	17850.0	United Kingdom
2	536365	84406B	CREAM CUPID HEARTS COAT HANGER	8	2010-12-01 08:26:00	2.75	17850.0	United Kingdom
3	536365	84029G	KNITTED UNION FLAG HOT WATER BOTTLE	6	2010-12-01 08:26:00	3.39	17850.0	United Kingdom
4	536365	84029E	RED WOOLLY HOTTIE WHITE HEART.	6	2010-12-01 08:26:00	3.39	17850.0	United Kingdom

If we take a closer look at the data, we can notice the following problems:

- The column names are in capital letters. This is a bit unusual, so we may lowercase them.
- Some of the transactions are returns: they are not of interest to us, so we should filter them out.
- Finally, some of the transactions belong to unknown users. We can assign some common ID for these users, for example, -1. Also, unknown users are encoded as `NaNs`, this is why the `CustomerID` column is encoded as float—so we need to convert it to an integer.

These problems can be fixed with the following code:

```
df.columns = df.columns.str.lower()
df =
df[~df.invoiceno.astype('str').str.startswith('C')].reset_index(drop=True)
df.customerid = df.customerid.fillna(-1).astype('int32')
```

Next, we should encode all item IDs (stockcode) with integers. One of the ways to do it is to build a mapping from each code to some unique index number:

```
stockcode_values = df.stockcode.astype('str')

stockcodes = sorted(set(stockcode_values))
stockcodes = {c: i for (i, c) in enumerate(stockcodes)}

df.stockcode = stockcode_values.map(stockcodes).astype('int32')
```

Now after we have encoded the items, we can split the dataset into train, validation, and test parts. Since we have e-commerce transactions data, the most sensible way to do the split is based on time. So we will use:

- **Training set**: before 2011.10.09 (around 10 months of data, approximately 378,500 rows)
- **Validation set**: between 2011.10.09 and 2011.11.09 (one month of data, approximately 64,500 rows)
- **Test set**: after 2011.11.09 (also one month, approximately 89,000 rows)

For that we just filter the dataframes:

```
df_train = df[df.invoicedate < '2011-10-09']
df_val = df[(df.invoicedate >= '2011-10-09') &
            (df.invoicedate <= '2011-11-09') ]
df_test = df[df.invoicedate >= '2011-11-09']
```

In this section, we will consider the following (very simplified) recommendation scenario:

1. The user enters the website.
2. We present five recommendations.
3. The user assesses the lists, maybe buys some things from there, and then continues shopping as usual.

So we need to build a model for the second step. To do so, we use the training data and then simulate the second and third steps using the validation set. To evaluate whether our recommendation was good or not, we count the number of recommended items that the user has actually bought.

Our evaluation measure is then the number of successful recommendations (the items the user has actually bought) divided by the number of total recommendations we made. This is called **precision**—a common measure of evaluating the performance of machine learning models.

For this project we use precision. Of course, it is a rather simplistic way of evaluating the performance, and there are different ways of doing this. Other metrics you may want to use include **MAP** (**Mean Average Precision**), **NDCG** (**Normalized Discounted Cumulative Gain**), and so on. For simplicity, however, we do not use them in this chapter.

Before we jump into using machine learning algorithm for this task, let us first establish a basic baseline. For example, we can calculate how many times each item was bought, then take the most frequent five items, and recommend these items to all the users.

With pandas it is easy to do:

```
top = df_train.stockcode.value_counts().head(5).index.values
```

This gives us an array of integers—stockcode codes:

```
array([3527, 3506, 1347, 2730,  180])
```

Now we use this array to recommend it to all the users. So we repeat the top array as many times as there are transactions in the validation dataset, and then we use this as the recommendations and calculate the precision metric to evaluate the quality.

For repeating we use the tile function from numpy:

```
num_groups = len(df_val.invoiceno.drop_duplicates())
baseline = np.tile(top, num_groups).reshape(-1, 5)
```

The tile function takes in an array and repeats it num_group times. After reshaping, it gives us the following array:

```
array([[3527, 3506, 1347, 2730,  180],
       [3527, 3506, 1347, 2730,  180],
       [3527, 3506, 1347, 2730,  180],
       ...,
       [3527, 3506, 1347, 2730,  180],
       [3527, 3506, 1347, 2730,  180],
       [3527, 3506, 1347, 2730,  180]])
```

Now we are ready to calculate the precision of this recommendation.

However, there is a complication: the way the items are stored makes it difficult to calculate the number of correctly classified elements per group. Using `groupby` from pandas is one way of solving the problem:

- Group by `invoiceno` (this is our transaction ID)
- For each transaction make a recommendation
- Record the number of correct predictions per each group
- Calculate the overall precision

However, this way is often very slow and inefficient. It may work fine for this particular project, but for slightly larger datasets it becomes a problem.

The reason it is slow is the way `groupby` is implemented in pandas: it internally performs sorting, which we do not need. However, we can improve the speed by exploiting the way the data is stored: we know that the elements of our dataframe are always ordered. That is, if a transaction starts at a certain row number `i`, then it ends at the number `i + k`, where `k` is the number of items in this transaction. In other words, all the rows between `i` and `i + k` belong to the same `invoiceid`.

So we need to know where each transaction starts and where it ends. For this purpose, we keep a special array of length `n + 1`, where `n` is the number of groups (transactions) we have in our dataset.

Let us call this array `indptr`. For each transaction `t`:

- `indptr[t]` returns the number of the row in the dataframe where the transaction starts
- `indptr[t + 1]` returns the row where it ends

This way of representing the groups of various length is inspired by the CSR algorithm—Compressed Row Storage (sometimes Compressed Sparse Row). It is used to represent sparse matrices in memory. You can read about it more in the Netlib documentation—`http://netlib.org/linalg/html_templates/node91.html`. You may also recognize this name from scipy—it is one of the possible ways of representing matrices in the `scipy.sparse` package: `https://docs.scipy.org/doc/scipy-0.14.0/reference/generated/scipy.sparse.csr_matrix.html`.

Creating such arrays is not difficult in Python: we just need to see where the current transaction finishes and the next one starts. So at each row index, we can compare the current index with the previous one, and if it is different, record the index. This can be done efficiently using the `shift` method from pandas:

```python
def group_indptr(df):
    indptr, = np.where(df.invoiceno != df.invoiceno.shift())
    indptr = np.append(indptr, len(df)).astype('int32')
    return indptr
```

This way we get the pointers array for the validation set:

```python
val_indptr = group_indptr(df_val)
```

Now we can use it for the `precision` function:

```python
from numba import njit

@njit
def precision(group_indptr, true_items, predicted_items):
    tp = 0

    n, m = predicted_items.shape

    for i in range(n):
        group_start = group_indptr[i]
        group_end = group_indptr[i + 1]
        group_true_items = true_items[group_start:group_end]

        for item in group_true_items:
            for j in range(m):
                if item == predicted_items[i, j]:
                    tp = tp + 1
                    continue

    return tp / (n * m)
```

Here the logic is straightforward: for each transaction we check how many items we predicted correctly. The total amount of correctly predicted items is stored in `tp`. At the end we divide `tp` by the total number of predictions, which is the size of the prediction matrix, that is, number of transactions times five in our case.

Note the `@njit` decorator from numba. This decorator tells numba that the code should be optimized. When we invoke this function for the first time, numba analyzes the code and uses the **just-in-time** (**JIT**) compiler to translate the function to native code. When the function is compiled, it runs multiple orders of magnitude faster—comparable to native code written in C.

 Numba's `@jit` and `@njit` decorators give a very easy way to improve the speed of the code. Often it is enough just to put the `@jit` decorator on a function to see a significant speed-up. If a function takes time to compute, numba is a good way to improve the performance.

Now we can check what is the precision of this baseline:

```
val_items = df_val.stockcode.values
precision(val_indptr, val_items, baseline)
```

Executing this code should produce 0.064. That is, in 6.4% of the cases we made the correct recommendation. This means that the user ended up buying the recommended item only in 6.4% cases.

Now when we take a first look at the data and establish a simple baseline, we can proceed to more complex techniques such as matrix factorization.

Matrix factorization

In 2006 Netflix, a DVD rental company, organized the famous Netflix competition. The goal of this competition was to improve their recommender system. For this purpose, the company released a large dataset of movie ratings. This competition was notable in a few ways. First, the prize pool was one million dollars, and that was one of the main reasons it became famous. Second, because of the prize, and because of the dataset itself, many researchers invested their time into this problem and that significantly advanced the state of the art in recommender systems.

It was the Netflix competition that showed that recommenders based on matrix factorization are very powerful, can scale to a large number of training examples, and yet are not very difficult to implement and deploy.

The paper Matrix factorization techniques for recommender systems by Koren and others (2009) nicely summarizes the key findings, which we will also present in this chapter.

Imagine we have the rating r_{ui} of a movie i rated by user u. We can model this rating by:

$$\hat{r}_{ui} = \mu + b_i + b_u + q_i^T p_u.$$

Here we decompose the rating into four factors:

- μ is the global bias
- b_i is the bias of the item i (in case of Netflix—movie)
- b_u is the bias of the user u
- $q_u^T p_i$ is the inner product between the user vector q_u and the item vector p_i

The last factor—the inner product between the user and the item vectors—is the reason this technique is called **Matrix Factorization**.

Let us take all the user vectors q_u, and put them into a matrix U as rows. We then will have an $n_u \times k$ matrix, where n_u is the number of users and k is the dimensionality of the vectors. Likewise, we can take the item vectors p_i and put them into a matrix I as rows. This matrix has the size $n_i \times k$, where n_i is the number of items, and k is again the dimensionality of the vectors. The dimensionality k is a parameter of the model, which allows us to control how much we want to compress the information. The smaller k is, the less information is preserved from the original rating matrix.

Lastly, we take all the known ratings and put them into a matrix R—this matrix is of $n_u \times n_i$ size. Then this matrix can be factorized as

$$R \approx U^T I.$$

Without the biases part, this is exactly what we have when we compute $\hat{r}_{ui}$ in the preceding formula.

To make the predicted rating $\hat{r}_{ui}$ as close as possible to the observed rating rating r_{ui}, we minimize the squared error between them. That is, our training objective is the following:

$$\text{minimize} \sum_{ui} (r_{ui} - \hat{r}_{ui})^2 + \lambda(\|p_u\|^2 + \|q_i\|^2)$$

This way of factorizing the rating matrix is sometimes called **SVD** because it is inspired by the classical Singular Value Decomposition method—it also optimizes the sum of squared errors. However, the classical SVD often tends to overfit to the training data, which is why here we include the regularization term in the objective.

After defining the optimization problem, the paper then talks about two ways of solving it:

- **Stochastic Gradient Descent (SGD)**
- **Alternating Least Squares (ALS)**

Later in this chapter, we will use TensorFlow to implement the SGD method ourselves and compare it to the results of the ALS method from the `implicit` library.

However, the dataset we use for this project is different from the Netflix competition dataset in a very important way—we do not know what the users do not like. We only observe what they like. That is why next we will talk about ways to handle such cases.

Implicit feedback datasets

In case of the Netflix competition, the data there relies on the explicit feedback given by the users. The users went to the website and explicitly told them how much they like the movie by giving it a rating from 1 to 5.

Typically it is quite difficult to make users do that. However, just by visiting the website and interacting with it, the users already generated a lot of useful information, which can be used to infer their interests. All the clicks, page visits, and past purchases tell us about the preferences of the user. This kind of data is called **implicit** - the users do not explicitly tell us what they like, but instead, they indirectly convey this information to us by using the system. By collecting this interaction information we get implicit feedback datasets.

The Online Retail Dataset we use for this project is exactly that. It tells us what the users previously bought, but does not tell us what the users do not like. We do not know if the users did not buy an item because they did not like it, or just because they did not know the item existed.

Luckily for us, with minor modification, we still can apply the Matrix Factorization techniques to implicit datasets. Instead of the explicit ratings, the matrix takes values of 1 and 0—depending on whether there was an interaction with the item or not. Additionally, it is possible to express the confidence that the value 1 or 0 is indeed correct, and this is typically done by counting how many times the users have interacted with the item. The more times they interact with it, the larger our confidence becomes.

So, in our case all values that the user has bought get the value 1 in the matrix, and all the rest are 0's. Thus we can see this is a binary classification problem and implement an SGD-based model in TensorFlow for learning the user and item matrices.

But before we do that, we will establish another baseline have stronger than the previous one. We will use the `implicit` library, which uses ALS.

 Collaborative Filtering for Implicit Feedback Datasets by Hu et al (2008) gives a good introduction to the ALS method for implicit feedback datasets. We do not focus on ALS in this chapter, but if you want to learn how ALS is implemented in libraries such as `implicit`, this paper is definitely a great source. At the time of writing, the paper was accessible via `http://yifanhu.net/PUB/cf.pdf`.

First, we need to prepare the data in the format `implicit` expects—and for that we need to construct the user-item matrix X. For that we need to translate both users and items to IDs, so we can map each user to a row of X, and each item—to the column of X.

We have already converted items (the column `stockcode`) to integers. How we need to perform the same on the user IDs (the column `customerid`):

```
df_train_user = df_train[df_train.customerid != -1].reset_index(drop=True)

customers = sorted(set(df_train_user.customerid))
customers = {c: i for (i, c) in enumerate(customers)}

df_train_user.customerid = df_train_user.customerid.map(customers)
```

Note that in the first line we perform the filtering and keep only known users there—these are the users we will use for training the model afterward. Then we apply the same procedure to the users in the validation set:

```
df_val.customerid = df_val.customerid.apply(lambda c: customers.get(c, -1))
```

Next we use these integer codes to construct the matrix X:

```
uid = df_train_user.customerid.values.astype('int32')
iid = df_train_user.stockcode.values.astype('int32')
ones = np.ones_like(uid, dtype='uint8')

X_train = sp.csr_matrix((ones, (uid, iid)))
```

The `sp.csr_matrix` is a function from the `scipy.sparse` package. It takes in the rows and column indicies plus the corresponding value for each index pair, and constructs a matrix in the Compressed Storage Row format.

Using sparse matrices is a great way to reduce the space consumption of data matrices. In recommender systems there are many users and many items. When we construct a matrix, we put zeros for all the items the user has not interacted with. Keeping all these zeros is wasteful, so sparse matrices give a way to store only non-zero entries. You can read more about them in the `scipy.sparse` package documentation at `https://docs.scipy.org/doc/scipy/reference/sparse.html`.

Now let us use `implicit` to factorize the matrix X and learn the user and item vectors:

```
from implicit.als import AlternatingLeastSquares

item_user = X_train.T.tocsr()
als = AlternatingLeastSquares(factors=128, regularization=0.000001)
als.fit(item_user)
```

To use ALS we use the `AlternatingLeastSquares` class. It takes two parameters:

- `factors`: this is the dimensionality of the user and item vectors, which we called previously k
- `regularization`: the L2 regularization parameter to avoid overfitting

Then we invoke the `fit` function to learn the vectors. Once the training is done, these vectors are easy to get:

```
als_U = als.user_factors
als_I = als.item_factors
```

After getting the *U* and *I* matrices, we can use them to make recommendations to the user, and for that, we simply calculate the inner product between the rows of each matrix. We will see soon how to do it.

Matrix factorization methods have a problem: they cannot deal with new users. To overcome this problem, we can simply combine it with the baseline method: use the baseline to make a recommendation to new and unknown users, but apply Matrix Factorization to known users.

So, first we select the IDs of known users in the validation set:

```
uid_val = df_val.drop_duplicates(subset='invoiceno').customerid.values
known_mask = uid_val != -1
uid_val = uid_val[known_mask]
```

We will make recommendations only to these users. Then we copy the baseline solution, and replace the prediction for the known users by values from ALS:

```
imp_baseline = baseline.copy()

pred_all = als_U[uid_val].dot(als_I.T)
top_val = (-pred_all).argsort(axis=1)[:, :5]
imp_baseline[known_mask] = top_val

prevision(val_indptr, val_items, imp_baseline)
```

Here we get the vectors for each user ID in the validation set and multiply them with all the item vectors. Next, for each user we select top five items according to the score.

This outputs 13.9%. This is a lot stronger baseline than our previous baseline of 6%. This should be a lot more difficult to outperform, but next, we nonetheless try to do it.

SGD-based matrix factorization

Now we are finally ready to implement the matrix factorization model in TensorFlow. Let us do this and see if we can improve the baseline by `implicit`. Implementing ALS in TensorFlow is not an easy task: it is better suited for gradient-based methods such as SGD. This is why we will do exactly that, and leave ALS to specialized implementations.

Here we implement the formula from the previous sections:

$$\hat{r}_{ui} = \mu + b_i + b_u + q_i^T p_u.$$

Recall that the objective there was the following:

$$\text{minimize} \sum_{ui} (r_{ui} - \hat{r}_{ui})^2 + \lambda(\|p_u\|^2 + \|q_i\|^2)$$

Note that in this objective we still have the squared error, which is no longer the case for us since we model this as a binary classification problem. With TensorFlow it does not really matter, and the optimization loss can easily be changed.

In our model we will use the log loss instead—it is better suited for binary classification problems than squared error.

The *p* and *q* vectors make up the *U* and *I* matrices, respectively. What we need to do is to learn these *U* and *I* matrices. We can store the full matrices *U* and *I* as a TensorFlow `Variable`'s and then use the embedding layer to look up the appropriate *p* and *q* vectors.

Let us define a helper function for declaring embedding layers:

```
def embed(inputs, size, dim, name=None):
    std = np.sqrt(2 / dim)
    emb = tf.Variable(tf.random_uniform([size, dim], -std, std), name=name)
    lookup = tf.nn.embedding_lookup(emb, inputs)
    return lookup
```

This function creates a matrix of the specified dimension, initializes it with random values, and finally uses the lookup layer to convert user or item indexes into vectors.

We use this function as a part of the model graph:

```
# parameters of the model
num_users = uid.max() + 1
num_items = iid.max() + 1

num_factors = 128
lambda_user = 0.0000001
lambda_item = 0.0000001
K = 5
lr = 0.005
```

```
graph = tf.Graph()
graph.seed = 1

with graph.as_default():
    # this is the input to the model
    place_user = tf.placeholder(tf.int32, shape=(None, 1))
    place_item = tf.placeholder(tf.int32, shape=(None, 1))
    place_y = tf.placeholder(tf.float32, shape=(None, 1))

    # user features
    user_factors = embed(place_user, num_users, num_factors,
        "user_factors")
    user_bias = embed(place_user, num_users, 1, "user_bias")
    user_bias = tf.reshape(user_bias, [-1, 1])

    # item features
    item_factors = embed(place_item, num_items, num_factors,
        "item_factors")
    item_bias = embed(place_item, num_items, 1, "item_bias")
    item_bias = tf.reshape(item_bias, [-1, 1])

    global_bias = tf.Variable(0.0, name='global_bias')

    # prediction is dot product followed by a sigmoid
    pred = tf.reduce_sum(user_factors * item_factors, axis=2)
    pred = tf.sigmoid(global_bias + user_bias + item_bias + pred)

    reg = lambda_user * tf.reduce_sum(user_factors * user_factors) + \
            lambda_item * tf.reduce_sum(item_factors * item_factors)

    # we have a classification model, so minimize logloss
    loss = tf.losses.log_loss(place_y, pred)
    loss_total = loss + reg

    opt = tf.train.AdamOptimizer(learning_rate=lr)
    step = opt.minimize(loss_total)

    init = tf.global_variables_initializer()
```

The model gets three inputs:

- place_user: The user IDs
- place_item: The item IDs
- place_y: The labels of each (user, item) pair

Then we define:

- `user_factors`: The user matrix U
- `user_bias`: The bias of each user b_u
- `item_factors`: The item matrix I
- `item_bias`: The bias of each item b_i
- `global_bias`: The global bias μ

Then, we put together all the biases and take the dot product between the user and item factors. This is our prediction, which we then pass through the sigmoid function to get probabilities.

Finally, we define our objective function as a sum of the data loss and regularization loss and use Adam for minimizing this objective.

The model has the following parameters:

- `num_users` and `num_items`: The number of users (items). They specify the number of rows in U and I matrices, respectively.
- `num_factors`: The number of latent features for users and items. This specifies the number of columns in both U and I.
- `lambda_user` and `lambda_item`: The regularization parameters.
- `lr`: Learning rate for the optimizer.
- `K`: The number of negative examples to sample for each positive case (see the explanation in the following section).

Now let us train the model. For that, we need to cut the input into small batches. Let us use a helper function for that:

```
def prepare_batches(seq, step):
    n = len(seq)
    res = []
    for i in range(0, n, step):
        res.append(seq[i:i+step])
    return res
```

This will turn one array into a list of arrays of specified size.

Recall that our dataset is based on implicit feedback, and the number positive instances—interactions that did occur—is very small compared to the number of negative instances—the interactions that did not occur. What do we do with it? The solution is simple: we use **negative sampling**. The idea behind it is to sample only a small fraction of negative examples. Typically, for each positive example, we sample K negative examples, and K is a tunable parameter. And this is exactly what we do here.

So let us train the model:

```
session = tf.Session(config=None, graph=graph)
session.run(init)

np.random.seed(0)

for i in range(10):
    train_idx_shuffle = np.arange(uid.shape[0])
    np.random.shuffle(train_idx_shuffle)
    batches = prepare_batches(train_idx_shuffle, 5000)

    progress = tqdm(total=len(batches))
    for idx in batches:
        pos_samples = len(idx)
        neg_samples = pos_samples * K

        label = np.concatenate([
                    np.ones(pos_samples, dtype='float32'),
                    np.zeros(neg_samples, dtype='float32')
                ]).reshape(-1, 1)

        # negative sampling
        neg_users = np.random.randint(low=0, high=num_users,
                                      size=neg_samples, dtype='int32')
        neg_items = np.random.randint(low=0, high=num_items,
                                      size=neg_samples, dtype='int32')

        batch_uid = np.concatenate([uid[idx], neg_users]).reshape(-1, 1)
        batch_iid = np.concatenate([iid[idx], neg_items]).reshape(-1, 1)

        feed_dict = {
            place_user: batch_uid,
            place_item: batch_iid,
            place_y: label,
        }
        _, l = session.run([step, loss], feed_dict)
        progress.update(1)
        progress.set_description('%.3f' % l)
```

```
progress.close()

val_precision = calculate_validation_precision(graph, session, uid_val)
print('epoch %02d: precision: %.3f' % (i+1, val_precision))
```

We run the model for 10 epochs, then for each epoch we shuffle the data randomly and cut it into batches of 5000 positive examples. Then for each batch, we generate $K * 5000$ negative examples ($K = 5$ in our case) and put positive and negative examples together in one array. Finally, we run the model, and at each update step, we monitor the training loss using tqdm. The tqdm library provides a very nice way to monitor the training progress.

This is the output we produce when we use the tqdm jupyter notebook widgets:

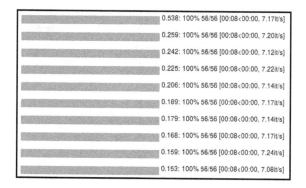

At the end of each epoch, we calculate precision—to monitor how our model is performing for our defined recommendation scenario. The calculate_validation_precision function is used for that. It is implemented in a similar way to what we did previously with implicit:

- We first extract the matrices and the biases
- Then put them together to get the score for each (user, item) pair
- Finally, we sort these pairs and keep the top five ones

For this particular case we do not need the global bias as well as the user bias: adding them will not change the order of items per user. This is how this function can be implemented:

```
def get_variable(graph, session, name):
    v = graph.get_operation_by_name(name)
    v = v.values()[0]
    v = v.eval(session=session)
    return v

def calculate_validation_precision(graph, session, uid):
```

```
U = get_variable(graph, session, 'user_factors')
I = get_variable(graph, session, 'item_factors')
bi = get_variable(graph, session, 'item_bias').reshape(-1)

pred_all = U[uid_val].dot(I.T) + bi
top_val = (-pred_all).argsort(axis=1)[:, :5]

imp_baseline = baseline.copy()
imp_baseline[known_mask] = top_val

return precision(val_indptr, val_items, imp_baseline)
```

This is the output we get:

```
epoch 01: precision: 0.064
epoch 02: precision: 0.086
epoch 03: precision: 0.106
epoch 04: precision: 0.127
epoch 05: precision: 0.138
epoch 06: precision: 0.145
epoch 07: precision: 0.150
epoch 08: precision: 0.149
epoch 09: precision: 0.151
epoch 10: precision: 0.152
```

By the sixth epoch it beats the previous baseline, and by the tenth, it reaches 15.2%.

Matrix factorization techniques usually give a very strong baseline solution for recommender systems. But with a small adjustment, the same technique can produce even better results. Instead of optimizing a loss for binary classification, we can use a different loss designed specifically for ranking problems. In the next section, we will learn about this kind of loss and see how to make this adjustment.

Bayesian personalized ranking

We use Matrix factorization methods for making a personalized ranking of items for each user. However, to solve this problem we use a binary classification optimization criterion—the log loss. This loss works fine and optimizing it often produces good ranking models. What if instead we could use a loss specifically designed for training a ranking function?

Of course, it is possible to use an objective that directly optimizes for ranking. In the paper *BPR: Bayesian Personalized Ranking from Implicit Feedback* by Rendle et al (2012), the authors propose an optimization criterion, which they call **BPR-Opt**.

Previously, we looked at individual items in separation from the other items. That is, we tried to predict the rating of an item, or the probability that the item i will be interesting to the user u. These kinds of ranking models are usually called "point-wise": they use traditional supervised learning methods such as regression or classification to learn the score, and then rank the items according to this score. This is exactly what we did in the previous section.

BPR-Opt is different. Instead, it looks at the pairs of items. If we know that user u has bought item i, but never bought item j, then most likely u is more interested in i than in j. Thus, when we train a model, the score $\hat{x}_{ui}$ it produces for i should be higher than the score $\hat{x}_{uj}$ for j. In other words, for the scoring model we want $\hat{x}_{ui} - \hat{x}_{uj} > 0$.

Therefore, for training this algorithm we need triples (user, positive item, negative item). For such triple (u, i, j) we define the pair-wise difference in scores as:

$$\hat{x}_{uij} = \hat{x}_{ui} - \hat{x}_{uj}$$

where $\hat{x}_{ui}$ and $\hat{x}_{uj}$ is scores for (u, i) and (u, j), respectively.

When training, we adjust parameters of our model in such a way that at the end item i does rank higher than item j. We do this by optimizing the following objective:

$$\text{minimize} - \sum \ln \sigma(\hat{x}_{uij}) + \lambda \|W\|^2$$

Where $\hat{x}_{uij}$ are the differences, σ is the sigmoid function, and W is all the parameters of the model.

It is straightforward to change our previous code to optimize this loss. The way we compute the score for (u, i) and (u, j) is the same: we use the biases and the inner product between the user and item vectors. Then we compute the difference between the scores and feed the difference into the new objective.

The difference in the implementation is also not large:

- For BPR-Opt we do not have `place_y`, but instead, we will have `place_item_pos` and `place_item_neg` for the positive and the negative items, respectively.
- We no longer need the user bias and the global bias: when we compute the difference, these biases cancel each other out. What is more, they are not really important for ranking—we have noted that previously when computing the predictions for the validation data.

Another slight difference in implementation is that because we now have two inputs items, and these items have to share the embeddings, we need to define and create the embeddings slightly differently. For that we modify the `embed` helper function, and separate the variable creation and the lookup layer:

```
def init_variable(size, dim, name=None):
    std = np.sqrt(2 / dim)
    return tf.Variable(tf.random_uniform([size, dim], -std, std),
name=name)

def embed(inputs, size, dim, name=None):
    emb = init_variable(size, dim, name)
    return tf.nn.embedding_lookup(emb, inputs)
```

Finally, let us see how it looks in the code:

```
num_factors = 128
lambda_user = 0.0000001
lambda_item = 0.0000001
lambda_bias = 0.0000001
lr = 0.0005


graph = tf.Graph()
graph.seed = 1

with graph.as_default():
    place_user = tf.placeholder(tf.int32, shape=(None, 1))
    place_item_pos = tf.placeholder(tf.int32, shape=(None, 1))
    place_item_neg = tf.placeholder(tf.int32, shape=(None, 1))
    # no place_y

    user_factors = embed(place_user, num_users, num_factors,
        "user_factors")
    # no user bias anymore as well as no global bias
```

```
item_factors = init_variable(num_items, num_factors,
    "item_factors")
item_factors_pos = tf.nn.embedding_lookup(item_factors, place_item_pos)
item_factors_neg = tf.nn.embedding_lookup(item_factors, place_item_neg)

item_bias = init_variable(num_items, 1, "item_bias")
item_bias_pos = tf.nn.embedding_lookup(item_bias, place_item_pos)
item_bias_pos = tf.reshape(item_bias_pos, [-1, 1])
item_bias_neg = tf.nn.embedding_lookup(item_bias, place_item_neg)
item_bias_neg = tf.reshape(item_bias_neg, [-1, 1])

# predictions for each item are same as previously
# but no user bias and global bias
pred_pos = item_bias_pos + \
    tf.reduce_sum(user_factors * item_factors_pos, axis=2)
pred_neg = item_bias_neg + \
    tf.reduce_sum(user_factors * item_factors_neg, axis=2)

pred_diff = pred_pos—pred_neg

loss_bpr =—tf.reduce_mean(tf.log(tf.sigmoid(pred_diff)))
loss_reg = lambda_user * tf.reduce_sum(user_factors * user_factors) +\
    lambda_item * tf.reduce_sum(item_factors_pos * item_factors_pos)+\
    lambda_item * tf.reduce_sum(item_factors_neg * item_factors_neg)+\
    lambda_bias * tf.reduce_sum(item_bias_pos) + \
    lambda_bias * tf.reduce_sum(item_bias_neg)

loss_total = loss_bpr + loss_reg

opt = tf.train.AdamOptimizer(learning_rate=lr)
step = opt.minimize(loss_total)

init = tf.global_variables_initializer()
```

The way to train this model is also slightly different. The authors of the BPR-Opt paper suggest using the bootstrap sampling instead of the usual full-pass over all the data, that is, at each training step we uniformly sample the triples (user, positive item, negative item) from the training dataset.

Luckily, this is even easier to implement than the full-pass:

```
session = tf.Session(config=None, graph=graph)
session.run(init)

size_total = uid.shape[0]
size_sample = 15000
```

```
np.random.seed(0)

for i in range(75):
    for k in range(30):
        idx = np.random.randint(low=0, high=size_total, size=size_sample)

        batch_uid = uid[idx].reshape(-1, 1)
        batch_iid_pos = iid[idx].reshape(-1, 1)
        batch_iid_neg = np.random.randint(
            low=0, high=num_items, size=(size_sample, 1), dtype='int32')

        feed_dict = {
            place_user: batch_uid,
            place_item_pos: batch_iid_pos,
            place_item_neg: batch_iid_neg,
        }
        _, l = session.run([step, loss_bpr], feed_dict)

    val_precision = calculate_validation_precision(graph, session, uid_val)
    print('epoch %02d: precision: %.3f' % (i+1, val_precision))
```

After around 70 iterations it reaches the precision of around 15.4%. While it is not significantly different from the previous model (it reached 15.2%), it does open a lot of possibilities for optimizing directly for ranking. More importantly, we show how easy it is to adjust the existent method such that instead of optimizing the point-wise loss it optimizes a pair-wise objective.

In the next section, we will go deeper and see how recurrent neural networks can model user actions as sequences and how we can use them as recommender systems.

RNN for recommender systems

A **recurrent neural networks (RNN)** is a special kind of neural network for modeling sequences, and it is quite successful in a number applications. One such application is sequence generation. In the article *The Unreasonable Effectiveness of Recurrent Neural Networks*, Andrej Karpathy writes about multiple examples where RNNs show very impressive results, including generation of Shakespeare, Wikipedia articles, XML, Latex, and even C code!

Since they have proven useful in a few applications already, the natural question to ask is whether we can apply RNNs to some other domains. What about recommender systems, for example? This is the question the authors of the recurrent neural networks *Based Subreddit Recommender System* report have asked themselves (see `https://cole-maclean.github.io/blog/RNN-Based-Subreddit-Recommender-System/`). The answer is yes, we can use RNNs for that too!

In this section, we will try to answer this question as well. For this part we consider a slightly different recommendation scenario than previously:

1. The user enters the website.
2. We present five recommendations.
3. After each purchase, we update the recommendations.

This scenario needs a different way of evaluating the results. Each time the user buys something, we can check whether this item was among the suggested ones or not. If it was, then our recommendation is considered successful. So we can calculate how many successful recommendations we have made. This way of evaluating performance is called Top-5 accuracy and it is often used for evaluating classification models with a large number of target classes.

Historically RNNs are used for language models, that is, for predicting what will be the most likely next word given in the sentence so far. And, of course, there is already an implementation of such a language model in the TensorFlow model repository located at `https://github.com/tensorflow/models` (in the `tutorials/rnn/ptb/` folder). Some of the code samples in the remaining of this chapter are heavily inspired by this example.

So let us get started.

Data preparation and baseline

Like previously, we need to represent the items and users as integers. This time, however, we need to have a special placeholder value for unknown users. Additionally, we need a special placeholder for items to represent "no item" at the beginning of each transaction. We will talk more about it later in this section, but for now, we need to implement the encoding such that the 0 index is reserved for special purposes.

Previously we were using a dictionary, but this time let us implement a special class, `LabelEncoder`, for this purpose:

```python
class LabelEncoder:
    def fit(self, seq):
        self.vocab = sorted(set(seq))
        self.idx = {c: i + 1 for i, c in enumerate(self.vocab)}

    def transform(self, seq):
        n = len(seq)
        result = np.zeros(n, dtype='int32')

        for i in range(n):
            result[i] = self.idx.get(seq[i], 0)

        return result

    def fit_transform(self, seq):
        self.fit(seq)
        return self.transform(seq)

    def vocab_size(self):
        return len(self.vocab) + 1
```

The implementation is straightforward and it largely repeats the code we used previously, but this time it is wrapped in a class, and also reserves 0 for special needs—for example, for elements that are missing in the training data.

Let us use this encoder to convert the items to integers:

```python
item_enc = LabelEncoder()
df.stockcode = item_enc.fit_transform(df.stockcode.astype('str'))
df.stockcode = df.stockcode.astype('int32')
```

Then we perform the same train-validation-test split: first 10 months we use for training, one for validation and the last one—for testing.

Next, we encode the user ids:

```python
user_enc = LabelEncoder()
user_enc.fit(df_train[df_train.customerid != -1].customerid)

df_train.customerid = user_enc.transfrom(df_train.customerid)
df_val.customerid = user_enc.transfrom(df_val.customerid)
```

Like previously, we use the most frequently bought items for the baseline. However, this time the scenario is different, which is why we also adjust the baseline slightly. In particular, if one of the recommended items is bought by the user, we remove it from the future recommendations.

Here is how we can implement it:

```
from collections import Counter

top_train = Counter(df_train.stockcode)

def baseline(uid, indptr, items, top, k=5):
    n_groups = len(uid)
    n_items = len(items)

    pred_all = np.zeros((n_items, k), dtype=np.int32)

    for g in range(n_groups):
        t = top.copy()

        start = indptr[g]
        end = indptr[g+1]
        for i in range(start, end):
            pred = [k for (k, c) in t.most_common(5)]
            pred_all[i] = pred

            actual = items[i]
            if actual in t:
                del t[actual]

    return pred_all
```

In the preceding code, `indptr` is the array of pointers—the same one that we used for implementing the `precision` function previously.

So now we apply this to the validation data and produce the results:

```
iid_val = df_val.stockcode.values
pred_baseline = baseline(uid_val, indptr_val, iid_val, top_train, k=5)
```

The baseline looks as follows:

```
array([[3528, 3507, 1348, 2731,  181],
       [3528, 3507, 1348, 2731,  181],
       [3528, 3507, 1348, 2731,  181],
       ...,
       [1348, 2731,  181,  454, 1314],
```

```
[1348, 2731,  181,  454, 1314],
[1348, 2731,  181,  454, 1314]], dtype=int32
```

Now let us implement the top-k accuracy metric. We again use the `@njit` decorator from numba to speed this function up:

```
@njit
def accuracy_k(y_true, y_pred):
    n, k = y_pred.shape

    acc = 0
    for i in range(n):
        for j in range(k):
            if y_pred[i, j] == y_true[i]:
                acc = acc + 1
                break

    return acc / n
```

To evaluate the performance of the baseline, just invoke with the true labels and the predictions:

```
accuracy_k(iid_val, pred_baseline)
```

It prints `0.012`, that is, only in 1.2% cases we make a successful recommendation. Looks like there is a lot of room for improvement!

The next step is breaking the long array of items into separate transactions. We again can reuse the pointer array, which tells us where each transaction starts and where it ends:

```
def pack_items(users, items_indptr, items_vals):
    n = len(items_indptr)—1

    result = []
    for i in range(n):
        start = items_indptr[i]
        end = items_indptr[i+1]
        result.append(items_vals[start:end])

    return result
```

Now we can unwrap the transactions and put them into a separate dataframe:

```
train_items = pack_items(indptr_train, indptr_train,
df_train.stockcode.values)

df_train_wrap = pd.DataFrame()
```

```
df_train_wrap['customerid'] = uid_train
df_train_wrap['items'] = train_items
```

To have a look at what we have at the end, use the `head` function:

```
df_train_wrap.head()
```

This shows the following:

	customerid	items
0	3439	[3528, 2792, 3041, 2982, 2981, 1662, 800]
1	3439	[1547, 1546]
2	459	[3301, 1655, 1658, 1659, 1247, 3368, 1537, 153...
3	459	[1862, 1816, 1815, 1817]
4	459	[818]

These sequences have varying lengths, and this is a problem for RNNs. So, we need to convert them into fixed-length sequences, which we can easily feed to the model later.

In case the original sequence is too short, we need to pad it with zeros. If the sequence is too long, we need to cut it or split it into multiple sequences.

Lastly, we also need to represent the state when the user has entered the website but has not bought anything yet. We can do this by inserting the dummy zero item—an item with index 0, which we reserved for special purposes, just like this one. In addition to that, we can also use this dummy item to pad the sequences that are too small.

We also need to prepare the labels for the RNN. Suppose we have the following sequence:

$$S = [e_1, e_2, e_3, e_4, e_5]$$

We want to produce a sequence of fixed length 5. With padding in the beginning, the sequence we use for training will look as follows:

$$X = [0, e_1, e_2, e_3, e_4]$$

Here we pad the original sequence with zero at the beginning and do not include the last element—the last element will only be included in the target sequence. So the target sequence—the output we want to predict—should look as follows:

$$Y = [e_1, e_2, e_3, e_4, e_5]$$

It may look confusing at the beginning, but the idea is simple. We want to construct the sequences in such a way that for the position i in X, the position i in Y contains the element we want to predict. For the preceding example we want to learn the following rules:

- $0 \rightarrow e_1$ - both are at the position 0 in X and Y
- $e_1 \rightarrow e_2$ —both are at the position 1 in X and Y
- and so on

Now imagine we have a smaller sequence of length 2, which we need to pad to a sequence of length 5:

$$S = [e_1, e_2]$$

In this case, we again pad the input sequence with 0 in the beginning, and also with some zeros at the end:

$$X = [0, e_1, e_2, 0, 0].$$

We transform the target sequence Y similarly:

$$Y = [e_1, e_2, 0, 0, 0].$$

If the input is too long, for example $[e_1, e_2, e_3, e_4, e_5, e_6, e_7]$, we can cut it into multiple sequences:

$$X = \begin{matrix} [0, e_1, e_2, e_3, e_4] \\ [e_1, e_2, e_3, e_4, e_5] \\ [e_2, e_3, e_4, e_5, e_6] \end{matrix} \text{ and } Y = \begin{matrix} [e_1, e_2, e_3, e_4, e_5] \\ [e_2, e_3, e_4, e_5, e_6] \\ [e_3, e_4, e_5, e_6, e_7] \end{matrix}$$

To perform such a transformation, we write a function `pad_seq`. It adds the needed amount of zeros at the beginning and at the end of the sequence. Then we `pad_seq` in another function - `prepare_training_data`—the function that creates the matrices X and Y for each sequence:

```
def pad_seq(data, num_steps):
    data = np.pad(data, pad_width=(1, 0), mode='constant')
```

```
    n = len(data)

    if n <= num_steps:
        pad_right = num_steps—n + 1
        data = np.pad(data, pad_width=(0, pad_right), mode='constant')

    return data

def prepare_train_data(data, num_steps):
    data = pad_seq(data, num_steps)

    X = []
    Y = []

    for i in range(num_steps, len(data)):
        start = i—num_steps
        X.append(data[start:i])
        Y.append(data[start+1:i+1])

    return X, Y
```

What is left to do is invoking the `prepare_training_data` function for each sequence in the training history, and then put the results together in `X_train` and `Y_train` matrices:

```
train_items = df_train_wrap['items']

X_train = []
Y_train = []

for i in range(len(train_items)):
    X, Y = prepare_train_data(train_items[i], 5)
    X_train.extend(X)
    Y_train.extend(Y)

X_train = np.array(X_train, dtype='int32')
Y_train = np.array(Y_train, dtype='int32')
```

At this point, we have finished data preparation. Now we are ready to finally create an RNN model that can process this data.

RNN recommender system in TensorFlow

The data preparation is done and now we take the produced matrices `X_train` and `Y_train` and use them for training a model. But of course, we need to create the model first. In this chapter, we will use a recurrent neural network with LSTM cells (Long Short-Term Memory). LSTM cells are better than plain RNN cells because they can capture long-term dependencies better.

 A great resource to learn more about LSTMs is the blog post "Understanding LSTM Networks" by Christopher Olah, which is available at `https://colah.github.io/posts/2015-08-Understanding-LSTMs/`. In this chapter, we do not go into theoretical details about how LSTM and RNN work and only look at using them in TensorFow.

Let us start with defining a special configuration class that holds all the important training parameters:

```
class Config:
    num_steps = 5

    num_items = item_enc.vocab_size()
    num_users = user_enc.vocab_size()

    init_scale = 0.1
    learning_rate = 1.0
    max_grad_norm = 5
    num_layers = 2
    hidden_size = 200
    embedding_size = 200
    batch_size = 20

config = Config()
```

Here the `Config` class defines the following parameters:

- `num_steps`—This is the size of the fixed-length sequences
- `num_items`—The number of items in our training data (+1 for the dummy 0 item)
- `num_users`—The number of users (again +1 for the dummy 0 user)
- `init_scale`—Scale of the weights parameters, needed for the initialization
- `learning_rate`—The rate at which we update the weights
- `max_grad_norm`—The maximally allowed norm of the gradient, if the gradient exceeds this value, we clip it
- `num_layers`—The number of LSTM layers in the network

- `hidden_size`—The size of the hidden dense layer that converts the output of LSTM to output probabilities
- `embedding_size`—The dimensionality of the item embeddings
- `batch_size`—The number of sequences we feed into the net in a single training step

Now we finally implement the model. We start off by defining two useful helper functions—we will use them for adding the RNN part to our model:

```
def lstm_cell(hidden_size, is_training):
    return rnn.BasicLSTMCell(hidden_size, forget_bias=0.0,
                state_is_tuple=True, reuse=not is_training)

def rnn_model(inputs, hidden_size, num_layers, batch_size, num_steps,
                is_training):
    cells = [lstm_cell(hidden_size, is_training) for
                                i in range(num_layers)]
    cell = rnn.MultiRNNCell(cells, state_is_tuple=True)

    initial_state = cell.zero_state(batch_size, tf.float32)
    inputs = tf.unstack(inputs, num=num_steps, axis=1)
    outputs, final_state = rnn.static_rnn(cell, inputs,
                                initial_state=initial_state)
    output = tf.reshape(tf.concat(outputs, 1), [-1, hidden_size])

    return output, initial_state, final_state
```

Now we can use the `rnn_model` function to create our model:

```
def model(config, is_training):
    batch_size = config.batch_size
    num_steps = config.num_steps
    embedding_size = config.embedding_size
    hidden_size = config.hidden_size
    num_items = config.num_items

    place_x = tf.placeholder(shape=[batch_size, num_steps], dtype=tf.int32)
    place_y = tf.placeholder(shape=[batch_size, num_steps], dtype=tf.int32)

    embedding = tf.get_variable("items", [num_items, embedding_size],
                dtype=tf.float32)
    inputs = tf.nn.embedding_lookup(embedding, place_x)

    output, initial_state, final_state = \
        rnn_model(inputs, hidden_size, config.num_layers, batch_size,
                num_steps, is_training)
```

```
W = tf.get_variable("W", [hidden_size, num_items], dtype=tf.float32)
b = tf.get_variable("b", [num_items], dtype=tf.float32)
logits = tf.nn.xw_plus_b(output, W, b)
logits = tf.reshape(logits, [batch_size, num_steps, num_items])

loss = tf.losses.sparse_softmax_cross_entropy(place_y, logits)
total_loss = tf.reduce_mean(loss)

tvars = tf.trainable_variables()
gradient = tf.gradients(total_loss, tvars)
clipped, _ = tf.clip_by_global_norm(gradient, config.max_grad_norm)
optimizer = tf.train.GradientDescentOptimizer(config.learning_rate)

global_step = tf.train.get_or_create_global_step()
train_op = optimizer.apply_gradients(zip(clipped, tvars),
               global_step=global_step)

out = {}
out['place_x'] = place_x
out['place_y'] = place_y
out['logits'] = logits
out['initial_state'] = initial_state
out['final_state'] = final_state

out['total_loss'] = total_loss
out['train_op'] = train_op

return out
```

In this model there are multiple parts, which is described as follows:

1. First, we specify the inputs. Like previously, these are IDs, which later we convert to vectors by using the embeddings layer.
2. Second, we add the RNN layer followed by a dense layer. The LSTM layer learns the temporary patters in purchase behavior, and the dense layer converts this information into a probability distribution over all possible items.
3. Third, since our model is multi-class classification model, we optimize the categorical cross-entropy loss.
4. Finally, LSTMs are known to have problems with exploding gradients, which is why we perform gradient clipping when performing the optimization.

The function returns all the important variables in a dictionary—so, later on, we will be able to use them when training and validating the results.

The reason this time we create a function, and not just global variables like previously, is to be able to change the parameters between training and testing phases. During training, the `batch_size` and `num_steps` variables could take any value, and, in fact, they are tunable parameters of the model. On the contrary, during testing, these parameters could take only one possible value: 1. The reason is that when the user buys something, it is always one item at a time, and not several, so `num_steps` is one. The `batch_size` is also one for the same reason.

For this reason, we create two configs: one for training, and one for validation:

```
config = Config()
config_val = Config()
config_val.batch_size = 1
config_val.num_steps = 1
```

Now let us define the computational graph for the model. Since we want to learn the parameters during training, but then use them in a separate model with different parameters during testing, we need to make the learned parameters shareable. These parameters include embeddings, LSTM, and the weights of the dense layer. To make both models share the parameters, we use a variable scope with `reuse=True`:

```
graph = tf.Graph()
graph.seed = 1

with graph.as_default():
    initializer = tf.random_uniform_initializer(-config.init_scale,
                config.init_scale)

    with tf.name_scope("Train"):
        with tf.variable_scope("Model", reuse=None,
                    initializer=initializer):
            train_model = model(config, is_training=True)

    with tf.name_scope("Valid"):
        with tf.variable_scope("Model", reuse=True,
                    initializer=initializer):
            val_model = model(config_val, is_training=False)

    init = tf.global_variables_initializer()
```

The graph is ready. Now we can train the model, and for this purpose, we create a `run_epoch` helper function:

```python
def run_epoch(session, model, X, Y, batch_size):
    fetches = {
        "total_loss": model['total_loss'],
        "final_state": model['final_state'],
        "eval_op": model['train_op']
    }

    num_steps = X.shape[1]
    all_idx = np.arange(X.shape[0])
    np.random.shuffle(all_idx)
    batches = prepare_batches(all_idx, batch_size)

    initial_state = session.run(model['initial_state'])
    current_state = initial_state

    progress = tqdm(total=len(batches))
    for idx in batches:
        if len(idx) < batch_size:
            continue

        feed_dict = {}
        for i, (c, h) in enumerate(model['initial_state']):
            feed_dict[c] = current_state[i].c
            feed_dict[h] = current_state[i].h

        feed_dict[model['place_x']] = X[idx]
        feed_dict[model['place_y']] = Y[idx]

        vals = session.run(fetches, feed_dict)
        loss = vals["total_loss"]
        current_state = vals["final_state"]

        progress.update(1)
        progress.set_description('%.3f' % loss)
    progress.close()
```

The initial part of the function should already be familiar to us: it first creates a dictionary of variables that we are interested to get from the model and also shuffle the dataset.

The next part is different though: since this time we have an RNN model (LSTM cell, to be exact), we need to keep its state across runs. To do it we first get the initial state—which should be all zeros—and then make sure the model gets exactly these values. After each step, we record the final step of the LSTM and re-enter it to the model. This way the model can learn typical behavior patterns.

Again, like previously, we use `tqdm` to monitor progress, and we display both how many steps we have already taken during the epoch and the current training loss.

Let us train this model for one epoch:

```
session = tf.Session(config=None, graph=graph)
session.run(init)

np.random.seed(0)
run_epoch(session, train_model, X_train, Y_train,
batch_size=config.batch_size)
```

One epoch is enough for the model to learn some patterns, so now we can see whether it was actually able to do it. For that we first write another helper function, which will emulate our recommendation scenario:

```
def generate_prediction(uid, indptr, items, model, k):
    n_groups = len(uid)
    n_items = len(items)

    pred_all = np.zeros((n_items, k), dtype=np.int32)
    initial_state = session.run(model['initial_state'])

    fetches = {
        "logits": model['logits'],
        "final_state": model['final_state'],
    }

    for g in tqdm(range(n_groups)):
        start = indptr[g]
        end = indptr[g+1]

        current_state = initial_state

        feed_dict = {}

        for i, (c, h) in enumerate(model['initial_state']):
            feed_dict[c] = current_state[i].c
            feed_dict[h] = current_state[i].h
```

```
prev = np.array([[0]], dtype=np.int32)

for i in range(start, end):
    feed_dict[model['place_x']] = prev

    actual = items[i]
    prev[0, 0] = actual

    values = session.run(fetches, feed_dict)
    current_state = values["final_state"]

    logits = values['logits'].reshape(-1)
    pred = np.argpartition(-logits, k)[:k]
    pred_all[i] = pred

return pred_all
```

What we do here is the following:

1. First, we initialize the prediction matrix, its size like in the baseline, is the number of items in the validation set times the number of recommendations.
2. Then we run the model for each transaction in the dataset.
3. Each time we start with the dummy zero item and the empty zero LSTM state.
4. Then one by one we predict the next possible item and put the actual item the user bought as the previous item—which we will feed into the model on the next step.
5. Finally, we take the output of the dense layer and get top-k most likely predictions as our recommendation for this particular step.

Let us execute this function and look at its performance:

```
pred_lstm = generate_prediction(uid_val, indptr_val, iid_val, val_model,
k=5)
accuracy_k(iid_val, pred_lstm)
```

We see the output 7.1%, which is seven times better than the baseline.

This is a very basic model, and there is definitely a lot of room for improvement: we can tune the learning rate and train for a few more epochs with gradually decreasing learning rate. We can change the batch_size, num_steps, as well as all other parameters. We also do not use any regularization—neither weight decay nor dropout. Adding it should be helpful.

But most importantly, we did not use any user information here: the recommendations were based solely on the patterns of items. We should be able to get additional improvement by including the user context. After all, the recommender systems should be personalized, that is, tailored for a particular user.

Right now our X_train matrix contains only items. We should include another input, for example U_train, which contains the user IDs:

```
X_train = []
U_train = []
Y_train = []

for t in df_train_wrap.itertuples():
    X, Y = prepare_train_data(t.items, config.num_steps)
    U_train.extend([t.customerid] * len(X))
    X_train.extend(X)
    Y_train.extend(Y)

X_train = np.array(X_train, dtype='int32')
Y_train = np.array(Y_train, dtype='int32')
U_train = np.array(U_train, dtype='int32')
```

Let us change the model now. The easiest way to incorporate user features is to stack together user vectors with item vectors and put the stacked matrix to LSTM. It is quite easy to implement, we just need to modify a few lines of the code:

```
def user_model(config, is_training):
    batch_size = config.batch_size
    num_steps = config.num_steps
    embedding_size = config.embedding_size
    hidden_size = config.hidden_size
    num_items = config.num_items
    num_users = config.num_users

    place_x = tf.placeholder(shape=[batch_size, num_steps], dtype=tf.int32)
    place_u = tf.placeholder(shape=[batch_size, 1], dtype=tf.int32)
    place_y = tf.placeholder(shape=[batch_size, num_steps], dtype=tf.int32)

    item_embedding = tf.get_variable("items", [num_items, embedding_size],
dtype=tf.float32)
    item_inputs = tf.nn.embedding_lookup(item_embedding, place_x)

    user_embedding = tf.get_variable("users", [num_items, embedding_size],
dtype=tf.float32)
    u_repeat = tf.tile(place_u, [1, num_steps])
    user_inputs = tf.nn.embedding_lookup(user_embedding, u_repeat)
```

```
    inputs = tf.concat([user_inputs, item_inputs], axis=2)

    output, initial_state, final_state = \
        rnn_model(inputs, hidden_size, config.num_layers, batch_size,
num_steps, is_training)

    W = tf.get_variable("W", [hidden_size, num_items], dtype=tf.float32)
    b = tf.get_variable("b", [num_items], dtype=tf.float32)

    logits = tf.nn.xw_plus_b(output, W, b)
    logits = tf.reshape(logits, [batch_size, num_steps, num_items])

    loss = tf.losses.sparse_softmax_cross_entropy(place_y, logits)
    total_loss = tf.reduce_mean(loss)

    tvars = tf.trainable_variables()
    gradient = tf.gradients(total_loss, tvars)
    clipped, _ = tf.clip_by_global_norm(gradient, config.max_grad_norm)
    optimizer = tf.train.GradientDescentOptimizer(config.learning_rate)

    global_step = tf.train.get_or_create_global_step()
    train_op = optimizer.apply_gradients(zip(clipped, tvars),
                global_step=global_step)

    out = {}
    out['place_x'] = place_x
    out['place_u'] = place_u
    out['place_y'] = place_y

    out['logits'] = logits
    out['initial_state'] = initial_state
    out['final_state'] = final_state

    out['total_loss'] = total_loss
    out['train_op'] = train_op

    return out
```

The changes between the new implementation and the previous model are shown in bold. In particular, the differences are the following:

- We add `place_u`—The placeholder that takes the user ID as input
- Rename `embeddings` to `item_embeddings`—not to confuse them with `user_embeddings`, which we added a few lines after that
- Finally, we concatenate user features with item features

The rest of the model code stays unchanged!

Initialization is similar to the previous model:

```
graph = tf.Graph()
graph.seed = 1

with graph.as_default():
    initializer = tf.random_uniform_initializer(-config.init_scale,
config.init_scale)

    with tf.name_scope("Train"):
        with tf.variable_scope("Model", reuse=None,
initializer=initializer):
            train_model = user_model(config, is_training=True)

    with tf.name_scope("Valid"):
        with tf.variable_scope("Model", reuse=True,
initializer=initializer):
            val_model = user_model(config_val, is_training=False)

    init = tf.global_variables_initializer()

session = tf.Session(config=None, graph=graph)
session.run(init)
```

The only difference here is that we invoke a different function when creating the model. The code for training one epoch of the model is very similar to the previous one. The only things that we change are the extra parameters of the function, which we add into the `feed_dict` inside:

```
def user_model_epoch(session, model, X, U, Y, batch_size):
    fetches = {
        "total_loss": model['total_loss'],
        "final_state": model['final_state'],
        "eval_op": model['train_op']
    }
```

```
num_steps = X.shape[1]
all_idx = np.arange(X.shape[0])
np.random.shuffle(all_idx)
batches = prepare_batches(all_idx, batch_size)

initial_state = session.run(model['initial_state'])
current_state = initial_state

progress = tqdm(total=len(batches))
for idx in batches:
    if len(idx) < batch_size:
        continue

    feed_dict = {}
    for i, (c, h) in enumerate(model['initial_state']):
        feed_dict[c] = current_state[i].c
        feed_dict[h] = current_state[i].h

    feed_dict[model['place_x']] = X[idx]
    feed_dict[model['place_y']] = Y[idx]
    feed_dict[model['place_u']] = U[idx].reshape(-1, 1)

    vals = session.run(fetches, feed_dict)
    loss = vals["total_loss"]
    current_state = vals["final_state"]

    progress.update(1)
    progress.set_description('%.3f' % loss)
progress.close()
```

Let us train this new model for one epoch:

```
session = tf.Session(config=None, graph=graph)
session.run(init)

np.random.seed(0)

user_model_epoch(session, train_model, X_train, U_train, Y_train,
batch_size=config.batch_size)
```

The way we use the model is also almost the same as previous:

```
def generate_prediction_user_model(uid, indptr, items, model, k):
    n_groups = len(uid)
    n_items = len(items)

    pred_all = np.zeros((n_items, k), dtype=np.int32)
    initial_state = session.run(model['initial_state'])
```

```
        fetches = {
            "logits": model['logits'],
            "final_state": model['final_state'],
        }

        for g in tqdm(range(n_groups)):
            start = indptr[g]
            end = indptr[g+1]
            u = uid[g]

            current_state = initial_state

            feed_dict = {}
            feed_dict[model['place_u']] = np.array([[u]], dtype=np.int32)

            for i, (c, h) in enumerate(model['initial_state']):
                feed_dict[c] = current_state[i].c
                feed_dict[h] = current_state[i].h

            prev = np.array([[0]], dtype=np.int32)

            for i in range(start, end):
                feed_dict[model['place_x']] = prev

                actual = items[i]
                prev[0, 0] = actual

                values = session.run(fetches, feed_dict)
                current_state = values["final_state"]

                logits = values['logits'].reshape(-1)
                pred = np.argpartition(-logits, k)[:k]
                pred_all[i] = pred

    return pred_all
```

Finally, we run this function to generate the predictions for the validation set, and calculate the accuracy of these recommendations:

```
pred_lstm = generate_prediction_user_model(uid_val, indptr_val, iid_val,
val_model, k=5)
accuracy_k(iid_val, pred_lstm)
```

The output we see is 0.252, which is 25%. We naturally expect it to be better, but the improvement was quite drastic: almost four times better than the previous model, and 25 better than the naive baseline. Here we skip the model check on the hold-out test set, but you can (and generally should) do it yourself to make sure the model does not overfit.

Summary

In this chapter, we covered recommender systems. We first looked at some background theory, implemented simple methods with TensorFlow, and then discussed some improvements such as the application of BPR-Opt to recommendations. These models are important to know and very useful to have when implementing the actual recommender systems.

In the second section, we tried to apply the novel techniques for building recommender systems based on Recurrent Neural Nets and LSTMs. We looked at the user's purchase history as a sequence and were able to use sequence models to make successful recommendations.

In the next chapter, we will cover Reinforcement Learning. This is one of the areas where the recent advances of Deep Learning have significantly changed the state-of-the-art: the models now are able to beat humans in many games. We will look at the advanced models that caused the change and we will also learn how to use TensorFlow to implement real AI.

Video Games by Reinforcement Learning

10

Contrary to supervised learning, where an algorithm has to associate an input with an output, in reinforcement learning you have another kind of maximization task. You are given an environment (that is, a situation) and you are required to find a solution that will act (something that may require to interact with or even change the environment itself) with the clear purpose of maximizing a resulting reward. Reinforcement learning algorithms, then, are not given any clear, explicit goal but to get the maximum result possible in the end. They are free to find the way to achieve the result by trial and error. This resembles the experience of a toddler who experiments freely in a new environment and analyzes the feedback in order to find out how to get the best from their experience. It also resembles the experience we have with a new video game: first, we look for the best winning strategy; we try a lot of different things and then we decide how to act in the game.

At the present time, no reinforcement learning algorithm has the general learning capabilities of a human being. A human being learns more quickly from several inputs, and a human can learn how to behave in very complex, varied, structured, unstructured and multiple environments. However, reinforcement learning algorithms have proved able to achieve super-human capabilities (yes, they can be better than a human) in very specific tasks. A reinforcement learning algorithm can achieve brilliant results if specialized on a specific game and if given enough time to learn (an example is AlphaGo `https://deepmind.com/research/alphago/`— the first computer program to defeat a world champion at Go, a complex game requiring long-term strategy and intuition).

In this chapter, we are going to provide you with the challenging project of getting a reinforcement learning algorithm to learn how to successfully manage the commands of the Atari game Lunar Lander, backed up by deep learning. Lunar Lander is the ideal game for this project because reinforcement learning algorithm can work successfully on it, the game has few commands and it can be successfully completed just by looking at few values describing the situation in the game (there is no need even to look at the screen in order to understand what to do, in fact, the first version of the game dates back to the 1960s and it was textual).

Neural networks and reinforcement learning are not new to each other; in the early 1990s, at IBM, Gerry Tesauro programmed the famous TD-Gammon, combining feedforward neural networks with temporal-difference learning (a combination of Monte Carlo and dynamic programming) in order to train TD-Gammon to play world-class backgammon, which a board game for two players to be played using a couple of dices. If curious about the game, you can read everything about the rules from the US Backgammon Federation: `http://usbgf.org/learn-backgammon/backgammon-rules-and-terms/rules-of-backgammon/`. At the time, the approach worked well with backgammon, due to the role of dices in the game that made it a non-deterministic game. Yet, it failed with every other game problem which was more deterministic. The last few years, thanks to the Google deep learning team of researchers, proved that neural networks can help solve problems other than backgammon, and that problem solving can be achieved on anyone's computer. Now, reinforcement learning is at the top of the list of next big things in deep learning and machine learning as you can read from Ian Goodfellow, an AI research scientist at Google Brain, who is putting it top of the list: `https://www.forbes.com/sites/quora/2017/07/21/whats-next-for-deep-learning/#6a8f8cd81002`.

The game legacy

Lunar Lander is an arcade game developed by Atari that first appeared in video game arcades around 1979. Developed in black and white vector graphics and distributed in specially devised cabinets, the game showed, as a lateral view, a lunar landing pod approaching the moon, where there were special areas for landing. The landing areas varied in width and accessibility because of the terrain around them, which gave the user different scores when the lander landed. The player was provided with information about altitude, speed, amount of fuel available, score, and time taken so far. Given the force of gravity attracting the landing pod to the ground, the player could rotate or thrust (there were also inertial forces to be considered) the landing pod at the expense of some fuel. The fuel was the key to the game.

The game ended when the landing pod touched the moon after running out of fuel. Until the fuel ran out, you kept on playing, even if you crashed. The commands available to the player were just four buttons, two for rotating left and right; one for thrusting from the base of the landing pod, pushing the module in the direction it is orientated; and the last button was for aborting the landing by rotating the landing pod upright and using a powerful (and fuel consuming) thrust in order to prevent the landing pod from crashing.

The interesting aspect of such a game is that there are clearly costs and rewards, but some are immediately apparent (like the quantity of fuel you are spending in your attempt) and others that they are all delayed until the time the landing pod touches the soil (you will know if the landing was a successful one only once it comes to a full stop). Maneuvering to land costs fuel, and that requires an economic approach to the game, trying not to waste too much. Landing provides a score. The more difficult and the safer the landing, the higher the score.

The OpenAI version

As stated in the documentation available at its website (`https://gym.openai.com/`), OpenAI Gym is a toolkit for developing and comparing reinforcement learning algorithms. The toolkit actually consists of a Python package that runs with both Python 2 and Python 3, and the website API, which is useful for uploading your own algorithm's performance results and comparing them with others (an aspect of the toolkit that we won't be exploring, actually).

The toolkit embodies the principles of reinforcement learning, where you have an environment and an agent: the agent can perform actions or inaction in the environment, and the environment will reply with a new state (representing the situation in the environment) and a reward, which is a score telling the agent if it is doing well or not. The Gym toolkit provides everything with the environment, therefore it is you that has to code the agent with an algorithm that helps the agent to face the environment. The environment is dealt by `env`, a class with methods for reinforcement learning which is instantiated when you issue the command to create it for a specific game: `gym.make('environment')`. Let's examine an example from the official documentation:

```
import gym
env = gym.make('CartPole-v0')
for i_episode in range(20):
        observation = env.reset()
        for t in range(100):
                    env.render()
                    print(observation)
```

```
# taking a random action
action = env.action_space.sample()
observation, reward, done, info = \
                            env.step(action)
If done:
    print("Episode finished after %i \
            timesteps" % (t+1))
    break
```

In this example, the run environment is `CartPole-v0`. Mainly a control problem, in the `CartPole-v0` game, a pendulum is attached to a cart that moves along a friction less track. The purpose of the game is to keep the pendulum upright as long as possible by applying forward or backward forces to the cart, and you can look at the dynamics of the game by watching this sequence on YouTube, which is part of a real-life experiment held at the Dynamics and Control Lab, IIT Madras and based on Neuron-like adaptive elements that can solve difficult control problems: `https://www.youtube.com/watch?v=qMlcsc43-lg`.

The Cartpole problem is described in *Neuron like adaptive elements that can solve difficult learning control problems* (`http://ieeexplore.ieee.org/document/6313077/`) by BARTO, Andrew G.; SUTTON, Richard S.; ANDERSON, Charles W. in IEEE transactions on systems, man, and Cybernetics.

Here is a brief explanation of the env methods, as applied in the example:

- `reset()`: This resets the environment's state to the initial default conditions. It actually returns the start observations.
- `step(action)`: This moves the environment by a single time step. It returns a four-valued vector made of variables: `observations`, `reward`, `done`, and `info`. Observations are a representation of the state of the environment and it is represented in each game by a different vector of values. For instance, in a game involving physics such as `CartPole-v0`, the returned vector is composed of the cart's position, the cart's velocity, the pole's angle, and the pole's velocity. The reward is simply the score achieved by the previous action (you need to total the rewards in order to figure out the total score at each point). The variable `done` is a Boolean flag telling you whether you are at a terminal state in the game (game over). `info` will provide diagnostic information, something that you are expected not to use for your algorithm, but just for debugging.

- `render( mode='human', close=False)`: This renders one time frame of the environment. The default mode will do something human-friendly, such as popping up a window. Passing the `close` flag signals the rendering engine to close any such windows.

The resulting effect of the commands is as follows:

- Set up the `CartPole-v0` environment
- Run it for 1,000 steps
- Randomly choose whether to apply a positive or negative force to the cart
- Visualize the results

The interesting aspect of this approach is that you can change the game easily, just by providing a different string to the `gym.make` method (try for instance `MsPacman-v0` or `Breakout-v0` or choose any from the list you can obtain by `gym.print(envs.registry.all())`) and test your approach to solving different environments without changing anything in your code. OpenAI Gym makes it easy to test the generalization of your algorithm to different problems by using a common interface for all its environments. Moreover, it provides a framework for your reasoning, understanding and solving of agent-environment problems according to the schema. At time *t-1* a state and reward are pushed to an agent, and the agent reacts with an action, producing a new state and a new reward at time *t*:

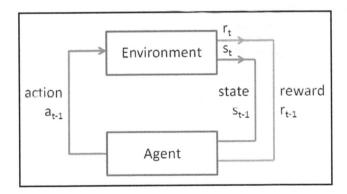

Figure 1: How the environment and agent interact by means of state, action, and reward

In every distinct game in OpenAI Gym, both the action space (the commands the agent responds to) and the `observation_space` (the representation state) change. You can see how they have changed by using some `print` commands, just after you set up an environment:

```
print(env.action_space)
print(env.observation_space)
print(env.observation_space.high)
print(env.observation_space.low)
```

Installing OpenAI on Linux (Ubuntu 14.04 or 16.04)

We suggest installing the environment on an Ubuntu system. OpenGym AI has been created for Linux systems and there is little support for Windows. Depending on the previous settings of your system, you may need to install some additional things first:

```
apt-get install -y python3-dev python-dev python-numpy libcupti-dev
libjpeg-turbo8-dev make golang tmux htop chromium-browser git cmake zlib1g-
dev libjpeg-dev xvfb libav-tools xorg-dev python-opengl libboost-all-dev
libsdl2-dev swig
```

We suggest of working with Anaconda, so install Anaconda 3, too. You can find everything about installing this Python distribution at `https://www.anaconda.com/download/`.

After setting the system requirements, installing OpenGym AI with all its modules is quite straightforward:

```
git clone https://github.com/openai/gym
cd gym
pip install -e .[all]
```

For this project, we are actually interested in working with the Box2D module, which is a 2D physics engine providing a rendering of real-world physics in a 2D environment, as commonly seen in pseudo-realistic video games. You can test that the Box2D module works by running these commands in Python:

```
import gym
env = gym.make('LunarLander-v2')
env.reset()
env.render()
```

If the provided code runs with no problem, you can proceed with the project. In some situations, Box2D may become difficult to run and, for instance, there could be problems such as those reported in `https://github.com/cbfinn/gps/issues/34`, though there are many other examples around. We have found that installing the Gym in a `conda` environment based on Python 3.4 makes things much easier:

```
conda create --name gym python=3.4 anaconda gcc=4.8.5
source activate gym
conda install pip six libgcc swig
conda install -c conda-forge opencv
pip install --upgrade tensorflow-gpu
git clone https://github.com/openai/gym
cd gym
pip install -e .
conda install -c https://conda.anaconda.org/kne pybox2d
```

This installation sequence should allow you to create a `conda` environment that's appropriate for the project we are going to present in this chapter.

Lunar Lander in OpenAI Gym

LunarLander-v2 is a scenario developed by Oleg Klimov, an engineer at OpenAI, inspired by the original Atari Lunar Lander (`https://github.com/olegklimov`). In the implementation, you have to take your landing pod to a lunar pad that is always located at coordinates $x=0$ and $y=0$. In addition, your actual x and y position is known since their values are stored in the first two elements of the state vector, the vector that contains all the information for the reinforcement learning algorithm to decide the best action to take at a certain moment.

This renders the task accessible because you won't have to deal with fuzzy or uncertain localization of your position with respect to the objective (a common problem in robotics).

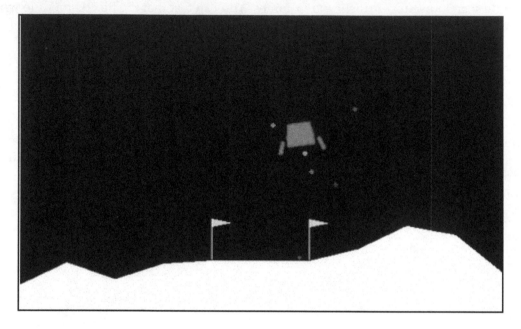

Figure 2: LunarLander-v2 in action

At each moment, the landing pod has four possible actions to choose from:

- Do nothing
- Rotate left
- Rotate right
- Thrust

There is then a complex system of reward to make things interesting:

- Reward for moving from the top of the screen to the landing pad and reaching zero speed ranges from 100 to 140 points (landing outside the landing pad is possible)

- If the landing pod moves away from landing pad without coming to a stop, it loses some of the previous rewards

- Each episode (the term used to point out a game session) completes when the landing pod crashes or it comes to rest, respectively providing additional -100 or +100 points
- Each leg in contact with the ground is +10
- Firing the main engine is -0.3 points per frame (but fuel is infinite)
- Solving the episode grants 200 points

The game works perfectly with discrete commands (they are practically binary: full thrust or no thrust) because, as the author of the simulation says, according to Pontryagin's maximum principle it's optimal to fire the engine at full throttle or completely turn it off.

 The game is also solvable using some simple heuristics based on the distance to the target and using a **proportional integral derivative** (**PID**) controller to manage the descending speed and angle. A PID is an engineering solution to control systems where you have feedback. At the following URL, you can get a more detailed explanation of how they work: `https://www.csimn.com/CSI_pages/PIDforDummies.html`.

Exploring reinforcement learning through deep learning

In this project, we are not interested in developing a heuristic (a still valid approach to solving many problems in artificial intelligence) or constructing a working PID. We intend instead to use deep learning to provide an agent with the necessary intelligence to operate a Lunar Lander video game session successfully.

Reinforcement learning theory offers a few frameworks to solve such problems:

- **Value-based learning**: This works by figuring out the reward or outcome from being in a certain state. By comparing the reward of different possible states, the action leading to the best state is chosen. Q-learning is an example of this approach.
- **Policy-based learning**: Different control policies are evaluated based on the reward from the environment. It is decided upon the policy achieving the best results.
- **Model-based learning**: Here, the idea is to replicate a model of the environment inside the agent, thus allowing the agent to simulate different actions and their consequent reward.

In our project, we will use a value-based learning framework; specifically, we will use the now classical approach in reinforcement learning based on Q-learning, which has been successfully controlled games where an agent has to decide on a series of moves that will lead to a delayed reward later in the game. Devised by C.J.C.H. Watkins in 1989 in his Ph.D. thesis, the method, also called **Q-learning**, is based on the idea that an agent operates in an environment, taking into account the present state, in order to define a sequence of actions that will lead to an ultimate reward:

$$s \xrightarrow{a} r, s\prime$$

In the above formula, it is described how a state s, after an action a, leads to a reward, r, and a new state s'. Starting from the initial state of a game, the formula applies a series of actions that, one after the other, transforms each subsequent state until the end of the game. You can then imagine a game as a series of chained states by a sequence of actions. You can then also interpret the above formula how an initial state s is transformed into a final state s' and a final reward r by a sequence of actions a.

In reinforcement terms, a **policy** is how to best choose our sequence of actions, a. A policy can be approximated by a function, which is called Q, so that given the present state, s, and a possible action, a, as inputs, it will provide an estimate of the maximum reward, r, that will derive from that action:

$$Q(s, a) = r$$

This approach is clearly greedy, meaning that we just choose the best action at a precise state because we expect that always choosing the best action at each step will lead us to the best outcome. Thus, in the greedy approach, we do not consider the possible chain of actions leading to the reward, but just the next action, a. However, it can be easily proved that we can confidently adopt a greedy approach and obtain the maximum reward using such a policy if such conditions are met:

- we find the perfect policy oracle, Q^*
- we operate in an environment where information is perfect (meaning we can know everything about the environment)
- the environment adheres to the *Markov principle (see the tip box)*

TIP

the Markov principle states that the future (states, rewards) only depends on the present and not the past, therefore we can simply derive the best to be done by looking at the present state and ignoring what has previously happened.

In fact, if we build the Q function as a recursive function, we just need to explore (using a breadth-first search approach) the ramifications to the present state of our action to be tested, and the recursive function will return the maximum reward possible.

Such an approach works perfectly in a computer simulation, but it makes little sense in the real world:

- Environments are mostly probabilistic. Even if you perform an action, you don't have the certainty of the exact reward.
- Environments are tied to the past, the present alone cannot describe what could be the future because the past can have hidden or long-term consequences.
- Environments are not exactly predictable, so you cannot know in advance the rewards from an action, but you can know them afterward (this is called an **a posteriori** condition).
- Environments are very complex. You cannot figure out in a reasonable time all the possible consequences of an action, hence you cannot figure out with certainty the maximum reward deriving from an action.

The solution is then to adopt an approximate Q function, one that can take into account probabilistic outcomes and that doesn't need to explore all the future states by prediction. Clearly, it should be a real approximation function, because building a search table of values is unpractical in complex environments (some state spaces could take continuous values, making the possible combinations infinite). Moreover, the function can be learned offline, which implies leveraging the experience of the agent (the ability to memorize becomes then quite important).

There have been previous attempts to approximate a Q function by a neural network, but the only successful application has been TD_Gammon, a backgammon program that learned to play by reinforcement learning powered by a multi-layer perceptron only. TD_Gammon achieved a superhuman level of play, but at the time its success couldn't be replicated in different games, such as chess or go.

That led to the belief that neural networks were not really suitable for figuring out a *Q* function unless the game was somehow stochastic (you have to throw a dice in backgammon). In 2013, a paper on deep reinforcement learning, *Playing Atari with deep reinforcement learning*(https://www.cs.toronto.edu/~vmnih/docs/dqn.pdf) Volodymyr Minh, et al, applied to old Atari games demonstrated the contrary.

Such paper demonstrates how a *Q* function could be learned using neural networks to play a range of Atari arcade games (such as Beam Rider, Breakout, Enduro, Pong, Q*bert, Seaquest, and Space Invaders) just by processing video inputs (by sampling frames from a 210 x 160 RGB video at 60 Hz) and outputting joystick and fire button commands. The paper names the method a **Deep Q-Network** (**DQN**), and it also introduces the concepts of experience replay and exploration versus exploitation, which we are going to discuss in the next section. These concepts help to overcome some critical problems when trying to apply deep learning to reinforcement learning:

- Lack of plenty of examples to learn from—something necessary in reinforcement learning and even more indispensable when using deep learning for it
- Extended delay between an action and the effective reward, which requires dealing with sequences of further actions of variable length before getting a reward
- Series of highly correlated sequences of actions (because an action often influences the following ones), which may cause any stochastic gradient descent algorithm to overfit to the most recent examples or simply converge non-optimally (stochastic gradient descent expects random examples, not correlated ones)

The paper, *Human-level control through deep reinforcement learning* (http://www.davidqiu.com:8888/research/nature14236.pdf), by Mnih and other researchers just confirms DQN efficacy where more games are explored by using it and performances of DQN are compared to human players and classical algorithms in reinforcement learning.

In many games, DQN proved better than human skills, though the long-term strategy is still a problem for the algorithm. In certain games, such as *Breakout*, the agent discovers cunning strategies such as digging a tunnel through the wall in order to send the ball through and destroy the wall in an effortless manner. In other games, such as *Montezuma's Revenge*, the agent remains clueless.

In the paper, the authors discuss at length how the agent understands the nuts and bolts of winning a Breakout game and they provide a chart of the response of the DQN function demonstrating how high reward scores are assigned to behaviors that first dig a hole in the wall and then let the ball pass through it.

Tricks and tips for deep Q-learning

Q-learning obtained by neural networks was deemed unstable until some tricks made it possible and feasible. There are two power-horses in deep Q-learning, though other variants of the algorithm have been developed recently in order to solve problems with performance and convergence in the original solution. Such new variants are not discussed in our project: double Q-learning, delayed Q-learning, greedy GQ, and speedy Q-learning. The two main DQN power-horses that we are going to explore are **experience replay** and the decreasing trade-off between **exploration and exploitation**.

With experience replay, we simply store away the observed states of the game in a queue of a prefixed size since we discard older sequences when the queue is full. Contained in the stored data, we expect to have a number of tuples consisting of the present state, the applied action, the consequently obtained state, and the reward gained. If we consider a simpler tuple made of just the present state and the action, we have the observation of the agent operating in the environment, which we can consider the root cause of the consequent state and of the reward. We can consider now the tuple (present state and action) as our predictor (x vector) with respect to the reward. Consequently, we can use the reward directly connected to the action and the reward that will be achieved at the end of the game.

Given such stored data (which we can figure out as the memory of our agent), we sample a few of them in order to create a batch and use the obtained batch to train our neural network. However, before passing the data to the network, we need to define our target variable, our y vector. Since the sampled states mostly won't be the final ones, we will probably have a zero reward or simply a partial reward to match against the known inputs (the present state and the chosen action). A partial reward is not very useful because it just tells part of the story we need to know. Our objective is, in fact, to know the total reward we will get at the end of the game, after having taken the action from the present state we are evaluating (our x value).

In this case, since we don't have such information, we simply try to approximate the value by using our existing Q function in order to estimate the residual reward that will be the maximum consequence of the (state, action) tuple we are considering. After obtaining it, we discount its value using the Bellman equation.

You can read an explanation of this now classic approach in reinforcement learning in this excellent tutorial by Dr. Sal Candido, a software engineer at Google: `http://robotics.ai.uiuc.edu/~scandido/?Developing_Reinforcement_Learning_from_the_Bellman_Equation`), where the present reward is added to the discounted future reward.

Using a small value (approaching zero) for discounting makes the Q function more geared toward short-term rewards, whereas using a high discount value (approaching one) renders the Q function more oriented to future gains.

The second very effective trick is using a coefficient for trading between exploration and exploitation. In exploration, the agent is expected to try different actions in order to find the best course of action given a certain state. In exploitation, the agent leverages what it learned in the previous explorations and simply decides for what it believes the best action to be taken in that situation.

Finding a good balance between exploration and exploitation is strictly connected to the usage of the experience replay we discussed earlier. At the start of the DQN algorithm optimization, we just have to rely on a random set of network parameters. This is just like sampling random actions, as we did in our simple introductory example to this chapter. The agent in such a situation will explore different states and actions, and help to shape the initial Q function. For complex games such as *Lunar Lander* using random choices won't take the agent far, and it could even turn unproductive in the long run because it will prevent the agent from learning the expected reward for tuples of state and action that can only be accessed if the agent has done the correct things before. In fact, in such a situation the DQN algorithm will have a hard time figuring out how to appropriately assign the right reward to an action because it will never have seen a completed game. Since the game is complex, it is unlikely that it could be solved by random sequences of actions.

The correct approach, then, is to balance learning by chance and using what has been learned to take the agent further in the game to where problems are yet to be solved. This resembles finding a solution by a series of successive approximations, by taking the agent each time a bit nearer to the correct sequence of actions for a safe and successful landing. Consequently, the agent should first learn by chance, find the best things to be done in a certain set of situations, then apply what has been learned and get access to new situations that, by random choice, will be also solved, learned, and applied successively.

This is done using a decreasing value as the threshold for the agent to decide whether, at a certain point in the game, to take a random choice and see what happens or leverage what it has learned so far and use it to make the best possible action at that point, given its actual capabilities. Picking a random number from a uniform distribution [0,1], the agent compares it with an epsilon value, and if the random number is larger than the epsilon it will use its approximate neural Q function. Otherwise, it will pick a random action from the options available. After that, it will decrease the epsilon number. Initially, epsilon is set at the maximum value, *1.0*, but depending on a decaying factor, it will decrease with time more or less rapidly, arriving at a minimum value that should never be zero (no chance of taking a random move) in order for there to always be the possibility of learning something new and unexpected (a minimal openness factor) by serendipity.

Understanding the limitations of deep Q-learning

Even with deep Q-learning, there are some limitations, no matter whether you approximate your Q function by deriving it from visual images or other observations about the environment:

- The approximation takes a long time to converge, and sometimes it doesn't achieve it smoothly: you may even witness the learning indicators of the neural network worsening instead of getting better for many epochs.
- Being based on a greedy approach, the approach offered by Q-learning is not dissimilar from a heuristic: it points out the best direction but it cannot provide detailed planning. When dealing with long-term goals or goals that have to be articulated into sub-goals, Q-learning performs badly.
- Another consequence of how Q-learning works is that it really doesn't understand the game dynamics from a general point of view but from a specific one (it replicates what it experienced as effective during training). As a consequence, any novelty introduced into the game (and never actually experienced during training) can break down the algorithm and render it completely ineffective. The same goes when introducing a new game to the algorithm; it simply won't perform.

Starting the project

After this long detour into reinforcement learning and the DQN approach, we are finally ready to start coding, having all the basic understanding of how to operate an OpenAI Gym environment and how to set a DQN approximation of a *Q* function. We simply start importing all the necessary packages:

```
import gym
from gym import wrappers
import numpy as np
import random, tempfile, os
from collections import deque
import tensorflow as tf
```

The `tempfile` module generates temporary files and directories that can be used as a temporary storage area for data files. The `deque` command, from the `collections` module, creates a double-ended queue, practically a list where you can append items at the start or at the end. Interestingly, it can be set to a predefined size. When full, older items are discarded in order to make the place for new entries.

We will structure this project using a series of classes representing the agent, the agent's brain (our DQN), the agent's memory, and the environment, which is provided by OpenAI Gym but it needs to be correctly connected to the agent. It is necessary to code a class for this.

Defining the AI brain

The first step in the project is to create a `Brain` class containing all the neural network code in order to compute a Q-value approximation. The class will contain the necessary initialization, the code for creating a suitable TensorFlow graph for the purpose, a simple neural network (not a complex deep learning architecture but a simple, working network for our project—you can replace it with more complex architectures), and finally, methods for fit and predict operations.

We start from initialization. As inputs, first, we really need to know the size of the state inputs (`nS`) corresponding to the information we receive from the game, and the size of the action output (`nA`) corresponding to the buttons we can press to perform actions in the game. Optionally, but strongly recommended, we also have to set the scope. In order to define the scope a string will help us to keep separate networks created for different purposes, and in our project, we have two, one for processing the next reward and one for guessing the final reward.

Then, we have to define the learning rate for the optimizer, which is an Adam.

 The Adam optimizer is described in the following paper: `https://arxiv.org/abs/1412.6980`. It is a very efficient gradient-based optimization method that requires very little to be tuned in order to work properly. The Adam optimization is a stochastic gradient descent algorithm similar to RMSprop with Momentum. This post, `https://theberkeleyview.wordpress.com/2015/11/19/berkeleyview-for-adam-a-method-for-stochastic-optimization/`, from the UC Berkeley Computer Vision Review Letters, provides more information. From our experience, it is one of the most effective solutions when training a deep learning algorithm in batches, and it requires some tuning for the learning rate.

Finally, we also provide:

- A neural architecture (if we prefer to change the basic one provided with the class)
- Input the `global_step`, a global variable that will keep track of the number of training batches of examples that have been feed to the DQN network up to that moment
- The directory in which to store the logs for TensorBoard, the standard visualization tool for TensorFlow

```
class Brain:
    """
    A Q-Value approximation obtained using a neural network.
    This network is used for both the Q-Network and the Target Network.
    """
    def __init__(self, nS, nA, scope="estimator",
                 learning_rate=0.0001,
                 neural_architecture=None,
                 global_step=None, summaries_dir=None):
        self.nS = nS
        self.nA = nA
        self.global_step = global_step
        self.scope = scope
        self.learning_rate = learning_rate
        if not neural_architecture:
            neural_architecture = self.two_layers_network
        # Writes Tensorboard summaries to disk
        with tf.variable_scope(scope):
            # Build the graph
            self.create_network(network=neural_architecture,
                                learning_rate=self.learning_rate)
```

```
if summaries_dir:
    summary_dir = os.path.join(summaries_dir,
                        "summaries_%s" % scope)
    if not os.path.exists(summary_dir):
        os.makedirs(summary_dir)
    self.summary_writer = \
                tf.summary.FileWriter(summary_dir)
else:
    self.summary_writer = None
```

The command `tf.summary.FileWriter` initializes an event file in a target directory (`summary_dir`) where we store the key measures of the learning process. The handle is kept in `self.summary_writer`, which we will be using later for storing the measures we are interested in representing during and after the training for monitoring and debugging what has been learned.

The next method to be defined is the default neural network that we will be using for this project. As input, it takes the input layer and the respective size of the hidden layers that we will be using. The input layer is defined by the state that we are using, which could be a vector of measurements, as in our case, or an image, as in the original DQN paper)

Such layers are simply defined using the higher level ops offered by the `Layers` module of TensorFlow (`https://www.tensorflow.org/api_guides/python/contrib.layers`). Our choice goes for the vanilla `fully_connected`, using the `ReLU` (rectifier) `activation` function for the two hidden layers and the linear activation of the output layer.

The predefined size of 32 is perfectly fine for our purposes, but you may increment it if you like. Also, there is no dropout in this network. Clearly, the problem here is not overfitting, but the quality of what is being learned, which could only be improved by providing useful sequences of unrelated states and a good estimate of the final reward to be associated. It is in the useful sequences of states, especially under the light of the trade-off between exploration and exploitation, that the key to not having the network overfit resides. In a reinforcement learning problem, you have overfitted if you fall into one of these two situations:

- Sub-optimality: the algorithm suggests sub-optimal solutions, that it is, our lander learned a rough way to land and it sticks to it because at least it lands
- Helplessness: the algorithm has fallen into a learned helplessness; that is, it has not found a way to land correctly, so it just accepts that it is going to crash in the least bad way possible

These two situations can prove really difficult to overcome for a reinforcement learning algorithm such as DQN unless the algorithm can have the chance to explore alternative solutions during the game. Taking random moves from time to time is not simply a way to mess up things, as you may think at first sight, but a strategy to avoid pitfalls.

With larger networks than this one, on the other hand, you may instead have a problem with a dying neuron requiring you to use a different activation, `tf.nn.leaky_relu` (https://www.tensorflow.org/api_docs/python/tf/nn/leaky_relu), in order to obtain a working network.

> A dead `ReLU` ends up always outputting the same value, usually a zero value, and it becomes resistant to backpropagation updates.

> The activation `leaky_relu` has been available since TensorFlow 1.4. If you are using any previous version of TensorFlow, you can create an ad hoc function to be used in your custom network:
>
> ```
> def leaky_relu(x, alpha=0.2):
>     return tf.nn.relu(x) - alpha * tf.nn.relu(-x)
> ```

We now proceed to code our `Brain` class, adding some more functions to it:

```
def two_layers_network(self, x, layer_1_nodes=32,
                                 layer_2_nodes=32):

    layer_1 = tf.contrib.layers.fully_connected(x, layer_1_nodes,
                                    activation_fn=tf.nn.relu)
    layer_2 = tf.contrib.layers.fully_connected(layer_1,
                                    layer_2_nodes,
                                activation_fn=tf.nn.relu)
    return tf.contrib.layers.fully_connected(layer_2, self.nA,
                                    activation_fn=None)
```

The method `create_network` combines input, neural network, loss, and optimization. The loss is simply created by taking the difference between the original reward and the estimated result, squaring it, and taking the average through all the examples present in the batch being learned. The loss is minimized using an Adam optimizer.

Also, a few summaries are recorded for TensorBoard:

- The average loss of the batch, in order to keep track of the fit during training
- The maximum predicted reward in the batch, in order to keep track of extreme positive predictions, pointing out the best-winning moves
- The average predicted reward in the batch, in order to keep track of the general tendency of predicting good moves

Here is the code for `create_network`, the TensorFlow engine of our project:

```
def create_network(self, network, learning_rate=0.0001):

    # Placeholders for states input
    self.X = tf.placeholder(shape=[None, self.nS],
                            dtype=tf.float32, name="X")
    # The r target value
    self.y = tf.placeholder(shape=[None, self.nA],
                            dtype=tf.float32, name="y")
    # Applying the choosen network
    self.predictions = network(self.X)
    # Calculating the loss
    sq_diff = tf.squared_difference(self.y, self.predictions)
    self.loss = tf.reduce_mean(sq_diff)
    # Optimizing parameters using the Adam optimizer
    self.train_op = tf.contrib.layers.optimize_loss(self.loss,
                    global_step=tf.train.get_global_step(),
                    learning_rate=learning_rate,
                    optimizer='Adam')
    # Recording summaries for Tensorboard
    self.summaries = tf.summary.merge([
        tf.summary.scalar("loss", self.loss),
        tf.summary.scalar("max_q_value",
                        tf.reduce_max(self.predictions)),
        tf.summary.scalar("mean_q_value",
                        tf.reduce_mean(self.predictions))])
```

The class is completed by a `predict` and a `fit` method. The `fit` method takes as input the state matrix, `s`, as the input batch and the vector of reward `r` as the outcome. It also takes into account how many epochs you want to train (in the original papers it is suggested using just a single epoch per batch in order to avoid overfitting too much to each batch of observations). Then, in the present session, the input is fit with respect to the outcome and summaries (previously defined as we created the network).

```python
def predict(self, sess, s):
    """
    Predicting q values for actions
    """
    return sess.run(self.predictions, {self.X: s})

def fit(self, sess, s, r, epochs=1):
    """
    Updating the Q* function estimator
    """
    feed_dict = {self.X: s, self.y: r}
    for epoch in range(epochs):
        res = sess.run([self.summaries, self.train_op,
                        self.loss,
                        self.predictions,
                        tf.train.get_global_step()],
                        feed_dict)
        summaries, train_op, loss, predictions,
                                self.global_step = res

    if self.summary_writer:
        self.summary_writer.add_summary(summaries,
    self.global_step)
```

As a result, `global step` is returned, which is a counter that helps to keep track of the number of examples used in training up so far, and then recorded for later use.

Creating memory for experience replay

After defining the brain (the TensorFlow neural network), our next step is to define the memory, that is the storage for data that will power the learning process of the DQN network. At each training episode each step, made of a state and an action, is recorded together with the consequent state and the final reward of the episode (something that will be known only when the episode completes).

Adding a flag telling if the observation is a terminal one or not completes the set of recorded information. The idea is to connect certain moves not just to the immediate reward (which could be null or modest) but the ending reward, thus associating every move in that session to it.

The class memory is simply a queue of a certain size, which is then filled with information on the previous game experiences, and it is easy to sample and extract from it. Given its fixed size, it is important that older examples are pushed out of the queue, thus allowing the available examples to always be among the last ones.

The class comprises an initialization, where the data structure takes origin and its size is fixed, the `len` method (so we know whether the memory is full or not, which is useful, for instance, in order to wait for any training at least until we have plenty of them for better randomization and variety for learning), `add_memory` for recording in the queue, and `recall_memory` for recovering all the data from it in a list format:

```python
class Memory:
    """
    A memory class based on deque, a list-like container with
    fast appends and pops on either end (from the collections
    package)
    """
    def __init__(self, memory_size=5000):
        self.memory = deque(maxlen=memory_size)
    def __len__(self):
        return len(self.memory)

    def add_memory(self, s, a, r, s_, status):
        """
        Memorizing the tuple (s a r s_) plus the Boolean flag status,
        reminding if we are at a terminal move or not
        """
        self.memory.append((s, a, r, s_, status))

    def recall_memories(self):
        """
        Returning all the memorized data at once
        """
        return list(self.memory)
```

Creating the agent

The next class is the agent, which has the role of initializing and maintaining the brain (providing the *Q-value* function approximation) and the memory. It is the agent, moreover, that acts in the environment. Its initialization sets a series of parameters that are mostly fixed given our experience in optimizing the learning for the Lunar Lander game. They can be explicitly changed, though, when the agent is first initialized:

- `epsilon = 1.0` is the initial value in the exploration-exploitation parameter. The `1.0` value forces the agent to completely rely on exploration, that is, random moving.
- `epsilon_min = 0.01` sets the minimum value of the exploration-exploitation parameter: a value of `0.01` means that there is a 1% chance that the landing pod will move randomly and not based on *Q* function feedback. This always provides a minimum chance to find another optimal way of completing the game, without compromising it.
- `epsilon_decay = 0.9994` is the decay that regulates the speed the `epsilon` diminishes toward the minimum. In this setting, it is tuned to reach a minimum value after about 5,000 episodes, which on average should provide the algorithm at least 2 million examples to learn from.
- `gamma = 0.99` is the reward discount factor with which the Q-value estimation weights the future reward with respect to the present reward, thus allowing the algorithm to be short- or long-sighted, according to what is best in the kind of game being played (in Lunar Lander it is better to be long-sighted because the actual reward will be experienced only when the landing pod lands on the Moon).
- `learning_rate = 0.0001` is the learning rate for the Adam optimizer to learn the batch of examples.
- `epochs = 1` is the training epochs used by the neural network in order to fit the batch set of examples.
- `batch_size = 32` is the size of the batch examples.
- `memory = Memory(memory_size=250000)` is the size of the memory queue.

Using the preset parameters, you are assured that the present project will work. For different OpenAI environments, you may need to find different optimal parameters.

The initialization will also provide the commands required to define where the TensorBoard logs will be placed (by default, the `experiment` directory), the model for learning how to estimate the immediate next reward, and another model to store the weights for the final reward. In addition, a saver (`tf.train.Saver`) will be initialized, allowing the serialization of the entire session to disk in order to restore it later and use it for playing the real game, not just learning how to play it.

The two mentioned models are initialized in the same session, using different scope names (one will be `q`, the next reward model monitored by the TensorBoard; the other one will be `target_q`). Using two different scope names will allow easy handling of the neuron's coefficients, making it possible to swap them with another method present in the class:

```python
class Agent:
    def __init__(self, nS, nA, experiment_dir):
        # Initializing
        self.nS = nS
        self.nA = nA
        self.epsilon = 1.0  # exploration-exploitation ratio
        self.epsilon_min = 0.01
        self.epsilon_decay = 0.9994
        self.gamma = 0.99  # reward decay
        self.learning_rate = 0.0001
        self.epochs = 1  # training epochs
        self.batch_size = 32
        self.memory = Memory(memory_size=250000)

        # Creating estimators
        self.experiment_dir =os.path.abspath\
                    ("./experiments/{}".format(experiment_dir))
        self.global_step = tf.Variable(0, name='global_step',
                                                trainable=False)
        self.model = Brain(nS=self.nS, nA=self.nA, scope="q",
                        learning_rate=self.learning_rate,
                        global_step=self.global_step,
                        summaries_dir=self.experiment_dir)
        self.target_model = Brain(nS=self.nS, nA=self.nA,
                                        scope="target_q",
                            learning_rate=self.learning_rate,
                                global_step=self.global_step)

        # Adding an op to initialize the variables.
        init_op = tf.global_variables_initializer()
        # Adding ops to save and restore all the variables.
        self.saver = tf.train.Saver()

        # Setting up the session
```

```
self.sess = tf.Session()
self.sess.run(init_op)
```

The `epsilon` dealing with the share of time devoted exploring new solutions compared to exploiting the knowledge of the network is constantly updated with the `epsilon_update` method, which simply modifies the actual `epsilon` by multiplying it by `epsilon_decay` unless it has already reached its allowed minimum value:

```
def epsilon_update(self, t):
    if self.epsilon > self.epsilon_min:
        self.epsilon *= self.epsilon_decay
```

The `save_weights` and `load_weights` methods simply allow the session to be saved:

```
def save_weights(self, filename):
    """
    Saving the weights of a model
    """
    save_path = self.saver.save(self.sess,
                            "%s.ckpt" % filename)
    print("Model saved in file: %s" % save_path)
def load_weights(self, filename):
    """
    Restoring the weights of a model
    """
    self.saver.restore(self.sess, "%s.ckpt" % filename)
    print("Model restored from file")
```

The `set_weights` and `target_model_update` methods work together to update the target Q network with the weights of the Q network (`set_weights` is a general-purpose, reusable function you can use in your solutions, too). Since we named the two scopes differently, it is easy to enumerate the variables of each network from the list of trainable variables. Once enumerated, the variables are joined in an assignment to be executed by the running session:

```
def set_weights(self, model_1, model_2):
    """
    Replicates the model parameters of one
    estimator to another.
    model_1: Estimator to copy the parameters from
    model_2: Estimator to copy the parameters to
    """
    # Enumerating and sorting the parameters
    # of the two models
    model_1_params = [t for t in tf.trainable_variables() \
                    if t.name.startswith(model_1.scope)]
```

```
        model_2_params = [t for t in tf.trainable_variables() \
                          if t.name.startswith(model_2.scope)]
        model_1_params = sorted(model_1_params,
                                key=lambda x: x.name)
        model_2_params = sorted(model_2_params,
                                key=lambda x: x.name)
        # Enumerating the operations to be done
        operations = [coef_2.assign(coef_1) for coef_1, coef_2 \
                      in zip(model_1_params, model_2_params)]
        # Executing the operations to be done
        self.sess.run(operations)
    def target_model_update(self):
        """
        Setting the model weights to the target model's ones
        """
        self.set_weights(self.model, self.target_model)
```

The `act` method is the core of the policy implementation because it will decide, based on `epsilon`, whether to take a random move or go for the best possible one. If it is going for the best possible move, it will ask the trained Q network to provide a reward estimate for each of the possible next moves (represented in a binary way by pushing one of four buttons in the Lunar Lander game) and it will return the move characterized by the maximum predicted reward (a greedy approach to the solution):

```
    def act(self, s):
        """
        Having the agent act based on learned Q* function
        or by random choice (based on epsilon)
        """
        # Based on epsilon predicting or randomly
        # choosing the next action
        if np.random.rand() <= self.epsilon:
            return np.random.choice(self.nA)
        else:
            # Estimating q for all possible actions
            q = self.model.predict(self.sess, s)[0]
            # Returning the best action
            best_action = np.argmax(q)
            return best_action
```

The `replay` method completes the class. It is a crucial method because it makes learning for the DQN algorithm possible. We are going, therefore, to discuss how it works thoroughly. The first thing that the `replay` method does is to sample a batch (we defined the batch size at initialization) from the memories of previous game episodes (such memories are just the variables containing values about status, action, reward, next status, and a flag variable noticing if the observation is a final status or not). The random sampling allows the model to find the best coefficients in order to learn the Q function by a slow adjustment of the network's weights, batch after batch.

Then the method finds out whether the sampling recalled statuses are final or not. Non-final rewards need to be updated in order to represent the reward that you get at the end of the game. This is done by using the target network, which represents a snapshot of the Q function network as fixed at the end of the previous learning. The target network is fed with the following status, and the resulting reward is summed, after being discounted by a gamma factor, with the present reward.

Using the present Q function may lead to instabilities in the learning process and it may not result in a satisfying Q function network.

```
def replay(self):
    # Picking up a random batch from memory
    batch = np.array(random.sample(\
            self.memory.recall_memories(), self.batch_size))
    # Retrieving the sequence of present states
    s = np.vstack(batch[:, 0])
    # Recalling the sequence of actions
    a = np.array(batch[:, 1], dtype=int)
    # Recalling the rewards
    r = np.copy(batch[:, 2])
    # Recalling the sequence of resulting states
    s_p = np.vstack(batch[:, 3])
    # Checking if the reward is relative to
    # a not terminal state
    status = np.where(batch[:, 4] == False)
    # We use the model to predict the rewards by
    # our model and the target model
    next_reward = self.model.predict(self.sess, s_p)
    final_reward = self.target_model.predict(self.sess, s_p)

    if len(status[0]) > 0:
        # Non-terminal update rule using the target model
        # If a reward is not from a terminal state,
        # the reward is just a partial one (r0)
```

```
            # We should add the remaining and obtain a
            # final reward using target predictions
            best_next_action = np.argmax(\
                            next_reward[status, :][0], axis=1)
            # adding the discounted final reward
            r[status] += np.multiply(self.gamma,
                    final_reward[status, best_next_action][0])

            # We replace the expected rewards for actions
            # when dealing with observed actions and rewards
            expected_reward = self.model.predict(self.sess, s)
            expected_reward[range(self.batch_size), a] = r

            # We re-fit status against predicted/observed rewards
            self.model.fit(self.sess, s, expected_reward,
                        epochs=self.epochs)
```

When the rewards of non-terminal states have been updated, the batch data is fed into the neural network for training.

Specifying the environment

The last class to be implemented is the Environment class. Actually, the environment is provided by the gym command, though you need a good wrapper around it in order to have it work with the previous agent class. That's exactly what this class does. At initialization, it starts the Lunar Lander game and sets key variables such as nS, nA (dimensions of state and action), agent, and the cumulative reward (useful for testing the solution by providing an average of the last 100 episodes):

```
class Environment:
    def __init__(self, game="LunarLander-v2"):
        # Initializing
        np.set_printoptions(precision=2)
        self.env = gym.make(game)
        self.env = wrappers.Monitor(self.env, tempfile.mkdtemp(),
                        force=True, video_callable=False)
        self.nS = self.env.observation_space.shape[0]
        self.nA = self.env.action_space.n
        self.agent = Agent(self.nS, self.nA, self.env.spec.id)

        # Cumulative reward
        self.reward_avg = deque(maxlen=100)
```

Then, we prepare the code for methods for `test`, `train`, and `incremental` (incremental training), which are defined as wrappers of the comprehensive `learning` method.

Using incremental training is a bit tricky and it requires some attention if you do not want to spoil the results you have obtained with your training so far. The trouble is that when we restart the brain has pre-trained coefficients but memory is actually empty (we can call this as a cold restart). Being the memory of the agent empty, it cannot support good learning because of too few and limited examples. Consequently, the quality of the examples being fed is really not perfect for learning (the examples are mostly correlated with each other and very specific to the few newly experienced episodes). The risk of ruining the training can be mitigated using a very low `epsilon` (we suggest set at the minimum, `0.01`): in this way, the network will most of the time simply re-learn its own weights because it will suggest for each state the actions it already knows, and its performance shouldn't worsen but oscillate in a stable way until there are enough examples in memory and it will start improving again.

Here is the code for issuing the correct methods for training and testing:

```
def test(self):
    self.learn(epsilon=0.0, episodes=100,
               trainable=False, incremental=False)

def train(self, epsilon=1.0, episodes=1000):
    self.learn(epsilon=epsilon, episodes=episodes,
               trainable=True, incremental=False)

def incremental(self, epsilon=0.01, episodes=100):
    self.learn(epsilon=epsilon, episodes=episodes,
               trainable=True, incremental=True)
```

The final method is `learn`, arranging all the steps for the agent to interact with and learn from the environment. The method takes the `epsilon` value (thus overriding any previous `epsilon` value the agent had), the number of episodes to run in the environment, whether it is being trained or not (a Boolean flag), and whether the training is continuing from the training of a previous model (another Boolean flag).

In the first block of code, the method loads the previously trained weights of the network for Q value approximation if we want:

1. to test the network and see how it works;
2. to carry on some previous training using further examples.

Then the method delves into a nested iteration. The outside iteration is running through the required number of episodes (each episode a Lunar Lander game has taken to its conclusion). Whereas the inner iteration is instead running through a maximum of 1,000 steps making up an episode.

At each time step in the iteration, the neural network is interrogated on the next move. If it is under test, it will always simply provide the answer about the next best move. If it is under training, there is some chance, depending on the value of epsilon, that it won't suggest the best move but it will instead propose making a random move.

```python
def learn(self, epsilon=None, episodes=1000,
          trainable=True, incremental=False):
    """
    Representing the interaction between the enviroment
    and the learning agent
    """
    # Restoring weights if required
    if not trainable or (trainable and incremental):
        try:
            print("Loading weights")
            self.agent.load_weights('./weights.h5')
        except:
            print("Exception")
            trainable = True
            incremental = False
            epsilon = 1.0

    # Setting epsilon
    self.agent.epsilon = epsilon
    # Iterating through episodes
    for episode in range(episodes):
        # Initializing a new episode
        episode_reward = 0
        s = self.env.reset()
        # s is put at default values
        s = np.reshape(s, [1, self.nS])

        # Iterating through time frames
        for time_frame in range(1000):
            if not trainable:
```

```
                # If not learning, representing
                # the agent on video
                self.env.render()
            # Deciding on the next action to take
            a = self.agent.act(s)
            # Performing the action and getting feedback
            s_p, r, status, info = self.env.step(a)
            s_p = np.reshape(s_p, [1, self.nS])

            # Adding the reward to the cumulative reward
            episode_reward += r

            # Adding the overall experience to memory
            if trainable:
                self.agent.memory.add_memory(s, a, r, s_p,
                                                    status)

            # Setting the new state as the current one
            s = s_p

            # Performing experience replay if memory length
            # is greater than the batch length
            if trainable:
                if len(self.agent.memory) > \
                        self.agent.batch_size:
                    self.agent.replay()

            # When the episode is completed,
            # exiting this loop
            if status:
                if trainable:
                    self.agent.target_model_update()
                break

        # Exploration vs exploitation
        self.agent.epsilon_update(episode)

        # Running an average of the past 100 episodes
        self.reward_avg.append(episode_reward)
        print("episode: %i score: %.2f avg_score: %.2f"
                "actions %i epsilon %.2f" % (episode,
                                    episode_reward,
                        np.average(self.reward_avg),
                                        time_frame,
                                        epsilon)
self.env.close()

if trainable:
```

```
# Saving the weights for the future
self.agent.save_weights('./weights.h5')
```

After the move, all the information is gathered (initial state, chosen action, obtained reward, and consequent state) and saved into memory. At this time frame, if the memory is large enough to create a batch for the neural network approximating the Q function, then a training session is run. When all the time frames of the episode have been consumed, the weights of the DQN get stored into another network to be used as a stable reference as the DQN network is learning from a new episode.

Running the reinforcement learning process

Finally, after all the digression on reinforcement learning and DQN and writing down the complete code for the project, you can run it using a script or a Jupyter Notebook, leveraging the `Environment` class that puts all the code functionalities together:

```
lunar_lander = Environment(game="LunarLander-v2")
```

After instantiating it, you just have to run the `train`, starting from `epsilon=1.0` and setting the goal to 5000 episodes (which corresponds to about 2.2 million examples of chained variables of state, action and reward). The actual code we provided is set to successfully accomplish a fully trained DQN model, though it may take some time, given your GPU's availability and its computing capabilities:

```
lunar_lander.train(epsilon=1.0, episodes=5000)
```

In the end, the class will complete the required training, leaving a saved model on disk (which could be run or even reprised anytime). You can even inspect the TensorBoard using a simple command that can be run from a shell:

```
tensorboard --logdir=./experiments --port 6006
```

The plots will appear on your browser, and they will be available for inspection at the local address `localhost:6006`:

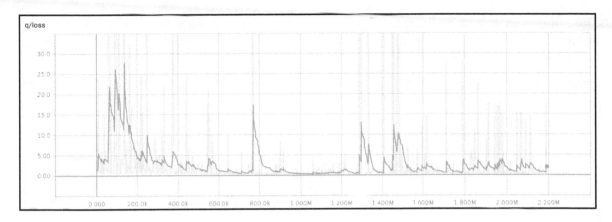

Figure 4: The loss trend along the training, the peaks represent break-thoughts in learning such as at 800k examples when it started landing safely on the ground.

The loss plot will reveal that, contrary to other projects, the optimization is still characterized by a decreasing loss, but with many spikes and problems along the way:

The plots represented here are the result of running the project once. Since there is a random component in the process, you may obtain slightly different plots when running the project on your own computer.

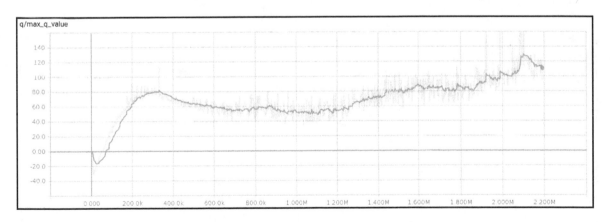

Figure 5: The trend of maximum q values obtained in a batch session of learning

The same story is told by the maximum predicted q value and the average predicted q value. The network improves at the end, though it can slightly retrace its steps and linger on plateaus for a long time:

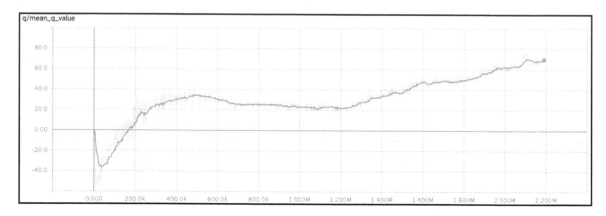

Figure 6: The trend of average q values obtained in a batch session of learning

Only if you take the average of the last 100 final rewards do you see an incremental path, hinting at a persistent and steady improvement of the DQN network:

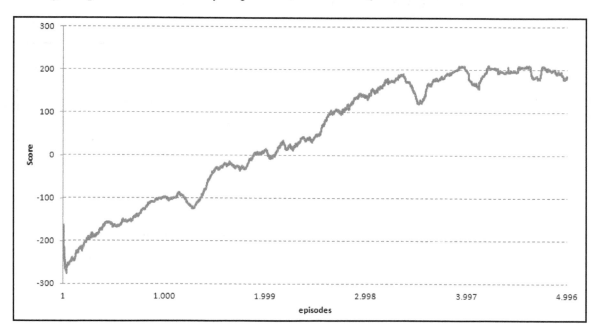

Figure 7: The trend of actually obtained scores at the end of each learning episode, it more clearly depicts the growing capabilities of the DQN

Using the same information, from the output, not from the TensorBoard, you'll also figure out that the number of actions changes on average depending on the `epsilon` value. At the beginning, the number of actions required to finish an episode was under 200. Suddenly, when `epsilon` is `0.5`, the average number of actions tends to grow steadily and reach a peak at about 750 (the landing pod has learned to counteract gravity by using its rockets).

In the end, the network discovers this is a sub-optimal strategy and when `epsilon` turns below `0.3`, the average number of actions for completing an episode drops as well. The DQN in this phase is discovering how to successfully land the pod in a more efficient way:

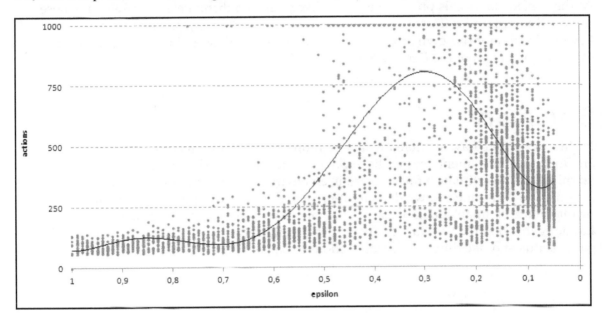

Figure 8: The relationship between the epsilon (the exploration/exploitation rate) and the efficiency of the DQN network, expressed as a number of moves used to complete an episode

If for any reason, you believe that the network needs more examples and learning, you can reprise the learning using the incremental `method`, keeping in mind that `epsilon` should be very low in this case:

```
lunar_lander.incremental(episodes=25, epsilon=0.01)
```

After the training, if you need to see the results and know, on average every 100 episodes, how much the DQN can score (the ideal target is a `score >=200`), you can just run the following command:

```
lunar_lander.test()
```

Acknowledgements

At the conclusion of this project, we would like to indeed thank Peter Skvarenina, whose project "Lunar Lander II" (`https://www.youtube.com/watch?v=yiAmrZuBaYU`) has been the key inspiration for our own project, and for all his suggestions and hints during the making of our own version of the Deep Q-Network.

Summary

In this project, we have explored what a reinforcement algorithm can manage to achieve in an OpenAI environment, and we have programmed a TensorFlow graph capable of learning how to estimate a final reward in an environment characterized by an agent, states, actions, and consequent rewards. This approach, called DQN, aims to approximate the result from a Bellman equation using a neural network approach. The result is a Lunar Lander game that the software can play successfully at the end of training by reading the game status and deciding on the right actions to be taken at any time.

Other Books You May Enjoy

If you enjoyed this book, you may be interested in these other books by Packt:

TensorFlow 1.x Deep Learning Cookbook

Antonio Gulli, Amita Kapoor

ISBN: 978-1-78829-359-4

- Install TensorFlow and use it for CPU and GPU operations
- Implement DNNs and apply them to solve different AI-driven problems.
- Leverage different data sets such as MNIST, CIFAR-10, and Youtube8m with TensorFlow and learn how to access and use them in your code.
- Use TensorBoard to understand neural network architectures, optimize the learning process, and peek inside the neural network black box.
- Use different regression techniques for prediction and classification problems
- Build single and multilayer perceptrons in TensorFlow

Deep Learning By Example
Ahmed Menshawy

ISBN: 978-1-78839-990-6

- Understand the fundamentals of deep learning and how it is different from machine learning
- Get familiarized with Tensorflow, one of the most popular libraries for advanced machine learning
- Increase the predictive power of your model using feature engineering
- Understand the basics of deep learning by solving a digit classification problem of MNIST
- Demonstrate face generation based on the CelebA database, a promising application of generative models
- Apply deep learning to other domains like language modeling, sentiment analysis, and machine translation

Leave a review - let other readers know what you think

Please share your thoughts on this book with others by leaving a review on the site that you bought it from. If you purchased the book from Amazon, please leave us an honest review on this book's Amazon page. This is vital so that other potential readers can see and use your unbiased opinion to make purchasing decisions, we can understand what our customers think about our products, and our authors can see your feedback on the title that they have worked with Packt to create. It will only take a few minutes of your time, but is valuable to other potential customers, our authors, and Packt. Thank you!

Index